Beyond Deconstruction

*The Uses and Abuses
of Literary Theory*

BEYOND DECONSTRUCTION

The Uses and Abuses of Literary Theory

HOWARD FELPERIN

CLARENDON PRESS · OXFORD
1985

Oxford University Press, Walton Street, Oxford OX2 6DP
London New York Toronto
Delhi Bombay Calcutta Madras Karachi
Kuala Lumpur Singapore Hong Kong Tokyo
Nairobi Dar es Salaam Cape Town
Melbourne Auckland
and associated companies in
Beirut Berlin Ibadan Mexico City Nicosia
Oxford is a trade mark of Oxford University Press

Published in the United States
by Oxford University Press, New York

British Library Cataloguing in Publication Data
Felperin, Howard
Beyond deconstruction: the uses and abuses
of literary theory.
1. Literature—Philosophy
I. Title
801   PN45
ISBN 0–19–812839–8

Library of Congress Cataloguing in Publication Data
Felperin, Howard.
Beyond deconstruction.
Includes index.
1. Criticism—history—20th century.   2. Deconstruction.
I. Title.
PN94.F45   1985   801'.95'09   84-23218
ISBN 0–19–812839–8

Set by Hope Services, Abingdon, Oxon
Printed in Great Britain
at the University Press, Oxford
by David Stanford
Printer to the University

For
Geoffrey Hartman,

and the memory of
Paul de Man:

τοῖς ἀνδράσι τοῖς ἀπόροις

Contents

The natural result of any investigation is that the investigators either discover the object of their search, or deny that it is discoverable . . . or persist in their search . . . Those who believe they have discovered it are the 'Dogmatists' . . . Other Academics treat it as inapprehensible; the Sceptics keep on searching. Hence it seems reasonable to hold that the main types of philosophy are three—the dogmatic, the academic, and the sceptic. Of the other schools it will best become others to speak: our task at present is to describe in outline the sceptic methodology, first stipulating that of none of our future statements do we positively affirm that the fact is exactly as we state it. Rather, we simply record each fact, like a chronicler, as it appears to us at the moment.

Sextus Empiricus, *Outlines of Pyrrhonism*, c.AD200.

Preface: A Guide to the Perplexed

Let me state at the outset, given the current rage for theory within our institutions of academic literary study, that this book is not aimed at promoting the claims of any of the theoretical schools it takes up. Still less does it claim to advance some new theory that would move us definitively into or beyond poststructuralism. While it begins in provisional sympathy with the far-reaching critique of humanist practices now in progress under the name of theory, it ends in reluctant scepticism towards that theoretical project—though not, it should also be stated straight away, a scepticism protective of our older humanism.

Without some initial sympathy, at the very least a willing suspension of disbelief, toward so radical a critique of institutional practice as that of contemporary theory, the book would doubtless have been different, more polemically defensive of tried and true liberal-humanist values and methods against the new barbarism. Yet its very identification with the continuing institutional critique has turned it, by the logic of that commitment, into a critique of the theoretical schools themselves. Nor is that critique without its own polemical side. Its polemic is directed not against one school or another, but against the purist or imperialist tendency of them all, their motivating belief that persistence in theory (their own in particular) will resolve the problems that have beset and debilitated past practice rather than throw up new ones just as debilitating.

Not least of the unforeseen problems entailed upon literary study by the current paradigm-shift toward theory is the problem of theory itself, the high but hidden costs that accompany the transformation of a humanist discourse, deriving its terms from the wider, broadly moral, cultural currency, into a more scientific and specialist, or philosophical and self-conscious, one. The problem of such a project, understandably repressed by the theorists busily engaged upon it, is that its success would only complete the process, long since under way, by which literary study gives up its centrality and prestige as the leisurely, indeed élitist, lingua franca of educated men and turns into the specialist discourse of a clerisy existing at the margin of the culture whose texts and contexts it sets out to explain. The very ambition of theory to oversee—the root meaning of the term—the operations of readers and texts with technical rigour would issue, if fulfilled, in a metadiscourse coherent perhaps in itself but for all practical and public purposes unintelligible and without influence within the wider culture. Within Anglo-American culture, just such a destiny has already overtaken philosophy, the discipline with which many theorists now seek closer ties. The dream of systematic transcendence would thus beget its own trivialization.

Fortunately for literary study, however, no such success is yet in sight. The search for a theoretical metadiscourse has so far yielded only a proliferation of sub-discourses that shows no sign of consolidating into a common language and methodology comparable to that which lends a semblance of coherence to the practices of science and some credence to the notion of a scientific community. (For structuralist theory in particular these have been the objects of institutional emulation.) Quite the contrary, as the discourses of theory continue to proliferate and recombine into new discourses, profound incompatibilities and mutual contradictions emerge in assumptions, aims, and methods, making it increasingly unlikely that any single meta- or master-discourse will achieve the desired condition of institutional domination. This, the present study argues, is not only the unavoidable destiny of textual study within a pluralist culture, but may not be an altogether unhappy fate. The unavailability of a common theoretical language may well save literary criticism from itself.

If the present study is *for* anything, it is for practice, now inevitably a *theoretical practice*, though not in Althusser's sense of a verified knowledge methodically purged of the false consciousness of rhetoric and ideology, but in the humbler, more sceptical or pragmatic, sense of an interpretive practice that thinks, in the terms available to it, what it is doing with the texts it takes up, even as it goes on taking them up. My own 'method', as the reader will discover, is the one commended long ago by Aristotle in a comment on Gorgias, known to us as a 'sophist' but actually an early master of deconstruction: 'Gorgias spoke rightly when he said one ought to lead the serious in one's opponent to its ruin in jest, and his jest to its ruin in seriousness.' The polemical purpose of the present study is thus carried forward by the mobile vehicle of parody, a 'singing beside', which from the viewpoint of contemporary theory is instinct with 'writing' itself. The sheer force of our emergent poststructuralisms, the very muscularity of their accounts of the operations of texts, can only too easily be turned against themselves or against one another, in order that something humbler, less muscle-bound or over-evolved, may have room to live.

The reader will also notice that my choice of theoretical antagonists excludes certain emergent contenders. The present study does not have much to say about feminist criticism, 'reader-response' criticsm, or post-freudian psychoanalytic criticism. I trust these omissions will not seem more idiosyncratic or dismissive than any such omission must be. In a book on so active and burgeoning a subject as contemporary literary theory, a certain bounding of the subject is as necessary as it is arbitrary, and my exclusion of these movements is not without its reasons. In their highly developed historicity, the schools I have discussed seem to me to exemplify, perhaps even to exhaust, the distinctive possibilities of thought available to contemporary theoretical discourse. They even retain an uncanny resemblance to the discursive models outlined by Sextus Empiricus eighteen hundred years ago and quoted as epigraph to this book, Sextus' dogmatists, academics, and sceptics corresponding to contemporary marxists, semiologists, and deconstructionists respectively. Of the other schools, as Sextus said, it will best become others to speak. To me they seem insufficiently distinctive and developed as theories, particularly as literary theories, to stand as exemplary and paradigmatic in their own right alongside the theories that are discussed. More on this in the final chapter.

Finally, what of my own 'implied' or 'ideal' reader? Just who is, or are, 'the perplexed' to whom this book offers its

unsolicited guidance? Here I must confess, that in the first
instance it was no one other than myself; indeed, the subtitle
of this Preface was my first choice, and remains my personal
preference, for that of the book as a whole. Some of the
circumstances of my own fall into perplexity in the face of an
emergent structuralism back in the sixties are briefly sketched
in the opening chapter. The work on Shakespeare, on which I
was then engaged and which was begun in a less perturbed
place and time, was not untouched by it. But a more direct
confrontation with theory, and my own anxiety of theory, still
seemed necessary; so for the past six years I have been
confronting both by teaching a seminar on literary theory.
While I cannot claim that the experience unperplexed me, I
did discover that I was not alone in my perplexity. My
students and colleagues at Melbourne, and others like them
elsewhere, who have listened patiently and responded intelli-
gently and theoretically to its self-help programme, are also
the implied readers of this book, the 'we' it sometimes ritually
invokes. Hence its occasional uncertainty as to whether it is a
synoptic introduction for those uninitiated in theory or a
sophisticated commentary for those already familiar with the
emerging field, that is to say, a work *on* literary theory or a
work *of* literary theory.

That question the reader must decide. While my intention
was to write a book *on* theory, to attain philosophical
command over the field so as to resolve its problems and limit
its spread, I fully accept that it has become a book *of* theory,
participating in the problems it set out to resolve and
perpetuating the perplexity it set out to dispel. To write
upon—or against—theory is to enter into and inhabit theory,
and thereby abandon all hope of resolving its problems from a
safe distance. That is the ultimate dilemma and destiny of the
theoretician, to be overtaken by the perplexity he wished to
oversee. So 'the perplexed' of the sub-title may have wider
reference still. It refers, as the inscription to my own former
colleagues and precursors in the field intimates, beyond
author and audience to the literary theorists themselves whose
work forms the subject of the book. For what but their own
perplexity in the face of texts would have moved them to
pursue the promise of theoretical transcendence in the first

place? Just as a poem is defined by one contemporary theorist, not as a resolved but as an 'achieved' anxiety, so a work of literary theory (this one at least) may be nothing other than an achieved perplexity, in so far as it puts naïve questions which issue in answers that become the occasion for more naïve questions. Such scepticism towards the theoretical adventure may be a far cry from the philosophical promise held out by the pre-socratics, and implicit in most post-platonic thought, that knowledge begins in wonder—as if it did not end there too! In defence of its admitted minimalism, I cite the remark of Walter Benjamin, fashionable nowadays among marxists and deconstructionists alike, on experiencing a strange city: 'The object is to learn, not how to find one's way, but how to lose it.'

1

Leavisism Revisited

Leopards break into the temple and drink to the dregs what is in the sacrificial pitchers; this is repeated over and over again; finally it can be calculated in advance, and it becomes a part of the ceremony.

Franz Kafka

I. THE MYSTIFICATIONS OF PLAIN TALK

When I joined the Yale English department in 1966, structuralism, or what I later came to identify as structuralism, was already in the air. There in New Haven, the 'new' criticism had been enshrined for twenty years, and like any ageing orthodoxy, had begun to seem routine and restrictive to the younger and older Turks among my new colleagues. Themselves Yale 'products'—in that very American term—they were more methodologically sophisticated than I, and when they spoke of 'binary oppositions,' '*bricolage*,' '*ostranenie*,' and 'Saussure', they seemed to know what they were talking about. Having just come down from Harvard, where literary criticism was still innocently regarded as a sub-genre of biography or history, I listened over coffee at the Yorkside and lunch at the Gourmet—talk about the arbitrariness of the sign!—to a mode of discourse as opaque and intimidating as a foreign language, which much of it in fact was.

To my ears it was all strange—this newest French criticism, not to mention the Russian formalism and Prague linguistics from which it was said to spring. After all, I was still struggling to master the techniques of the old new criticism, Yale formalism to be precise, which I only then discovered, like M. Jourdain, was what I had been practising at Harvard without realizing it. Harvard provincialism being what it is, I

resisted the outlandish theoretical babble of New Haven in the
name of plain talk and common sense. Until, that is, Yale
provincialism had had time to displace the Harvard kind in
my admirably open and independent mind. Gradually, the
principles of plain talk and common sense began to seem more
like fallacies of univocal expression and unmediated perception, and soon I could have been taken for a native speaker.

This reminiscence is what used to be termed, in the familiar
language of an older criticism, a 'flashback' or beginning *in
medias res*. In the terminology of the new science of 'narrat-
ology', it is an 'anachrony', or more precisely still, an
'analepsis', the characteristic feature of a narrative that is not
straightforward, or in structuralist parlance once again, one in
which story (*histoire*) and discourse (*discours*) do not coincide.
Because the story I want to tell—that of the coming of age of
literary criticism over the past twenty years as a mature
discipline—is by no means straightforward, and because that
story is inseparable from my personal and institutional
experience of it, I beg the reader's indulgence for the self-
critical nostalgia with which I proceed. After all, if criticism is,
as Oscar Wilde once wrote, 'the most civilized form of
autobiography', the converse may also hold true, and autobiography prove an advanced form of criticism. And since every
author is the hero of his own script, all falls that occur therein
must be fortunate. This principle applies not merely to a fall
from Cambridge to New Haven, but even to a fall so far south
as to make one almost disappear off the map. This second fall,
this second cultural and intellectual dislocation at the very
least, occurred in 1977 when I took up a chair of English
literature in Australia.

Indeed, when I first arrived in Australia, language was once
again the problem. Although my difficulties with basic
Australian largely disappeared through prolonged exposure—
it turned out after all to be merely an inflection of English—
my difficulties with the technical language of literary criticism
as I found it, did not. In some respects my language problem
in Melbourne was the opposite of the one I experienced on
arriving in New Haven. At Yale I had encountered a number
of strange jargons that came in time to seem, if never quite
natural, at least intelligible and defensible as the contending

discourses of a technical discipline in the making. At Melbourne I encountered what seemed plain speaking itself, an educated, middle-class idiom as clear as the BBC. Yet I soon became aware that this same idiom, rather than being transparent, hid a thousand mysteries, and was in consequence of dubious utility for a discipline with any claim or aspiration to make sense. My initiation into the mysteries of this—to me—novel jargon occurred in two stages. It began in my sense of present perplexity during the painfully genteel conversations over tea in the department library, only to deepen into thorough bewilderment when I read the essays published by my colleagues in the departmental organ *The Critical Review*.

What I discovered was that an author's prose can be 'crisp', or if he is not careful, 'brittle'; his moral outlook 'buoyant' and 'life-affirming' (unless of course it is 'life-denying'); his work 'central' or 'essential' or 'marginal'. (To what and for whom was not made explicit, unless it was 'life' or the 'great tradition'.) The only authors who seemed to be consistently regarded as 'central' and 'essential,' for whatever it is worth, were Shakespeare and Jane Austen. The critic, in turn, supposed himself to write out of his 'inward possession' of the work, to seek a 'realised experience' in it, to strive for 'completeness of response' to it, but most often seemed to entertain 'worries' about its artistic, and especially, its moral status until he could finally dismiss it as 'easy' or 'unearned' or 'self-indulgent'. He thereby proved himself a reader or critic—never an interpreter or scholar or even student—of 'sensibility' and 'judgement,' superior by implication to the author he had just put in his place.[1]

My own 'worries' with this school of criticism—and allowing for the economy of caricature, I think I have offered a fair sample of its characteristic terms and procedures—had to do with its curious combination of self-proclaimed democracy and undeclared authoritarianism. Here was a 'natural language,' a critical idiom drawn from common parlance and apparently aimed at an audience of 'common readers'; yet its

---

[1] The full lexicon of local usage, from which I have drawn only a representative sample of 'terms', was actually compiled by a visiting Canadian scholar, Dr Robert Rawson Wilson. To his fresh, estranged, and appalled perception of this last outpost of Leavisite imperialism I owe a great deal.

vocabulary was deployed in such a way as to create a tone as dreadfully earnest and a protocol as predictable and formulaic as a religious ritual. Indeed, the critical practices parodied above may be seen as so many narrative functions of an underlying mythic structure: a hard-working faithful follow their inner lights into a kingdom of eternal and unmediated life, a kingdom earned and enjoyed only by that handful of writers and critics who constitute the elect. (Who is qualified to decide who qualifies for this elect is a problem better left aside for the moment.) Whether this literary puritanism (whence its paradoxical combination of democracy and authoritarianism), with its self-righteous scrupulosity and unflinching last judgements, owes more to the tradition of Scottish book-reviewing or religion can also be left aside. The overwhelming impression at the time was of a mode of criticism that had stiffened, despite its original impulse to be democratic and plain-spoken, into the ritual moves and postures of a priestly élite. Moreover, to the extent that the 'plain style' I found in Melbourne had become the expression of an unconscious reflex rather than independent or considered or even informed reflection, it was more truly a jargon than anything I had ever heard on an ordinary evening in New Haven.

II. THE LOWER EVANGELICISM

There is a story told of the James household that William one morning at breakfast suggested, as a frontispiece to his father's latest opus on Swedenborgianism, a picture of a man beating a dead horse. The reader, having recognized by now the critical fashion I have been mocking, may wish to object in similar terms. It might be urged that Leavis is dead and the 'practical criticism' he championed moribund, so why raise these ghosts only to vex them, particularly when they take so provincial and etiolated a form? Even if there are Leavisite epigones alive and well and living in Australia, as well as parts of Canada, the UK, and indeed America, they cannot any longer be considered influential or representative within the local community of letters, let alone the international one. While acknowledging the general point, I raise the problem of

Leavisism, not simply because it struck me forcibly upon my arrival in Melbourne, but because our present and larger critical situation cannot be understood except as the outcome of contradictions within its underlying philosophical—or aggressively *anti*-philosophical—position.

That present situation, to anticipate the course of our argument momentarily, may be characterized as the attempt to address questions begged or repressed by new and practical criticism alike. Is the language of literature a privileged language, a language of moral instruction, of organic unity, of fullness and precision, a language redeemed from the divisions and duplicities that bedevil 'ordinary' language? Is there even such a thing as poetic or literary language in the first place, a language authentically different from 'ordinary' language? Then too, what is the proper language of literary criticism? What relation does criticism bear to its object of study, namely, literature or language, or the language of literature? To the die-hard practical critic these questions—questions that disturb, not to say obsess, all schools of contemporary criticism—would be rhetorical at best. It is on the unquestioned assumption—it has been all but a matter of faith—that literary language both exists and is privileged that criticism has traditionally proceeded, and that practical criticism in particular has gone about its business of constructing its great traditions and revaluing the authors who compose them.

This idealism is precisely what has been called into question by marxism, structuralism, and deconstruction alike. Though each of these movements approaches its task of demystification from a different angle, a central target of each is the myth of literary privilege of which practical criticism in England and new criticism in America were the last pure (and purist) manifestations: once upon a time there was a special category of works designated as Literature, within which an even more privileged group of works was set apart and conscientiously re-edited, reinterpreted, and taught. This latter group was known as the 'canon' or the 'great tradition'. All of these 'works' were thought of as 'created' by 'authors' endowed with godlike powers of originality, wisdom and clairvoyance. But because the demi-divine poetic word, eternal essence that it is, is sometimes obscure to mere mortal ears, critics of special sensibility and authority akin, but by no means equal, to that of the authors themselves, are needed to sort out the sheep and the goats, the genuine works of literature from the pretenders or look-alikes, and to extract from the genuine article its universal moral truths for the benefit of a wide audience of 'common readers,' ranging from laymen to students to literati. Hence the need to repeat the truth of literature in a plain-spoken idiom intelligible to all, so that all might understand and be saved.

All of the dominant schools of contemporary criticism—marxism, structuralism, and deconstruction—have converged upon this myth, and in dismantling it of its idealist and metaphysical yearnings and trappings, its Arnoldian inheritance of displaced religion, have inevitably raised another set of questions. If the nature of literature is put into question, so too must be the nature of criticism. At the very least, a new critical language has to be invented, once the notion of a privileged literary language (which is what had prescribed after all, the terms and level of our critical discourse, as a king sets the standard for his kingdom) can no longer be taken for granted. The *ancien régime* having been overthrown, the various critical ideologies abroad in the land, each with its own discourse and programme, now jostle for place, and in so doing, constitute our present institutional confusion.

No one has been better placed than Raymond Williams to observe how the internal contradictions of practical criticism could not have helped but lead to its defeat:

The claim of literature to be the central human study has rested . . . 'on practical criticism,' which deserves attention in itself and because it is from this, paradoxically, that much of the English work in literary sociology has come. I know Goldmann would have been surprised—every visitor is surprised—to meet the full intensity, the extraordinary human commitment, of this particular and local allegiance. In his attack on 'scientism' he might for a moment have assumed that there were Cambridge allies, who had attacked the same thing in the same word. But this wouldn't have lasted long. Goldmann's attack on scientism—the uncritical transfer of method from the physical to the human sciences—was above all in the name of a critical sociology; whereas that word 'sociology' has only to be mentioned, in practical-critical circles, to provoke the last sad look at the voluntarily damned. And I would give it about fifteen minutes, as Goldmann began to describe his own methodology, for that crushing quotation to be brought out from Lawrence: 'We judge a work of art by its effect on our sincere and vital emotion, and nothing else. All the critical twiddle-twaddle about style and form, all this pseudo-scientific classifying and analysing of books in an imitation-botanical fashion, is mere impertinence and mostly dull jargon.'

So no methodology here, thank you; only sincere and vital emotion. But who decides the sincerity and vitality? If you need to ask that you couldn't begin to understand the answer. People decide it, in themselves and in an active and collaborative critical process. But which people, in what social relationships, with each other and with others? That, at whatever risk of damnation, is the necessary question of the sociologist. Practical criticism is vulnerable at several points: in its hardening into an apparently objective method which is based, even defiantly, on subjective principles; in its isolation of texts from contexts; in its contemplative aspects, which have often made it hostile to new literary work. But all these weaknesses are most apparent, we say, when it is badly done: well or badly being again an internal criterion. In fact, however, all these weaknesses, or potential weaknesses, follow from the specific social situation of its practitioners. The real answer to that question—which people, in what social relationships?—was, as we all know, precise and even principled: the informed critical minority. What began as the most general kind of claim, a visibly human process centred on the apparently absolute qualities of sincerity and vitality, ended, under real pressures, as a self-defining group.[2]

The limitations of practical criticism discerned by Williams, then, are limitations of self-blindness, or more pointedly, of unself-scrutiny. Even under challenge by René Wellek, Leavis and the *Scrutiny* group were reluctant—indeed, made a virtue of their reluctance—to examine the premisses and presuppositions of their own activity,[3] a reluctance that lends all their work, the so-called 'best,' as well as the 'worst', an air of unwitting circularity. For all their professed concern with

[2] 'Literature and Sociology: in memory of Lucien Goldmann', *New Left Review*, 67 (May–June 1971), pp. 8–9.

[3] See Leavis's 'Literary Criticism and Philosophy: A Reply', *Scrutiny*, vi. i (June 1937), pp. 59–70.

relations between social conditions and 'sensibility' (I continue to put this term in quotation marks because to this day I am not sure what it means), particularly but not exclusively before its fall in the seventeenth century into disunity and alienation, the Leavisites remained cavalierly complacent about scrutinizing the historical nature of their own enterprise. To do so would have been to relativize that revelation which they would have liked to believe absolute. By the time they began to examine and shore up their own 'paradigm' or 'episteme' in the sixties, it had already broken down beyond repair.

'Cavalier' and 'complacent'—no doubt the last words they would ever have imagined could be applied to their nervy and embattled endeavour. Yet when one does scrutinize their social conditioning, their tastes, prejudices, judgements, their 'sensibilities' do indeed seem in retrospect the only too predictable product of the particular cultural moment within which Leavis and his followers came to maturity. Their consistent claim to be vigorous, independent, discerning minds making free discriminations among the best and the less than best that has been thought and said could appear, with great plausibility, to be nothing other than a conditioned reflex, the by-product of a social process long in train and distinctively English. Their precious 'sensibility' could be described, sociologically, as the reaction (or reaction–formation) of a puritan petite-bourgeoisie (seemingly forever on the rise since the Middle Ages), against a growing mass culture on the one side, and an academic culture still dominated by aristocratic amateurs, on the other: the groups already identified by Arnold, with anxious wit, as Philistines, Populace, and Barbarians respectively. (Can it be that 'sensibility' means, after all, nothing other than ideology or neurosis?) So practical criticism turns out to be a form of social revolution acting itself out under the guise of intellectual reform against a Cambridge backdrop that looks more like a Hollywood set than a part of that vulgar post-industrial—what Leavis termed 'technologico-Benthamite'—world, from which our revolutionaries recoiled in aesthetic distaste. Transistors on Cambridge Common! Perhaps the reaction could only have taken place, the ideology only have taken form, within the anachronism of such a setting.[4]

III. THE POLITICS OF INTERPRETATION

The prescription arising from this diagnosis, the specific needed, according to Williams and others, to restore a failing practical criticism, is some form of literary sociology. After all, the hypostatization of 'literature' into a pure essence uncontaminated by the dross of history and modernity, a process of which practical criticism represents only one by-product, is nothing if not historical and 'modern':

What has then to be traced is the attempted and often successful specialization of 'literature' to certain kinds of writing. . . . Clearly, the major shift, represented by the modern complex of 'literature', *art, aesthetic, creative,* and *imaginative* is a matter of social and cultural history. 'Literature' itself must be seen as a late medieval and Renaissance isolation of the skills of reading and of the qualities of the book; this was much emphasized by the development of printing. . . . Then 'literature' was specialized towards *imaginative writing,* within the basic assumptions of Romanticism. . . .

Significantly in recent years 'literature' and 'literary', though they still have effective currency in post-C18 senses, have been increasingly challenged, on what is conventionally their own ground, by concepts of *writing* and *communication* which seek to recover the most active and general senses which the extreme specialization had seemed to exclude.[5]

Given this shift in the historical designation of 'literature' away from such social acceptations as 'learning' and 'communication' toward the more subjective and specialized acceptation of fictional and imaginative writing, it is not surprising that the modern study of literature has come to

---

[4] Leavis's reaction against technology, modernity, America (which epitomizes both), and their encroachment upon a mythical England, finds its fullness in *Nor Shall My Sword* (London: Chatto and Windus, 1972). In this work, incidentally, Leavis meets the charge of 'literarism' levelled against him by a far-flung Melbourne disciple in the journal mentioned above, inaccurately cited as the *'Melbourne Quarterly'* (pp. 96–7).

[5] Raymond Williams, *Keywords: A Vocabulary of Culture and Society* (London: Croom Helm, 1976), pp. 152–4.

concentrate on its formal and textual aspect at the expense of the historical and contextual. Nor is it surprising—let this too be acknowledged at the outset—that after a long sequence of academic formalisms—Russian, Anglo-American, and most recently French—the resuscitation of interest in historical and political contexts—not least that of the institution itself—should have come to seem to many such an urgent *desideratum*. As the French structuralist Gérard Genette, writing in the mid-sixties on the excesses of Russian formalism, put it, 'literature had been regarded for so long as a message without a code that it became necessary to regard it for a while as a code without a message.'[6] That 'while' has prolonged itself to the point where it once again seems 'necessary', at least to some, to recover the 'message', assumed, as it usually is, to exist 'outside' literature in its formal, fictive sense. The wheel of cultural history seems to be coming full circle.

It is little wonder then that literary studies have turned their attention over the past decade, in the effort to break out of the textual and institutional self-enclosure that limited new and practical criticism, toward the wider social process within which texts are written and read. This diverse inquiry has included not only the literary sociology, the 'left Leavisism'[7] prescribed and practised by Williams, but the full-dress historical critique of a revivified marxism and emergent feminism, interdisciplinary excursions into an ever-present popular culture and the newer visual media, and the history and phenomenology of reception and response on the part of readers and audiences. While each of these movements has developed its own special theories and discourses, they have at least one motive and justification in common: to open up the closed and self-supporting economy of evaluative textual criticism, what marxism would term the commodity-fetischism of the text-as-object, and promote that commerce between the literary text and its social context which new and practical

---

[6] *Figures I* (Paris: Seuil, 1966), p. 150. Translation mine, in accordance with my practice throughout of translating all quotations from texts which have not been translated into English.

[7] The term, highly appropriate, is Terry Eagleton's. See his brilliantly ambivalent critique of the work of his master, Williams, and of that of his master's master, Leavis, in *Criticism and Ideology* (London: New Left Books, 1976), pp. 11–43.

criticism had all but embargoed under the twin fallacies of intentionalism and affectivism in its definition of and dealings with 'literature.' All these developments are readily understandable as attempts to supply the increasingly visible defects of our institutional practice and restore its integrity as an activity of wide social and political, not to mention personal, import and consequence.

Yet none of these developments seems to me likely to supplant, though they are bound to transform, new and practical criticism. Predictions of this kind are admittedly risky, particularly in so unsettled a climate as that of contemporary criticism, and I venture this one only with reluctance. With reluctance, not out of nostalgia for the new criticism with which I grew up, and still less out of the belief that practical criticism 'at its best' offered something worth retaining, often identified with its close encounters with the 'words-on-the-page'. (As if a pure, close attentiveness were separable from the ideology that guides it, or other interpretive modes were inattentive to the text!) On the contrary, the Leavisite privileging of intuition over intellect, morality over form, evaluation over interpretation, conscience over consciousness, and the rush to judgement toward which these priorities predisposed it—as distinct from the more principled procedures and inverse priorities of new criticism—still seem to me fundamentally misguided. Rather, I make so sweeping a pronouncement because the various contextual strategies designed to supplant the older textual tactics have not squarely faced, much less negotiated or transcended, the ground resistance on which the older tactics foundered to be sure, but foundered only because they actually engaged it: the difficult question of what constitutes 'literary' or 'poetic' as against 'ordinary' language. Without addressing the specific problem of literary language more openly and explicitly than did the older textual criticism, no contextual criticism can hope to succeed where its predecessor failed. Yet this is precisely the kind of problem, in so far as it involves linguistic and aesthetic as distinct from social and historical issues, that the move from text to context seems unlikely, on the face of it, to succeed in resolving. Unless, of course, the linguistic and aesthetic aspects of textuality are ignored or repressed or subsumed in the flush of a resurgent historicism, under such social concepts as 'discourse', 'practice', or 'ideology'.

That is exactly what happens in the most radical version of the new contextualism, namely the post-Althusserian marxism that informs the literary criticism of Pierre Macherey and Terry Eagleton, among others. In this view, the 'literary' text is regarded as an indirect and elliptical expression of 'ideology', i.e. group subjectivity or collective self-deception, and 'explained'—as distinct from 'interpreted'—by reference to a social and historical ideology about which it is silent but by which it is 'produced'.[8] Yet the problem of the language of literature as something distinct from the language of history, which has been neatly sidestepped, makes its embarrassing return the moment we ask how the study of literature can be founded on or explained by history, when what constitutes history may be nothing other than literature, since both are 'inscriptions' of 'ideology'. How can fiction be 'explained' by reference to what is only another fiction, or the explicator's explanations extricate themselves from the ideological torsions and coercions that produced the fictions he sets out to explain? The concept of ideology, begging as it does the question of its linguistic status as history or fiction (since it seems to be capable of being defined as either or both), introduces a radical circularity into the project of 'explanation', a circularity no less self-enclosing than that of the moral formalism and formal moralism that characterized practical criticism.

Suffice it to say for the moment—we shall return later to the new marxism—that without a working concept of writing capable of distinguishing in even the most preliminary way between 'literary' or 'poetic' on the one hand, and 'ordinary' or 'referential' or communicative uses of language on the other, we have no way of distinguishing those linguistic constructs which are fictive and ideological from those which are non-fictive and non-ideological, or of telling literary texts from the 'historical documents' that are supposed to be

---

[8] See Macherey, *A Theory of Literary Production*, trans. Geoffrey Wall (London: Routledge and Kegan Paul, 1978); Terry Eagleton, *Marxism and Literary Criticism* (London, Methuen, 1976) and *Criticism and Ideology* (London: New Left Books, 1976). For sympathetic discussion and critique, see Catherine Belsey, *Critical Practice* (London: Methuen, 1980), and John Frow, 'Structuralist Marxism', *Southern Review*, xv. 2 (July 1982), pp. 208–17.

ultimately able to 'explain' them. Without such a theory of language and textuality, we doom ourselves to the absurd labour of explaining the subjective and deceptive by the equally subjective and deceptive and leave ourselves without a reliable frame or ground of reference against which the potential extravagances of textuality can be recognized and read as such. In the absence of such a ground distinction, there is nothing to prevent my writing off Eagleton's re-plotting of 'the great tradition' as the fiction or fantasy of a special interest group pursuing its own institutional promotion and political power in the name of something high and noble, in the same way Eagleton writes off Leavis's. The moment 'history' is recognized as 'discourse-specific', as having no location outside language, i.e. as neither past nor present nor even the presence of a past, but as a *myth* of presence, a *mediation*, it ceases to be a reliable *ground* for literary criticism, let alone for political action, since a mediation can never be a ground but only a problem, an occasion for more discourse. At the same time, I would have to write off or at least bracket off my own deprivileging of the Leavisite ideology of the text as a late displacement of puritanism, a re-plotting of the pilgrim's progress in secular literary terms, on the same lack of 'grounds', since the status of the critical texts on which it is 'based', not to mention that of the present text which bears ambiguous witness to them, remains precarious.

The foregoing argument, even in so summary a form, will be recognizable as 'deconstructionist' or 'textualist', and reflects the view of marxism's mighty opposite within contemporary literary theory. The extreme language-scepticism of deconstruction casts a cold eye on any critical enterprise that seeks access to the constructs of history and society while bypassing direct confrontation with the difficulties and duplicities of their textual mode of existence. Yet paradoxically, it was out of a recognition of the central importance of linguistic structures for the study of culture that all emergent modes of contemporary criticism, marxist as well as decon-structionist, may be said to have arisen. That common provenance was structuralism, the multidisciplinary move-ment of the fifties and sixties which sought nothing less than a methodology formed on the model of linguistics for all the human sciences. In the writings of Lévi-Strauss, Althusser, Lacan, and Foucault, methodological strategies were developed with the aim of correcting the distortions of ethnocentricity, ideology, the metaphysics of the self that mystify the study of society, history, and the mind, and arriving at their 'objective' structures. These 'objective' structures were conceived on the analogy of the linguistic structures of grammar and syntax that underlie the system of language, the enabling and conditioning structures which the chatter and noise of everyday speech, the 'knowledge-effects' of conventional wisdom, simultaneously depend on, point to, and conceal.

There is, then, an 'interested' component in our unprocessed understanding of human and social phenomena, oriented toward the political action—or inaction—of maintaining the status quo, of passing off the historical formations of discourse and culture as the eternally 'given' forms of nature. This ideological aspect of cultural texts, which bears analogy to the suasive and deceptive processes of rhetorical figuration in language, is therefore to be methodically mistrusted and reconstituted through a 'theoretical practice', subjected to the demystifying law of system, in order that their objective meaning can be extrapolated and true knowledge released from the mystified form in which it meets the naïve but uninnocent eye.[9] This multidisciplinary attempt to read cultural texts in a way that strips them of the ideological vested interests in which they come packaged, and which traditional bourgeois interpretation only reinforces, held obvious appeal for a marxist tradition originating in a demystifying materialism and committed to cultural change. The methodical procedures enabling the texts that constitute cultural history to be translated into an object-language,

---

[9] The terms 'knowledge-effects' and 'theoretical practice', though specific to the work of Louis Althusser (see note 19 below), could be extended to designate the cultural raw materials and the mode of its intellectual processing within structuralism generally. Within the already vast literature of and on structuralism, Fredric Jameson's *The Prison-House of Language* (Princeton: Princeton University Press, 1972) still seems to me the sharpest general discussion. On the ways in which structuralist methodology was adopted or co-opted by marxist and psychoanalytic schools of thought, see Alan Sheridan, *Michel Foucault: The Will to Truth* (London: Tavistock, 1980), pp. 195–226.

whose meaning could be reliably and unequivocally read, seemed tailor-made for a marxism ever ready to ground its vision of social progress on the claim to objective, materialist, scientific truth. The structuralist destabilization of the meaning of the text as held in place by an unself-conscious but disingenuous bourgeois tradition of interpretation thus provided a new potential and means for the restabilization of the meaning of the text on systematic, objective, and (in the marxist version) materialist principles.

As long as the texts under scrutiny were 'cultural' in the broadest sense, that is to say, the relatively unself-conscious products of a society that could regard itself as nature or 'second nature'—historical documents, myths, the mass media, even fashion or cuisine—the methods developed by structural linguistics for the study of 'natural languages, could be applied with some promise of objective results. After all, such social constructs could be plausibly if not perfectly, likened to the constructs of 'natural languages', with their implicit norms of competence and performance, and both could be plausibly likened, in turn, to the natural world that forms the object of scientific investigation. The underlying laws, the regulating syntax, the conditions of meaning that govern those systems of exchange beneath superficially idiosyncratic, tendentious, and ideological appearances could then be methodically extrapolated. Such an approach, based as it was on a series of analogies that are by no means identities, was not without problems, of which its practitioners were not unaware. But it was only when structuralism turned its attention in the early sixties to literary texts, stretching still further the chain of analogy on which it had always depended, that the limitations of the method became apparent as never before.

What stance was the earnest investigator to adopt before a body of texts, especially but by no means exclusively modernist or 'writerly' texts, that flaunt their *unnaturalness*, a textual mode in which linguistic deviation is conspicuously cultivated and rhetorical extravagance the self-advertised norm? Given such a complex literary system—second-order in relation to ordinary language, and third-order in relation to previous literature—could its conditioning and governing laws ever be realiably objectified or consensually formalized? Can a system that thrives on self-conscious figuration ever be fully disfigured and reduced, by any conceivable series of operations, to the status of a natural, given, or literal object? Where does the process of reconstituting the text so as to reveal the laws of its functioning, once activated by structuralist method, logically come to rest? Where, given the text's origin in the figurative, i.e. generative, potential of language, does it even begin? Could not the 'object-language' which purports to be the goal and product of that method, be subjected in turn to a further operation, through which its supposed objectivity would be put into question?

Here the characteristic marxist move to return the text to history as its ground, to demystify the 'literary' text by revealing it as the product of material determinants, is of no help: for what is that 'history' but another figurative, rhetorical construct, capable in turn of still further demystification? At what point, in fine, does the process of destabilizing or denaturalizing ideological acceptations become aware of *its own rhetoricality*, of the inescapable figuration of its own methods, manœuvres, and meanings? In so far as its own constructs are made of language, and language is not a material object except at the initial level of the signifier, are not all methodological procedures susceptible to a destabilization and demystification that never ceases the moment they begin their march on signified meaning? Can any technology of the text, marxist or structuralist, ever attain the status of a hermeneutics of the text without participating in the metaphysics of traditional interpretation, the metaphor-making built into language, the exorcism of which had motivated and justified its invention? These questions, though unanswered, are not merely rhetorical, and I shall address them at greater length in the chapters that follow. Suffice it to say for the moment that they become most peremptory and perplexing for structuralist method in general, and its marxist version in particular, at the point of confrontation with literary language. In that confrontation, the object of intended demystification displays its full capacity to demystify its would-be demystifiers, to reveal their supposedly objective procedures as yet another mystification.

IV. FROM PHILOLOGY TO THEORY

In drawing attention to the founding presupposition of recent structuralist and marxist theories—that some discourse (namely their own) can transcend the rhetorical duplicities of idealism and ideology—and to the special power of literary language to reveal the vulnerability of that presupposition, I realize I am laying myself open to the charges, by now familiar and ever-ready, of aestheticism and élitism. To maintain 'literature' as a category apart, existing in hygenic— and sterile—isolation from all other verbal and non-verbal experience is to risk returning its study to the ivory-towered domain of a mandarin academic class. I could be—no doubt will be, given the slipperiness of discourse and the free-play of interpretability that I am arguing to be inescapable—accused of perpetuating, under the guise. of an avant-garde methodology, the most regressive aspects of practical and new criticism: its squeamishness before historical and social change, and withdrawal into a precious self-enclosure. Whether conceived as describing 'life', as it once was, or being inscribed by 'life', as it now is, it does not seem possible any longer to regard 'literature' as a category apart. After all, to maintain the integrity and autonomy of literary language, would mean embodying that category in a canon of texts, which would have to be the invention of some institution or group, the product of an undeniably social and political decision. To deny the political nature of canon-formation could only smack of an anachronistic essentialism in which the category of literary language was an eternal and universal given, its embodiment in a particular canon the merest concession, at most a token gesture, to history, a spectral historicism indeed. And why would we wish to do so, when it was precisely our dissatisfaction with just such an ideology of the text that moved us to re-examine our new-critical predispositions in the first place?

To answer that question, let us turn once again to history and inspect more closely the process that has led to our present pass (or impasse), the specialization, in Raymond Williams's term, of literature 'towards imaginative writing, within the basic assumptions of Romanticism.' And having already expressed doubts, by no means unique or original, about the rhetorical disinterestedness of historical constructs, I can scarcely claim for the one I am about to outline exemption from the pathos of that ineluctable dubiety. All that I can do is try to make its own vested interests explicit and test its credit with the body whose story it purports to trace: the interpretive community itself. A poor and divided thing perhaps, but our own, and the only body available to pronounce on it. Its pronouncement, moreover, will not be—according to my own argument—on its truth or validity in any absolute or trans-historical sense, but owing to the diversity of its own interests, on the value and utility of this historical account for its own future development. So it is very much a history in brackets that is offered. Whether that is as it should be, it is only as it can be, since it can lie with no other body than the existing institution of literary study to project the form of its own survival within the community at large and the social pressures that derive from it. And to judge from the rhetoric of crisis that has come to seem inseparable from criticism itself over the past decade, nothing less than its survival seems to be at issue.

When it began in the nineteenth century, the study of European vernacular literature modelled itself on the long-established study of Biblical and classical texts, taking over the methods of its precursors, while adapting them to new aims.[10] That is to say, its method was historical and philological, regarding the texts it addressed as documents in the history of a culture and a language, while its aim was to contribute to a new-found sense of modern European national identity. The study of vernacular literature, according to the century's foremost literary historians from Herder to Taine, was ultimately bound up with 'race, milieu, and moment'. What gradually emerged from this initial phase of historical and philological inquiry was a contradiction. In scrutinizing the historical and philological aspects of vernacular texts, scholars became aware, some intensely and obsessively aware, of patterns of meaning and form that transcended or eluded

[10] See D. J. Palmer, *The Rise of English Studies* (New York: Oxford University Press, 1965). Several of the essays in *Re-Reading English*, ed. Peter Widdowson (London: Methuen, 1982) offer an alternative, i.e. marxist, account of this institutional history.

specification in terms of 'race, milieu, moment' or national language, patterns that seemed capable of being described as universal. The texts under study, or some of them, seemed to inscribe a language that spoke to their readers in an autonomous idiom that, while it engaged personal and ethical issues, transcended the English, French, German, or Russian in which these texts were written. To such readers—as diverse as Victor Shklovsky, F. R. Leavis, and Cleanth Brooks— something like a *language of literature* seemed to exist in these texts, a language whose forms could be codified and whose meanings communicated to the humblest individual, however unerudite in history or philology he might be. The ultimate embodiment of this realization was the discipline of General and Comparative Literature, heir to the linguistic and national compartmentalization of literary study earlier institutionalized in the *MLA*.

At that point, literary criticism entered its hermeneutic or interpretive phase. The 'language of literature', whether conceived as a language of 'defamiliarization', 'realization' and 'enactment', or 'paradox, irony, and ambiguity', was hypostatized into an eternal and universal essence, which was in turn canonized into a tradition of texts which embodied that essence most purely, which were in turn regarded as objects offering resistance to interpreting subjects, who in turn methodically read out of them more or less personal, more or less communal meanings, for the enrichment and understanding of 'life'. This burgeoning activity was known in England and America as 'practical' and 'new' criticism respectively, and gradually came to dominate the increasingly institutionalized study of literature in schools and universities, as well as the editorial policies of the learned journals and academic publishers, previously given to historical and philological scholarship, to the point where a given author's works became the objects of numerous critical studies. A new paradigm for literary research was firmly in place.

It is important to note that the older historical and philological preoccupations were not altogether abandoned, but rather were carried over into the hermeneutic phase, in more subtle forms. The older concern with texts as documenting linguistic and cultural development was sublated in the

Leavisite preoccupation with canon-formation and great traditions, based on implicit myths of historical development and decline, of the special cultural conditions that were supposed to bring literature of eternal value into being. The best illustration of this implicit historicism is the organicist myth of 'unified sensibility' that underwrites Leavis's and the new critics' promotion of metaphysical and demotion of romantic poetry. The Leavisite version of Henry James's pronouncement that 'it takes a lot of history to make a little literature' (this might serve as slogan for the philological phase) was modified into the principle that 'it takes special historical conditions to make any literature at all.'

At the height of the hermeneutic or interpretive phase of the development of literary studies, which I would date in the early to mid-sixties to coincide with the emergence of Fryean and French structuralist poetics, new contradictions became apparent and a new restlessness began to be felt. These took the form of an informed and reflective dissatisfaction with interpretation itself. Perhaps it could only have occurred as the by-product of the vast institutionalized industry that interpretation had become, but amid all that busy productivity, a certain doubt came to be felt, often by its most gifted practitioners, concerning the apparent haphazardness of the process by which the meaning of literary texts was divined and promulgated. How could such a vast establishment have grown up around so intuitive, unsystematic, and unverifiable a set of attitudes and operations? With so many interpretations of the same canonical texts abroad in the land, all jostling for place and competing for acceptance, how could one or another be established as more valid than its rivals? What with the same texts being interpreted and reinterpreted, a certain wearisome repetition came to seem inseparable from the process of interpretation itself, its moves and procedures having become increasingly familiar and predictable but no more verifiable. Critics began to write 'against interpretation' and to project hopes of going 'beyond' the dominant formalism.

At first, this discontent took the form of avant-garde journalism, as in Susan Sontag's essays of the early sixties, but it would soon take more academic, even pseudo-scientific forms. The need to test those procedures or discover new ones began to be felt, and the redirection of critical attention to neglected, unfamiliar, or 'sub-literary' texts offered itself as one means of doing so, if only as a way of clarifying to ourselves what we had been so busily and often blindly engaged in doing for so long. All this is implicit in Frye's *Anatomy of Criticism*, with its promise of systematic totalization. The idea of a canon of literature, for so long the unquestioned pretext and justification for all this questionable activity, now came into question. A new demand for scientific or philosophical rigour, whether to be sought in structural linguistics, marxist historicism, or phenomenological critique, as a control upon the subjectivity and ideology that had unwittingly vitiated our too familiar habits of interpretation, entered the discourse. Literary studies had entered upon its theoretical phase.

V. THE TRIUMPH OF THEORY

This latest transition from a hermeneutic to a semiotic conception of the subject, which coincides roughly with the decade of the seventies, was of course accompanied by acute institutional anxiety and marked by a new rhetoric of crisis. Beneath the polemical exchanges between avant-garde schools and movements, not to mention new and old guard within particular departments—exchanges, that is, that occurred at every level of institutional life, from the pages of the learned journals to the appointments committees of universities (the MacCabe affair at Cambridge was only a belated, if spectacular, instance of a process of ideological infighting long since under way in Paris and New Haven)—beneath these superficial tremors, a profound institutional upheaval was indeed occurring. The shift involved nothing less than the promotion of literary theory from a peripheral to a central and commanding status within the discipline. Literary theory had of course been around for some time. René Wellek, W. K. Wimsatt, and Northrop Frye—all of whom I have identified with various aspects of the hermeneutic phase—had all written books of literary theory. The difference between the older and the newer theorizing is that the former conceived and represented itself as a logical formulation of the principles underlying a literary-critical practice already in place and operating on an accepted canon of 'literary texts'; the latter as the logical foundation or prescription for a new and revolutionary practice that would put the very notion of 'literature' into question. Theory of literature had given way to theory of criticism.

Theory was now to be reinvented for the purpose of displacing a critical practice that had got out of hand in its wayward empiricism and happy-go-lucky intuitiveness and replacing it with something more philosophically demanding or scientifically austere. As far back as the late fifties, Northrop Frye had already likened contemporary criticism to a mystery-religion without a gospel, or to chemistry in its alchemical stage. Anglo-American evangelists of structuralist poetics like Jonathan Culler were fond of quoting these dicta as prefigurations of the sweet science finally and fully revealed in their own theoretical gospel. There were even older prophets of this new and grateful hegemony of theory. The marxists, die-hard avatars of a positively enlightenment rationalism and perennial defenders of the scientific nature of their enterprise, could hardly have done other than invest heavily in the theoretical bull-market. Had not Marx, the founder himself, rewriting Kant, written that 'practice without theory is blind'? The complementary clause seemed at the time less relevant: 'theory without practice is empty.' It was during this heady period too that 'empiricism', usually preceded by the epithet 'Anglo-Saxon' or 'Anglo-American', became a term of disdain. After all, if you had the right paradigm, the particulars would take care of themselves, for all practical purposes fall into place.[11] (For the new discipline was paying increased attention to the history and philosophy of science as an alter ego or role model for itself.) Since when has a paradigm, from that of Ptolemy to that of Einstein,

---

[11] The concept of the 'paradigm', or dominant institutional and epistemological model determining the nature of research at a given historical moment, is advanced by Thomas S. Kuhn, *The Structure of Scientific Revolutions* (Chicago: University of Chicago Press, 1962). As a means of understanding the structure of a discipline and its discourse, the 'paradigm', along with Michel Foucault's analogous concept of the 'episteme', has played a major role in recent literary theory, and will be discussed more fully in the following chapters, particularly Chapter Three.

failed to discover or generate the particulars to fill itself out?

For what was at stake was the capacity of theory, not merely to describe, not even to control and correct, but to dictate practice, to *prescribe* it in the fullest sense of the word. And by the end of the decade, to judge from book-titles, attendances at *MLA* panels, the titles and table of contents of learned (and some not-so-learned) journals, the battle had been all but won, the triumph of theory assured. Theory, that is, had established itself as not only a legitimate literary-critical activity, but as its guiding light. Hardly more than the mopping-up action now seems to remain of bringing the few wayward practical interpreters, not to mention the odd, regressive reader, into one or another theoretical camp. Or short of such total control, at least to get them to load every rift of their practice (if practice they must) with the rich ore of theory, now widely available in the form of brief, inexpensive paperback introductions to all the once avant-garde movements. For the various theories that comprise theory, no longer battling each other for precedence with an all but religious sense of rectitude and mission, have reached concordat. The field having been won, our theoretical schools now seem content to divide the spoils of an expanding market of students and their teachers. The question pressing on the young academic or graduate student, as he stands perplexed before the array of polysyllabic titles on the shelves of his university bookstore, is no longer whether or not to go theoretical but which theory to go with.

VI. THE TWO FACES OF POSTSTRUCTURALISM

By the early seventies, then, the handwriting was already on the institutional wall, its message clear to the sharp-eyed interpreter: 'In this sign (i.e. the sign of theory [i.e. the theory of signs]), thou shalt conquer.' Somewhere within the polysyllabic patois of an emerging poststructuralism lay the potent 'open sesame' which would unlock the secrets of the world's textuality. But it was also becoming clear that this poststructuralism, for all its promise, was something of an umbrella term covering a number of distinct developments, and begging a number of questions. What these developments have in common, and perhaps justifies the shared label, despite their different ambitions, was the conceptual and terminological inheritance of structuralism. It might appear, for example, that Derrida's or de Man's tricky hyper-reflections on texts, and Foucault's metadiscursive archaeologies of discourse, not to mention the works of their numerous followers, march to the sounds of different drummers. The work of Foucault, with its relentless exposure of the will to power within the will to knowledge, is nothing if not political in its implications, however elusive or unprogrammatic Foucault's own politics may be. The work of Derrida and his Yale associates, by contrast, in its single-minded concentration on the duplicities of language and textuality, is usually regarded as explicitly a- or post-political, whatever political quiescence or conservatism such an attitude may imply, so that superficially, poststructuralism seems to present at least two distinct family resemblances: the deconstructive textualism centred at Yale, and the political contextualism to be found in various manifestations almost everywhere else. These types of poststructuralism can be assigned not only different presiding, patriarchal geniuses but opposed rubrics for their activities: for the former, Derrida's dictum that '*il n'y a pas de hors-texte*' ('there is nothing outside the text');[12] for the latter, the slogan—I do not know whether any critic has actually written it, but it would be surprising indeed if one has not—that 'all texts are political.'

The foregoing authorless, or at least unattributed, statement illustrates, in precisely its authorlessness, at least one common point of departure, and perhaps a common destination, of these two apparently antithetical types of poststructuralist theory. That is the attack on the traditional conceptions of authorship, authority, and the authorial self, which is part and parcel of the notion of intertextuality. If sources and origins can never be fixed in the flux of discursive formations or the freeplay of infinite textuality, if the author himself is only an intersection of texts or discourses, the concept of author becomes meaningless. The obvious precedent for this attack is to be found in structuralist approaches to such

[12] Jacques Derrida, *Of Grammatology*, trans. Gayatri Chakravorty Spivack (Baltimore: Johns Hopkins University Press, 1976), p. 158.

authorless constructs as language and myth, where a socially generative or productive power seems to operate above or beyond or through the individual author, or at least, *the romantic and post-romantic conception of authorship does not seem to apply*. One may use the language to coin neologisms, but to the extent that neologisms work only by analogy with known and familiar forms—otherwise, no neologism could be understood —can one be said to *author* them? Similarly with myth, one may write, like Sophocles, a version of the Oedipus myth, but it seems to be in the nature of myth that it precede and survive any particular version of it. In that sense, it consumes or eclipses its individual authors and puts into question the idea of authorship itself. Lévi-Strauss even goes so far, in his classic essay on the Oedipus myth, as to identify the myth not with any preferred or privileged version of it but with nothing less than the sum total of all its versions.[13]

The implication is that as long as a myth remains culturally alive, its authorship is somehow collective; that is, cultural authority and individual authorship seem to be inversely related. This is not really a surprising principle, given the pre-literate nature of the social texts that form the object of study for structural anthropology: oral narratives, rituals, games, kinship structures, social customs. Authorship is a liminal and problematic concept in Homeric Greece or medieval Europe, where anonymity in the arts was the norm; it becomes important only retrospectively, from the viewpoint of the literate cultures that succeeded. The attribution of certain poems to Homer (as distinct from Sophocles) or even to Chaucer (as distinct from Milton; Shakespeare is a transitional case), is belated, post-literate, and still highly problematic. 'The notion of the author', Foucault wrote, 'constitutes a strong moment of individualization in the history of ideas, knowledge, and literature, as well as in the history of philosophy and science.'[14] It is also inseparable, as Foucault

---

[13] See Claude Lévi-Strauss, *Structural Anthropology*, trans. Claire Jacobson and Brooke Grundfest Schoepf (London: Allen Lane, 1968), pp. 206–18. 'Myth is the part of language', writes Lévi-Strauss, 'where the formula *traduttore, tradittore* reaches its lowest truth value. From that point of view it should be placed in the gamut of linguistic expressions at the end opposite to that of poetry . . .' (p. 210).

[14] Michel Foucault, 'What is an Author?' in *Textual Strategies*, ed. Josué V. Harari (London: Methuen, 1979), pp. 141–60.

was well aware, from the invention of writing, and *a fortiori*, of printing.

Poststructuralism, in both its textualist and contextualist variants, may be seen as the extension, *mutatis mutandis*, into the domain of post-literate culture of some of the characteristic manœuvres developed by structuralism for the study of pre-literate cultures. One such manœuvre is the attempt to disjoin authority, in the sense of official or socially legitimate power, from authorship (individual power or influence deriving from knowledge) and disperse it into an impersonal and collective intertextuality, whether that intertextuality is conceived as a function of language and writing, or of the discursive formations and conformations of institutions and ideologies. The former, textualist intertextuality follows upon the Heideggerian notion of language as that which speaks us rather than, or at least as much as, that which we speak. A given text is determined, indeed overdetermined, by other texts, from which it has no independent existence. There is no text 'in itself'. This phenomenon of intertextuality has so far generated two distinctive descriptions. In its 'Parisian' version, by which I refer to the work published by Roland Barthes and Jacques Derrida in the late sixties and seventies, texts resemble so many Pacific islands in a vast coral reef of textuality, all outwardly distinct yet uncertainly connected with and supported by each other in an elaborate submarine network.

For Harold Bloom, by contrast, the text is the battleground of Oedipal agon, the hard-won or hard-lost site of an ever-problematic selfhood and originality, the place where three or more than three roads meet.[15] Whereas the writerly text for Barthes is a blissful surrender of the authorial self to the irresistible siege of textuality, for Bloom it is characterized by an anxious resistance to the infiltrations and betrayals of a burdensome, domineering, even castrating tradition and enveloping contemporaneity. So for Bloom something like an older romantic conception of authorship, is still possible, even if, as the product of consuming struggle, it is deeply problematic, fraught with losses as well as gains. For Bloom,

[15] Bloom's theory of poetic influence or 'misprision' has unfolded through a continuing series of books and articles beginning with *The Anxiety of Influence* (New York: Oxford University Press, 1973).

and to some extent for all his Yale colleagues, the author is no longer a definitive source of meaning, but a site of contending meanings. Yet there is a dignity and prestige in this agon. Still viable too is the traditional conception of a canon or great tradition, or in Bloom's terms, 'line of vision'. Dr Johnson is as much Bloom's strong precursor as Freud or Frye. After all, the battle for emergence as self and poet in Bloom, though gloomy, hard-fought, and doubtful, is always all in the family, whereas for the late Barthes and Derrida the family is so extended as to risk the collapse of any permanent or ultimate distinction between the literary and the non-literary text. By the time Barthes, for example, has exposed the multiple 'codes' of realism on which 'Sarrasine' depends and which it manipulates or scrambles, it is an open question whether Balzac's novella can be considered different in kind from other—traditionally regarded as lesser—formulations of those codes.

Even more explicitly (though not necessarily more profoundly) anti-authorial and anti-canonical than textualist intertextuality in any of its versions is contextualist intertextuality. This too takes many forms, or as its adherents prefer to say, 'formations', the latter term suggesting a man-made historical construct while the former smacks of an eternal platonic essence, 'essences' being the bane of this school's existence. If 'all texts are political', i.e. products or inscriptions of the discursive formations of institutions and ideologies, that is, the site of a political rather than personal or familial power struggle, then claims on behalf of a category of literary language, and the canon of texts that embodies it, represent no more than the will-to-power of an interest group—be it a class, a gender, a race, or a clerisy.

This knowledge carries with it its own potential power, and issues in interpretations bearing in turn the stamp of their own discursive formation (be it marxist, feminist, or whatever) and attempting to make their own intervention on its behalf. Apprised as he is of the text's own political designs—all texts are, after all, political—the politicized reader can still gain the upper hand over the text in the power game that reading has now become, can turn (as in Aikido) the text's force against itself, can rough it up, so to speak, until it says what is ideologically required by the interpreter's community. For whatever the text's *apparent* politics, it can always be made over, through certain devices we shall inspect more closely in a later chapter, into the mouthpiece for the reader's own politics. Even such apparently aloof or well-bred texts as *Paradise Lost, Clarissa, Middlemarch,* or *The Waste Land,* sophisticated in technique and canonical in standing as they are, can still be made the spokesman of interests quite alien to those usually ascribed to its author. The process is one of systematic misconstruction, a kind of textual harassment.

At this point, the contextualist assault on authorship and canonicity joins forces with the textualist. If the text has no existence 'in itself', independent of its interpretations or misinterpretations, but exists only within a discursive formation or ideological configuration, and if both text and interpretation are the product of power relations, then the 'correct' interpretation is nothing other than that which expresses the vested interests of the powers that be, of the 'authorities'. Might makes right. Rhetoric, central to the formal preoccupation of textualism, thus regains a new prestige for contextualism as well, since the misconstructed meaning of a text now stands or falls only on the persuasive power, numbers, and aggressiveness of its partisans. In fairness to those whose work I have designated textualist, it should be emphasized that I am describing not so much their own practice but the use to which their practice has been put by more politically determined critics. When Roland Barthes employs political metaphors of insurrection and assassination at the end of 'The Death of the Author',[16] he is motivated by the explicit desire to protect the open-endedness of writing and reading, however readily his work can be enlisted in an ideological power struggle between tyrant authors and insurgent readers. Nor do the processes of political misconstruction have much to do with those of 'strong misprision', as described by Harold Bloom, by means of which poets wrest from the work of their precursors newly or potentially canonical texts and their own claim to authority.

By contrast, the thrust of political misconstruction is anti-

[16] *Image-Music-Text*, trans. Stephen Heath (New York: Hill and Wang, 1977), pp. 142–8.

authorial and anti-canonical. Its aim is the carnivalization of the canon, by means of which literary study turns into a free-for-all, in which the high are brought low and the low upraised, the hegemony of authors and canons and the 'essentialist thinking' that holds them in place overturned to make room—for what? For the writerly fluidity of a Barthes, the post-romantic agonism of a Bloom, the learned scepticism of a Foucault? Or for a new hegemony of the political, in effect as 'essentialist' and totalitarian as the old formalism it would replace, with its older hegemony of authors and canons? Though advanced under the banner of de-essentializing the concept of literature by re-historicizing and politicizing it, contextualist criticism repeatedly falls into the very attitudes it condemns in the older and newer textualism. When the marxist/feminist critic claims that 'all texts are political', he or she is *not* saying that all texts are available to or susceptible of a political approach. Who would take issue with that? Political readings of texts are commonplace indeed in the history of interpretive practice. Nor would the purest deconstructive textualist, by his own principles, disagree. What he would challenge is that a political—or historical, or psychological, or philological—approach to texts constitutes literary criticism at all, let alone a privileged or valid form of criticism.[17]

But that is not, as we have begun to see, the rhetorical implication of the slogan. On hearing that all texts are political, we are meant—are we not?—to understand with the force of revelation that something fundamental to textuality itself has been disclosed: to wit, that texts are not merely *susceptible* to political readings, but that texts, as political products themselves, *demand* political reading. Politics, in sum, is *of the essence* of textuality, and those who ignore this in their critical practice do so at peril of being stigmatized as remiss, culpable, reactionary, or simply as having missed the point. It follows that those texts to which attention repeatedly returns

[17] See, for example, Paul de Man, *Blindness and Insight* (New York: Oxford University Press, 1971), p. 8: 'In periods that are not periods of crisis, or in individuals bent on avoiding crisis at all cost, there can be all kinds of approaches to literature: historical, philological, psychological, etc., but there can be no criticism. For such periods or individuals will never put the act of writing into question by relating it to its specific intent.'

in enlightened (i.e. politicized) critical practice will eventually and inevitably have special claims made for them as epitomizing textuality itself, much as the poems of Donne were once thought to epitomize poeticity with their paradoxical wit.

The novels of X or Y are more overtly, or more profoundly political (i.e. better) than the poems of Z. Gradually, a new or regained authority will be conferred on these writers, and a new or reconstituted canon will emerge. We have seen such a process at work over the past decade in the quickened attention paid to such writers as Conrad, the Brontës, and Virginia Woolf—all of whom, incidentally and ironically, had strong claims made for them before colonialism and feminism became fashionable topics. This institutional process (if my account of it rings any bells at all) looks uncannily like the essentialist thinking about literature it was supposed to supersede, a new essentialism having simply replaced the old. Have the exponents of popular culture, of women's or black or colonial writing been able to refrain from forming their own counter-canons and exalting their own shadow 'authors'? It makes little sense to rule out as 'essentialist' the claims of a canon formed on a presumption of intrinsic 'literariness' only to replace it with a new one formed on the presumption of intrinsic 'politicality'.

A similar pattern of relapse into vilified ways can be observed in the manœuvres of deconstructive textualism, particularly in its increasingly routinized forms. Derridean textualism was conceived as a critique—and transcendence— of the metaphysics of presence supposed to imprison European thought, the logocentric, ultimately religious, superstitious, or nostalgic, impulse to ground or centre discourse in an originary author, response in a unitary subject, and textuality on a re-presentable world, when all are nothing other than effects and functions of linguistic differences. That unforecloseable difference or deferral (*différance*) is what is apparently· closed, but actually only occluded or repressed, in speech as opposed to writing, where difference is foregrounded. Hence the supposed privileging from Plato onward of speech over writing, when it is actually writing, with its foregrounding of *différance*, that offers a model for the way all language (including speech) works. Similarly with systems of thought, such as materialism or empiricism, that attempt illicitly to privilege their own claim to grasp or represent 'reality' over that of some opponent system, such as 'idealism'.

Such myths of metaphysical or materialist presence can be deconstructed in terms of the linguistic difference on which they rest but which they conceal from themselves. For the materialist, for example, the concept of the subjective 'self', worse yet the 'free individual', is a bourgeois mystification, a metaphor that works to obscure the actual, i.e. material determinations that constitute all individuals in society, a sign that must be decoded into its 'real' meaning. For the 'idealist', by contrast, these material determinants are themselves metaphors, signs, or symbols whose meaning is a moral or psychological selfhood more 'real' than its material manifestations, much as in an earlier religious or neo-Platonic system the soul's reality outweighed its material incarnation. In each case, it could be argued, it is language, the system of differences and oppositions that constitutes a particular discourse, that is determining the nature of the object of study, rather than the object that determines the nature of the discipline and discourse: 'There is nothing outside the text.' Does man speak language or language speak man?

Yet this critique of metaphysics, so boldly avant-garde in its understanding of the indirections of writing and textuality, bears an uncanny resemblance to some of the oldest, most flagrantly metaphysical and religious notions of poetic composition. For the idea that language speaks us goes back beyond Heidegger, Derrida's immediate 'source', indeed beyond Freud, for whom our deepest selves are revealed not in the language we consciously manipulate but in the uncanny wisdom of that language which speaks us: the puns, slips, malapropisms of joke, dream, and fantasy. The idea goes all the way back to Plato and Homer, for whom poetic composition, like prophecy, was anything but a matter of authorial intent present to itself—*pace* Derrida—but rather a matter of semi-involuntary possession from without. Whether the 'muse' is conceived as divine prompter or simply as a memory device for poetic tradition, the role of the poet as a humble mediator of an authority much larger than and exterior to himself, a role to which he is 'called' or has thrust upon him, is very ancient indeed. While such a conception of the poet's role contrasts dramatically with the post-romantic conception of original authorship, it is not very far from the understanding of Derrida and the textualists of all writing as a kind of ghost-writing, be the ghost the 'absent presence' (the phrase is Sir Philip Sidney's) of epic or lyric convention or that of language itself. Nor is the concept of the world as book, of a textuality without walls, a new concept when enunciated by Mallarmé; it is one of the oldest commonplaces of Christian and Greek thought.[18] The newest theory seems also to be one of the oldest.

VII. BRIGHT PARADIGMS, OR THE THEORY OF THEORY

My purpose in pointing out textualism's—and contextualism's—affinities with older, now vilified modes of thought is not to confute or invalidate them. For that would be to admit the assumption that the 'mystifications' that recent theory seeks to transcend—essentialism, metaphysics, idealism, authorship, the canon—are the wretched things they are held to be and ought to be put behind us as quickly as possible. On the contrary, that view seems to me itself a mystification, though not a despicable one, since I do not believe it would be undesirable to emerge into the pure good of theory, if only it could be done. My scepticism, however, tells me that it cannot, and my pragmatism tells me that this is not altogether regretable, since our burden of mystification has not prevented learned and intelligent people from saying and writing learned and intelligent things—of both a textualist and contextualist kind—about the books they read, or if you prefer, read them, and this without benefit or warranty of recent theory, and indeed while labouring under that burden.

Does it matter whether Shakespeare is regarded as a person, an empirical or biographical self, who 'created' or 'crafted' his plays out of the diverse raw materials, textual and contextual, available to him, or as a point of intersection or space of interaction of equally diverse economic, ideological, and linguistic formations and forces? From either point of

[18] See E. R. Curtius, 'The Book of Nature', *European Literature and the Latin Middle Ages*, tr. Willard R. Trask (Princeton: Princeton University Press, 1953), pp. 319–26.

departure, the study of those texts printed (by virtue of western bibliographical, economic, and ideological structures) under the name of Shakespeare will lead in many different directions, involve countless complex relations and irresolvable issues, and lead (on those issues and relations regarded at a particular moment as most peremptory) to no definitive theoretical principles but to a great deal of rich and wayward interpretive practice. Unless it really were possible to specify 'objectively' the myriad texts and contexts (each determined by myriad texts and contexts) which constitute the image or illusion of the 'personal' author and to which he is subject, as well as the precise way in which he is constituted and subject, there is little positive gain in doing away with that notion and calling it an outmoded mystification. Except, of course, the work the new project occasions and the energy it generates to perform it. But unless the mystification 'Shakespeare' can be replaced by an economic or ideological or linguistic explanatory system with a genuine claim to completeness and precision, we are still in the realm of mystification, and on that criterion, might as well hang on to 'Shakespeare'. To my knowledge, no such systematic reduction of authorship to inter- or con-textuality, despite all our theorizing towards it, has achieved anything like consensual acceptance, though it has generated a great deal of debate and polemic.

This is not surprising, since the role and status of the author are always a function of cultural ideology, as is the attack on the author now being mounted under the banner of theory. Within western culture, the name 'Shakespeare' has functioned innocently enough as the signifier of a corpus of texts—though even here there is the taint of private property—and less innocently as the signified of those texts, the controlling consciousness to which they seem to give access, or which they bring to mind, as we attend to them. At a moment in history correlative, as Foucault and many others have reminded us, with the rise of empiricism, mercantilism, puritanism, and individualism—and coinciding with Shakespeare's career—the consciousness inhabiting a text began to be individualized and privatized in complicity with these larger movements into that of the author. This moment of individualization in the history of ideas marked the upward mobility, in every sense, of the author, and in the case of Shakespeare, issued by the end of the nineteenth century in the full flowering of 'bardolatry'. (The simultaneous emergence of a 'disintegrationist' textual scholarship and various anti-Stratfordian cults, both of which attempted to parcel out Shakespeare's texts to other candidates, in no way contradicts this historical account, since each ascribes the same monumental prestige and centrality to authorship.) This process of canonization had the unfortunate effect of transfiguring Shakespeare—and other authors in varying degrees—into a kind of world-cultural object, a transcendent form of extra-textual life, a life of allegory whose works were the comments on it. The author had become an extra- or supra-interpretive reference-point, an independent origin and autonomous source of the creative decisions that had issued in his texts, and to which our own interpretive decisions concerning their meaning could be referred in order to validate them or overrule those of other commentators.

All this might seem in retrospect an inversion or perversion of our actual experience of reading, in which the author is a function, rather than the determinant, of the text. And so it is by the lights of contemporary literary theory. But because 'our actual experience of reading' is not value-free but highly ideological, the contemporary demotion of the author into a contextual or intertextual function does not signal an epistemological breakthrough into some 'actual' or absolute truth about reading but an ideological shift in the way we now read that reflects a wider cultural deprivileging of individualism. To the extent that the post-romantic, personal author could never live up to the role assigned to him as source and resting-point of subsequent interpretive activity, the transcendent embodiment of textual meaning and arbitrator of textual interpretation, the contemporary demystification of authorship is a welcome corrective. But to the extent that it seeks to replace the author as the transcendent determinant of his text with other determinants, no less transcendent for being depersonalized, it remains a mystification and an idolatry, albeit of a transcendent textual anonymity, to paraphrase Foucault. Though less than a demi-god, the author, in so far as that term is still meaningful, remains more than the sum of his constituent parts, if only because those parts are not finite, material, and objective but themselves remain a matter of ideology, and of course, interpretation.

That is my smaller claim, that in the study of literature there is no end of making theories and theories of theories and little gain in any positive or progressive sense upon some fundamental epistemological truth. This is by no means to deny the brilliance of particular theoretical performances or, dare I say it, *practices*.[19] Indeed, the synoptic history of literary study offered above seems to suggest just such a procession of bright paradigms, advanced and taken up for the promise they hold out of resolving the problems of textuality in general. On the basis of these paradigms a great deal is written until they are literally and figuratively written out, until, that is, several things become clear to the interpretive community that has adopted them: to wit, that the 'problems' identified, addressed, and 'resolved' by a given paradigm are a function of that particular paradigm and not absolute or universal (they may not emerge as problems at all within another paradigm); that a given paradigm merely adumbrates new and unforeseen problems which it proves, in time, powerless to resolve, and for which a new paradigm will have to be invented.[20] For example, while literature was studied historically and biographically, as mimetic or expressive of something outside it, such problems as how many children Lady Macbeth might have had, or whether Shakespeare was a recusant Catholic or had been a lawyer, were real for literary scholars. When his plays came to be regarded as formal and conventional constructs, they ceased to be so. When the formalist orthodoxy came firmly into place the problem of an author's personal views and experience was momentarily 'resolved' with the invention of the 'persona', or more

[19] The term 'theoretical practice' is employed by Louis Althusser in *For Marx* (Harmondsworth: Allen Lane, 1969) and *Lenin and Philosophy* (London: New Left Books, 1971), to designate the process by which 'knowledge-effects' are converted into 'Knowledge'. Perhaps needless to say, this is not the sense in which I employ the term here and in my final chapter. Rather, I am urging a 'theoretical practice' that is philosophically informed, reflective, and critical, but purged of all epistemological or quasi-scientific claims or pretensions to truth, something much closer to what Frank Kermode, in a recent review–article of that title, provocatively terms 'intelligent theory' (*London Review of Books*, 7–20 October 1982, pp. 8–9).

[20] As in Kuhn's account of the succession and demise of scientific paradigms: *The Structure of Scientific Revolutions*, Ch. 1.

accurately, 'dissolved' into it through the potent reagent of 'the intentional fallacy'. But once textual authority came no longer to be identified with the tense formal coherence of the particular work, as is now the case with both contextualist and textualist poststructuralism, but sought elsewhere, in its contextual relations and intertextual differences the 'persona' had to be discarded as yet another mystification.

The procession of bright and promising theoretical paradigms seems to have no end, each serving a temporary and particular purpose before yielding its claim to privilege and falling victim in turn to theoretical critique. The corollary of this sceptical claim is of course that no such theoretical critique (including the present one) can be in its own right definitive, since that would presuppose that some more authentically privileged position is available from which to conduct such a critique and on which to erect some master-theory, some ultimate theory of theories. The sad moral of our history seems to be that no such theoretical vantage point exists outside of practice, from which practice might be objectively described, let alone prescribed. Theory seems to be only another version of practice, subject, alas, to the same vagaries and mystifications. Put another way, the history or philosophy toward which literary theory regularly turns in search of a 'ground' for the study of literature—or writing—turns out to be only more literature—or writing—requiring, in turn, another 'ground' on which to ground it. Turtles standing one on another, all the way down!

The moral is indeed sad, our vision hopelessly mystified, our claims and ambitions necessarily small—as long, that is, as literature and literary criticism are viewed, by analogy with science, as a body of knowledge. But this is not the only way they can be, or have been, viewed. For my larger, more consequential and practical claim is that what must seem dark indeed when viewed as a body of systematic or positive knowledge may appear from another viewpoint a source of insight. If literary activity is conceived not as issuing in a body of knowledge but in a mode of being, the absence of certainty or consensus in the study of texts is no longer a disability. Whatever may have determined the temporal and precarious condition of all textual existence and understanding, it is our

style of address to the uncertainties we cannot avoid that
defines the activity of an interpretive community in its
distinctiveness and lends that activity its unique value. If a
body of knowledge were the goal of our activity, as it is in the
sciences, we would be in serious trouble indeed, given the
apparent unavailability of a stable and reliable paradigm
under which to pursue our 'research'. But if our goal is a mode
of being rather than a method of knowing, a kind of 'power', in
De Quincey's terms, rather than a body of knowledge,[21] then
we are going to need our authors and canons, which must
remain matters of critical debate precisely to the extent that
they cannot be matters of scientific rigour. The question of the
truth-claims of science has itself been reopened in recent
decades, and I shall have to return to it in those subsequent
chapters which attempt to evaluate the contemporary critical
movements that lay claim to scientific status.

Suffice it to say for the moment that whatever the truth-
claims of science, those of literature and literary study are
even more dubious. A recent study by the National Science
Foundation of the process of peer-evaluation of journal–article
and grant submissions revealed that about a third of the
submissions in a large sample would have met opposite
destinies had they been evaluated by different, but equally
qualified, experts. On my reporting this to a literary scholar at

[21] De Quincey's distinction takes the form of a proto-deconstruction of the
opposition between 'instruction' and 'delight' in classical poetics, and is highly
relevant to contemporary theoretical discussion: 'It is difficult to construct the idea of
"literature" with severe accuracy . . . in fact, a severe construction of the idea must be
the *result* of a philosophical investigation into this subject, and cannot precede it . . . .
I have said that the antithesis of Literature is Books of Knowledge. Now, what is that
antithesis to *knowledge* which is here implicitly latent in the word literature? The
vulgar antithesis is *pleasure* ("aut prodesse volunt, aut delectare poetae"). Books, we
are told, propose to *instruct* or to *amuse. Indeed!* . . . *The true antithesis to knowledge, in this
case, is not pleasure,* but *power.*' And again: 'The reason why the broad distinctions
between the two literatures of power and knowledge so little fix the attention lies in
the fact that a vast proportion of books,—history, biography, travels, miscellaneous
essays, etc.—lying in a middle zone, confound these distinctions by interblending
them. All that we call "amusement" or "entertainment" is a diluted form of the power
belonging to passion, and also a mixed form; and, where threads of direct *instruction*
intermingle in the texture with these threads of *power*, this absorption of the duality
into one representative *nuance* neutralizes the separate perception of either. Fused into
a *tertium quid*, or neutral state, they disappear to the popular eye as the repelling forces
which, in fact, they are.' *The Collected Writings of Thomas de Quincey*, ed. David Masson
(Edinburgh: Adam and Charles Black, 1890), x, p. 49 and xi, p. 59.

Columbia, he replied that had such a study been conducted in our field, the variation would have been more like two-thirds! Whereas the scientific community aspires to a godlike rule of method and principle—here, if anywhere, it is the discourse, not men nor subjects nor personalities, that speaks through researchers subdued to their element—the literary community knows no such impersonality. Whereas it is commonplace for scientific articles, as the products of team-research, to bear the names of five or more 'authors', to multiply and disperse authorship to the point where the very concept well and truly dies away, or radically diminishes in importance, no such disappearance of individual testimony or diminishing of individual responsibility, and of the authorship that identifies them, seems imminent or even conceivable in literary activities, whatever the dreams of some theoretical schools. We do not seem able, even in the most strenuous and rigorous theoretical discussion, to dispense with the names of authors or their extension into canons. And to an Anglophone ear at least, such exotic, even vaguely obscene or allegorical names as Barthes, Lacan, Foucault, Derrida, de Man. Names to conjure with indeed, and to what effect but to conjure up these *genii* as authoritative presences?

Why should this be? What is it about literary study that prevents the attainment of an ultimately impersonal or fully communal discourse, an authorless authority? Why should it continue to matter, to paraphrase Beckett and Foucault, who is speaking? Can it be that in our dealings with language and literature, the idea of authorship and the metaphysics of presence it carries with it, if only as a trace, is unavoidable? This is not to say that a sustained awareness of that connection is not desirable. The authority that such figures as Barthes, de Man, Derrida, Foucault *et al.* have exercised over literary studies in the past decade, that is, may itself be charismatic, authorial, quasi-religious *even as they argue for the compelling power of an impersonal textuality*. What could be more ironic than that these textualists and contextualists have acquired the status of *presences*? Does not their writing bear a kind of personal witness—note the religious terminology—to their unique and exemplary experience of writing? To what scientist, however influential, would such terms be even remotely applicable? It follows that our argument should not be that the sciences are at base epistemologically the same as literary studies—the argument mounted by some contemporary theorists to win back from science some of the cultural prestige that literary studies have lost to it—but that literary studies are defined by a further, unrecuperable difference from science. That difference consists not in their epistemological basis, but in their institutional practice, in the personal, indeed authorial, stance that characterizes the man of letters in relation to the echoing discourse of the institution, in precisely his persistent pursuit of difference. The relation of author to discourse, however these are conceived, is inescapably that of figure to ground.[22]

While the humanities may have grown up alongside the sciences within the university, and not surprisingly, acquired some of the same habits as the sciences—their characteristic aims and ambitions are notoriously different. If the end of science is the understanding, prediction, and control of nature, that traditionally projected for literary studies, at least in their liberal humanist phase since Arnold, has been the understanding, transmission, and extension of culture, which is not (unless you are a structuralist) assimilable to nature. In restating this traditional goal amid the current redefinition of the discipline, I trust it is still shared by those engaged in the teaching of literature with relatively little initial dissent. The disagreement begins when we attempt to specify what is meant by 'culture' and how it might best be understood, transmitted, and extended. Even when the definition of 'culture' is further sharpened to mean 'literacy'—and which of us would deny that *that* is currently at stake—as distinct, on the one hand, from an older, more exclusive and class-bound notion of culture, and on the other, from the systematic

---

[22] Thus Richard Rorty, commenting on Lionel Trilling's resistance to the tendency of post-romantic literary culture to make 'figures' out of writers, points to its underlying democratic rejection of 'a sacred wisdom which takes precedence over the common moral consciousness . . . [and which is] purchased at the price of his separation from his fellow-humans.' Rorty recognizes that 'this moral objection states the really important issue about textualism' and admits that he has 'no ready way to dispose of it': *Consequences of Pragmatism* (Minneapolis: University of Minnesota Press, 1982), pp. 157–8.

knowledge of facts and principles that constitute a *Wissenschaft* or a pedantry. My point is that the culture of literacy is not a *product* in any Arnoldian or Leavisite sense of a time-capsule containing the 'best' that has been thought and said—for that invites its fetishization or sacralization into a fixed canon— nor in the philological sense of a positive body of 'facts' empirically collected and related through 'objective' or quasi- scientific methods of analysis—and certainly not in an outmoded aristocratic sense of what the 'best' people have.

Rather, it is a continuing and restless *process* of thinking and being, ultimately unprogrammatic and unverifiable because its grounds and principles are themselves always in question. Hence the inbuilt disposition toward self-differentiation in which writing, and its study and transmission in more writing, thrives. Such a process, because it consists in a constant begging-to-differ from institutional models, conventional norms, and discursive conformations is necessarily subjective and individualistic. Whereas the institution of science cultivates normalcy, that of literature is abnormal from the beginning, arising as it does in the self-differentiation of personal witness. Yet when that difference—individual, subjective, and subver- sive by definition—is publicly perceived as such, it too will become an institutional norm and thereby lose its differential character. Roland Barthes designates this paradox of writing as the 'institutionalization of subjectivity', though it is only a special case of the larger processes of institutionalization described by Max Weber as the 'routinization of charisma'.[23]

That routinization of charisma is precisely what we see at work in the dubious triumph of contemporary literary theory. Kafka's parable of high modernism, *The Leopards in the Temple*, projects just such a process of authorial transgression and

[23] 'Our age produces a bastard-type: the author–writer. His function is inevitably paradoxical: he provokes and exorcises at the same time; formally, his language is free, screened from the institution of literary language, and yet, enclosed in this very freedom . . . . And naturally it is not surprising that such a conflict (or such a contract, if you prefer) should be joined on the level of language; for language is this paradox: the institutionalization of subjectivity.' 'Authors and Writers' in *Critical Essays*, trans. Richard Howard (Evanston: Northwestern University Press, 1972), pp. 149–50. See also Max Weber, *Wirtschaft und Gesellschaft*, Part I, trans. A. M. Henderson and Talcott Parsons, *The Theory of Social and Economic Organization* (New York: The Free Press, 1964), pp. 363–73.

institutional routinization. There, the profanation of religious ritual—the leopards' breaking into the temple and defiling the sacred offerings—issues in a resacralization when this repeated action becomes incorporated into the ritual. Substitute the professors of historical scholarship and traditional interpretation for the temple priests, and the poststructuralist demystifiers for the leopards, and you have a representation of contemporary institutional process, of the legitimation of textual transgression through the assimilation of potentially destructive agents. At the present moment, that is, poststructuralist literary theory, perceived during the seventies as a subversive threat to literary studies, is being naturalized and legalized into a respectable member of the community. More than that, as courses on literary theory proliferate in the curriculum and special centres for its study are established, the institution has conferred on its sometime antagonist its highest honour: canonization. Would that Bernard Shaw were living at this hour to do justice to the institutional high comedy of the process.

Yet there is more than rueful irony in the spectacle of the institution's welcoming in through the front door what it had tried so hard to keep out the back. In so far as the contemporary theory now being canonized is profoundly anti-canonical in most of its aspects, it puts into question the very idea of an institution. The concordat with theory, so slow in coming, may now be too readily embraced. For like the question of authorship, the question of the canon goes to the heart of the institution's peculiar existence. Just as a certain kind of writing, the kind that has come to be known as 'literature', is inconceivable without authorship, so the institutional study of that writing is inconceivable without a canon. Without a canon, a corpus or cynosure of exemplary texts, there can be no interpretive community, no more than there can be a faith-community without a gospel. What the interpretive community has in common, what makes it a *community*, is precisely the canon. Dispense with the canon, and you have effectively fragmented or disbanded the community as a community of interests, whatever institutional superstructure may remain standing, just as the Christian church as an institution was dependent on the stabilization of its canonical gospels out of numerous competing texts by the early fathers.[24]

Here, however, a crucial difference between religious and secular interpretive communities—and by extension the difference between the Leavisite and my own understanding of the institution of literary study—emerges. In a fully secular (i.e. non-Leavisite) interpretive community, the formation of a canon is a means, a necessary and enabling condition, a pretext for the work of interpretation rather than its end. The argument for a canon derives, that is, not from the importance of our reading the *right* texts, whatever our criteria of rectitude (moral, political, historical, rhetorical), but from the necessity of our reading the *same* texts, or enough of the same texts, to enable the discourse of the interpretive community to go on. The object of the exercise is not agreement, some purely hypothetical and ever elusive 'true judgement' or correct interpretation, but that continuing discussion which enables continuing self-differentiation. In the politics of literary study, as distinct from the politics of politics, of religion, or of science—doctrinal consensus or soundness or normalcy is not the aim. Only enough consensus is required to enable us to go on differing. *Pace* some contemporary schools, do we really want a criticism that tells us how to vote? Rather, we need to vote in order that we may practice criticism in the first place. It is only the fundamentalist—and as I have been arguing, superstitious—belief that posits resting-points (always illusory) for institutional discourse, that would prescribe a canon of texts as if it were the source or goal, rather than the occasion, of cultural value.

Two potential and related objections come to mind. One is that the provisional and minimal consensus required for the activity of interpretation is not so easily obtained. Why, after all, would literary study be in its currently divided state if it were? The other is that the nomination of interpretive process as its proper aim is precisely what contemporary theory has put into question. Are not the enabling conditions, determin-

---

[24] The parallels and divergences between scriptural and literary interpretation, and their sponsoring institutions are succinctly but suggestively drawn by Frank Kermode, 'Institutional Control of Interpretation', *Salmagundi*, No. 43 (Winter 1979), pp. 72–86.

ants, and structures of interpretation what now need to be explored, and that is the domain of theory rather than interpretation? In so far as these objections involve pragmatic choices, my responses to them will be cast in pragmatic terms. Given the necessity of canon-formation as the precondition for the institutional study of writing, the arguments for a conservative approach to that process seem to me very strong. Whatever the dangers of reification and fetishization that accompanied the pre-structuralist cultivation of a 'great tradition', that tradition is substantially the one with which most members of the institution grew up and which comprises the object of study for them. Whatever redefinition of the canon is to be negotiated, among contending interests, it is bound to include a number of these traditional texts. 'Let us have the old poets,' wrote Keats, 'and Robin Hood.'

While 'Robin Hood' may assume the guise of popular, women's, or ethnic literature in response to special historical interests, it seems unlikely that a fully institutional canon could ever be formed out of them, simply because the interests they represent are special or sectarian, and hence, exclusive. Robin Hood has even donned the robe of theory, as what were once regarded as strictly philosophical texts command an increasing share of attention in departmental curricula. In so far as this change represents an expansion of our definition of literary language, and the canon that exemplifies it, it is a welcome change. The canon, except to a fundamentalist few, has never been an unchanging essence but a cultural and institutional convention, a working typification of qualities agreed to be 'literary' at a particular historical moment. The danger is not theory but theoretical expansionism, the grand illusion that theory, and the theory of theory, and the theory of theory of theory, can rise above the need for common texts of reference which orient and maintain institutional discourse.

The brief answer—it will grow longer in the chapters to follow—to those who would see interpretation give way to poetics or theory is that interpretation can never be escaped or transcended by going theoretical. Even when theory or poetics becomes the object, its study can never work itself free from the subjectivity of the interpreter or from an interpretive subject-matter. That impulse is wholly misguided within contemporary theory to rid itself of the bad habits of interpreting texts by rising, through self-reflection, above interpretation, and by implication, steering clear of the canonical texts which have attracted so much interpretation in the past. In seeking out the ghostly paradigm of a meta- or post-interpretive poetics, not only do we risk falling into yet another platonic idealism, but losing for instruction a rich repository of moves, procedures, yes errors. The avoidance of the history of interpretation, like that of history itself, can only result in its unconscious repetition.

For the theory we wish to distinguish from practice, like all utopian dreams, is itself historical. Theory will turn out to be only another practice, from which there can be no escape or transcendence. Ironically, it was Leavis himself who recognized this back in the thirties when he refused, under challenge by René Wellek, to theorize his own practice. He was right to do so, not for his mock-humble pretext that he had better leave it to philosophers (like Wellek himself!) to do what he, as a mere practitioner, could not do. He was right, because the philosophers cannot do it either. That Leavis could not know; but we can. For since Leavis's time, the philosophers themselves, so long preoccupied with 'ordinary' language and establishing a first philosophy of it, have grown more humble. That first- or ground-philosophy, so long sought as a kind of master-key to all understanding, has come increasingly to be regarded as an illusion, an institutional mirage or myth, and the work done toward it as more 'literature'. The energy of that pursuit is now being redirected toward the interrogation of 'literary' language. That much of this labour will be, indeed already is, highly intelligent and sophisticated is beyond doubt. But there is no reason to believe that the philosophers of literature will have any more success in finding a key to all mythologies, and thereby cut short our long interpretive fumbling at the locks of literary texts, than the philosophers of ordinary language did in finding a positive and logical master-key to the processes of thought and communication, or for that matter, than did the interpreters themselves.

2

Marxism *Redivivus*

> Always historicize! This slogan—the
> one absolute and we may even say
> 'transhistorical' imperative of all dia-
> lectical thought.
>
> Fredric Jameson

I. FROM REFLECTION TO INSCRIPTION

Marxist literary criticism will be with us as long as its *raisons
d'être*, literature and the poor, are with us. This is not offered
as prophecy or aphorism, but historical observation. For
whatever the outcome of any social revolution that might take
place—be it slow or sudden, abortive or apocalyptic—marxism
itself will persist, either as a newly established political system
or an oppositional ideology as at present, and in either case, so
will marxist criticism. For all the methodological novelty of its
recent manifestations, marxist criticism is by far the oldest of
the avant-garde movements currently vying for place, and
that seems reason enough to deal with it first. Moreover, the
problems that beset it at present seem to have done so from its
inception in Marx's own sporadic comments upon literature,
and these problems have as much to do with the elusive
reserve of its literary object as with the questionable validity,
in view of the uncanny resilience of capitalism to survive
repeated crises, of its theory of history.[1] Those problems, in
fine, arise from the dubious potential of a materialist
understanding of history to engage what seems from a post-
romantic viewpoint a phenomenon so im- or trans-material,
or even in marxist terms so 'superstructural', as literature.

---

[1] Marx's and Engels's scattered comments on literary–historical relations are
discussed by Terry Eagleton, *Marxism and Literary Criticism* (London: Methuen, 1976),
pp. 1–18.

Is a marxist poetics, from which a revivified critical practice might spring, even possible? Can a theory of fiction-making and textuality be formulated which is genuinely literary, i.e. capable of accounting for such features as form and style, while remaining genuinely historical, that is, materialist? Until recently, marxist critics have been rather inclined—particularly within Anglo-American empirical tradition—to put aside their politics when actually engaging a literary text, or to put aside the text when expounding their politics. This compartmentalization is no less characteristic of that large body of marxist criticism which avoids questions of literary language and form—the work of Lukács is the classic example —by confining itself to texts, mainly nineteenth-century novels, that appear to be transparent upon a pre-existing historical world. The social, economic, and political aspects of that world are then discussed directly, as if the form of words that yields the illusion of this-worldliness were not itself a stylistic as well as a bourgeois convention, and consequently a linguistic and formal issue rather than simply a historical given. For a marxist criticism determined to advance its political cause, this problem was repressed in favour of an unself-questioning preference for realism and mistrust of modernism in its dealings with literature.

There were no doubt historical reasons for this repression. The absence of a sustained tradition of linguistic reflection within earlier marxism—though the work of M. M. Bakhtin is a striking exception[2]—along with the present hope of positive social change following the Russian Revolution, the First World War, and the Great Depression, may help to explain its reluctance to be distracted from its primary historical task by the complexities of literary form. Such factors may also account for the rhetorical over-confidence or unself-consciousness that characterizes so much marxist criticism, whatever doubts or anxieties might emerge in particular practitioners, as belonging to an earlier, more insouciant world. After all,

[2] See Tony Bennett, *Formalism and Marxism* (London: Methuen, 1979), pp. 79–92, and Michael Holquist, ed., *The Dialogic Imagination: Four Essays by M. M. Bakhtin* (Austin: University of Texas Press, 1981), pp. xv–xxxiv. The promise of mediation between fictional and social context recently rediscovered in Bakhtin's 'dialogism,' still to be fully developed, is searchingly qualified by Paul de Man, 'Dialogue and Dialogism,' *Poetics Today*, iv, 1 (1983), pp. 99–107.

the innocence I have been describing is fully present in Trotsky's literary essays, despite the modernist challenge posed by the Russian formalists, whose work he tried with such polemical verve to dismiss. (Rhetorical suasion gave way to political suppression a few years later.) Until that challenge was faced, however, it was not really possible for marxist criticism to progress beyond regarding a literary text or career as a more or less direct reflection or rejection of a given social reality, and valuing it accordingly, regarding it, in sum, as precisely what the formalists had argued, with formidable sophistication, it was not.[3]

Within a context of renewed linguistic and formal interest (in which the work of the Russian formalists has figured prominently), that challenge has now been taken up, and the marxist criticism that once refused it labelled as 'vulgar' by the marxists themselves, with something of the embarrassment of university-educated children of *parvenus* over their parents' taste. These latest 'sophisticated' marxists have tried to develop a theory of textuality and practice of reading capable of negotiating the formal indirections of literary modernism and attuned to the methodological preoccupations of contemporary poetics. The older errors are attributed to an over-simplified application to literary history of such fundamental marxist concepts as the reflection of the economic base in the cultural superstructure, the determination of consciousness by social being, and of literary form by social content. The new marxism, by contrast, focuses on the concept of ideology as it is elaborated in the political and philosophical writings of Louis Althusser—the tissue of 'ideas, values and feelings by which men experience their societies at various times'—and examined in relation to literary texts in the work of Pierre Macherey and Terry Eagleton.[4] 'Literature', in this

---

[3] Reflectionism at its most naïve or vulgar is typified in T. A. Jackson, *Dickens: The Progress of a Radical* (London: Lawrence and Wishart, 1937), the *ne plus ultra* in literary biography for many marxists of my father's generation, but it still persists. See, for example, Michael Wilding, *Political Fictions* (London: Routledge and Kegal Paul, 1980), in which such non- or anti-realistic forms as dream-vision and utopian fable are seen as mirroring in their 'radicalism' a presumed radicalism of theme or vision, once the necessary adjustments are made. Several major texts in the marxist debate over realism are collected in *Aesthetics and Politics* (London: New Left Books, 1977).

[4] Pierre Macherey, *Pour une théorie de la production littéraire* (Paris: Francois Maspero, 1966); trans. Geoffrey Wall as *A Theory of Literary Production* (London: Routledge and

view, is no longer simply an ideological or superstructural reflection of the productive modes and relations of an economic base, but itself a product on which the general mode of production of society remains ideologically 'inscribed'. Criticism turns into the technique of reading this 'inscription', the 'impress' of its material conditions of production, the ideology that the text carries encoded within, or as we shall see, between its lines.

In contrast to its status in vulgar marxist criticism, the text ceases to be regarded as a transparent medium, giving direct access to the historical world in all its social and economic objectivity, and becomes itself a material object bearing the imprint of social ideology. Nor is that ideology itself directly accessible; it too must be 'read' as the impression left by the pressures of changing material relations within society, since it is the nature of ideology to mask or distort its material causes. The text, that is, has come to be regarded as a product bearing the stamp of its material mode of production, but it can be so regarded only by negative and indirect means. In the study of literary texts, it seems, two fictional negatives begin to make a historical positive. Thus, Eagleton discusses the formal fragmentation of *The Waste Land*, or the ethical and characterological focus of the nineteenth-century novel, and Macherey, the labyrinthine structures of Borges's stories, not as technical mutations making it possible to bring to light some aspect of universal human experience—as formalist criticism or even their authors themselves might have us take them— but as the inscriptions in the text of particular crises in the history of capitalism, the strains and cracks of which capitalist ideology can only conceal. It is through the fissures, gaps, or silences of the literary text, that is, that we are able to read the changing material relations of society, the stresses of which have been glossed over in the dominant or official ideology of that society. The form of the text, in such a theory, can then be *explained*—as distinct, it is repeatedly insisted, from *interpreted*—as an expression of its mode of production.[5] This highly indirect and mediated process of reading historical

Kegan Paul, 1978); Terry Eagleton, *Criticism and Ideology* (London: New Left Books, 1976).

[5] See Eagleton, *Marxism and Literary Criticism*, pp. 18–19.

truth out of fissured texts and inverted ideologies might be likened to holding the apparently straightforward text up to a mirror to produce its ideological transposition, then subjecting that image to a second mirror-reading to reproduce its basic material meaning.

Whether or not this last analogy is valid, some form of the theory of reflection seems to have been saved after all. How could it be otherwise, for if Marxist criticism were to dispense altogether with mimeticism, it would only turn into formalism? But the theory of reflection has been saved at the cost of a complexity that is, if I have understood it correctly, almost mind-boggling, and, if I have not, a complexity that is mind-boggling indeed. A less sympathetic critic might compare it with the proliferation of epicycles brought in to prop up a faltering Ptolemaicism. Such methodological complexity has been attacked from within marxism itself as an 'orrery of errors', a Rube Goldberg or Heath Robinson contraption of misguided ingenuity, the byzantine academicism of which has the self-defeating effect, if not the intention, of obscuring what ought to be a liberating knowledge.[6]

There is a parallel here with the Lacanian development of freudian theory. In the aspiring of both movements to a new sophistication and respectability as intellectual disciplines, an earlier aspiration to therapeutic and social effectiveness has been all but lost in the process. However institutionally necessary, such absorption in methodological self-legitimation cannot but be counter-productive in some degree for any discipline—be it marxist or freudian—whose initial *raison d'être* was moral and therapeutic, and which still claims value as a social *praxis*. In the case of marxism, this justification is not only the modest institutional aim of establishing a demystified, non-élitist alternative to practical criticism enabling the humblest student to understand texts of all kinds, but a larger political ambition to bring about revolutionary social change. It is difficult to imagine any but the most apt or eager or credulous student finding guidance in so oblique and perplexing a method of analysis, let alone any wider audience of readers.

[6] See E. P. Thompson, *The Poverty of Theory* (London: Merlin Press, 1978), pp. 193–398.

II. THE MYSTIFICATIONS OF MATERIALISM

It would be more interesting, however, if the complexity of this recent marxist criticism arises, not out of inadvertent scholasticism but out of authentic mystification. The more so, because marxist criticism stakes its claims to validity on the ground that it is a demystification of the idealist and metaphysical tendencies of bourgeois formalism. Those tendencies are apparent in the institutionalization of a category of works that compose *literature*, within which an even more privileged set of works, the *canon* or the *great tradition*, occupy special pedestals. These 'works' are 'created' by 'authors', who are endowed or inspired with godlike or prophetic powers. The demystifying corrective offered by the new marxism is to historicize, and thereby relativize, these categories as cultural and temporal rather than universal and timeless, to speak not of a class of works born to privilege, but of 'texts' created equal—or rather *produced* instead of created, since the demi-divine status of the individual author, working in splendid romantic isolation, is replaced by a more impersonal concept of authorship as a convergence of specifiable historical forces and relations toward specifiable social purposes. The role of the critic—if that is still an appropriate term for him—is no longer to *interpret* the text—interpretation being the ideological fetish of bourgeois individualism—but to *explain* the text, to read its specific social formations out of its gaps and silences. The marxist critic is thus at base a historian, though not a bourgeois, liberal, eclectic historian, a 'Whig' historian, for this new criticism is a historiography that is nothing if not objective, materialist, and scientific.

How, then, does this bold and radical demystification of bourgeois literary culture turn into yet another mystification? One marxist critic sees the enterprise of these Althusserians as doomed from the start through their having adopted what he terms the 'legacy of aesthetics', the categories and concerns of bourgeois criticism.[7] Consider, for example, the problem of 'the great tradition'. One cannot but be a bit surprised that despite his critique of Leavisism, left and right, Eagleton goes

---

[7] Tony Bennett, *Formalism and Marxism*, pp. 127–42.

on to retain the concept of a great tradition, and in many cases the particular texts that traditionally compose it. To replace Leavis's great tradition of Austen, Eliot, James, Conrad, and Lawrence with another composed of Arnold, George Eliot, Conrad, James, T. S. Eliot, Yeats, Joyce, and Lawrence is not much of a revolution, even if the basis of selection and valuation is different. In fact, Eagleton's principle of valorization can be seen as a simple inversion of Leavis's, Eagleton valuing what he terms 'the fissuring of organic form' and the 'destruction of corporate and organist ideologies' that his writers exemplify in precisely the degree that Leavis deplores it.[8] As Tony Bennett puts it, 'his comments on the problem of literary value become successively more contorted as he attempts to reconcile this realization (that a text cannot be valued *because of* the circumstances of its production) with the conviction that there is something specific about the works which comprise the "great tradition" which he does not wish to surrender to those forms of populism which would claim the parity or equivalence of all writing.'[9]

Despite his ambitions towards 'a scientific knowledge of the literary past',[10] Eagleton's rewriting of the great tradition does not escape or transcend but only inverts the value-structure of its arch-conservator. The work of Pierre Macherey, on which Eagleton openly bases his own study, avoids this idealism, by focusing the 'practical' side of its project on texts by Conan Doyle, Jules Verne, and Jorge Luis Borges, texts

---

[8] *Criticism and Ideology*, p. 161.

[9] *Formalism and Marxism*, p. 154.

[10] *Criticism and Ideology*, p. 161. Given Eagleton's extraordinary flair for parody (already well developed even in this early work), it is difficult to gauge the tone in which the 'scientific' formulas relating the literary to the general mode of production ('LMP' to 'GMP') and the general to the authorial to the aesthetic ideologies ('GI' to 'AuI' to 'AI') are put forward in Ch. 2, 'Categories for a Materialist Criticism', and Ch. 3, 'Towards a Science of the Text'. These chapters could be read as parody of the solemn pseudo-scientificity of Louis Althusser's schematizations of 'Knowledge', 'Knowledge-Effects', 'Theory', and 'Science' (capitals his) in *For Marx* (Harmondsworth: Allen Lane, 1969) and *Lenin and Philosophy* (London: New Left Books, 1971), or perhaps as a mischievous attempt to *épater le bourgeois* 'mystery' of literature. Such tonal uncertainties, whether or not they are regarded as unfathomable mysteries, are precisely the sort of radical complication or deferral that no writing can escape and much writing cultivates in its signifying process, and that embarrasses attempts to explain it scientifically. The tone of Althusser and Macherey, varying only between the straight-faced and the shrill, admittedly presents no such difficulty in gauging.

that might be termed sub- or para- or meta-literary respectively, and that in any case have not yet become canonical. Macherey's choice of texts is at least witty and provocative in the context of French institutionalized literary study, if not particularly revolutionary by more flexible Anglo-American norms. In the case of Eagleton, however, it seems you can take the boy out of Cambridge, but you cannot take Cambridge out of the boy.

There is, however, a more fundamental source of mystification in the work of both critics, and that is the belief—it amounts to a lingering nineteenth-century faith or superstition —that the study of literary texts can be, should be, or, in the case of their own work, *is* 'scientific'. Obviously, such a claim or ambition is the *sine qua non* of a marxist literary criticism, in so far as marxism itself has claimed to be a materialist science. And it is on this claim to scientific status that the 'explanations' offered by Macherey and Eagleton must be judged:

When we explain the work, instead of ascending to a hidden centre which is the source of life (the interpretive fallacy is organicist and vitalist), we perceive its actual decentredness. We refuse the principle of an intrinsic analysis (or an immanent criticism) which would artificially circumscribe the work, and deduce the image of a 'totality' (for images too can be deduced) from the fact that it is *entire*. The structure of the work, which makes it available to knowledge, is this internal displacement, this caesura, by which it corresponds to a reality that is also incomplete, which it shows without reflecting. The literary work gives the meaning of a difference, reveals a determinate absence, resorts to an eloquent silence.[11]

In taking over this concept of explanation from Macherey, Eagleton is surely right in claiming that 'much non-Marxist criticism would reject a term like "explanation", feeling that it violates the "mystery" of literature.'[12] But even if it is not the 'mystery' of literature we wish to preserve, which of us would not accept, at this late stage in the development of criticism, the relevance of this general objection. 'Interpretation' as impressionism—Macherey elsewhere calls it '*la critique comme*

[11] *A Theory of Literary Production*, p. 79.
[12] *Marxism and Literary Criticism*, p. 77 n.

appréciation'—not to mention the loose and casual interpretation, still very much with us, of literature as an expression of
its author's . life, times, or state of mind, is certainly a
bourgeois and sentimental mystification and would seem to fit
only too well the description of it as an ideological distortion, a
refusal of the text as it is, that Machery and Eagleton hold
against it. We have had more than enough of that kind of
'interpretation', and no doubt will have a great deal more.

My own resistance to the marxist dream of 'explanation' as
a successor to interpretation does not proceed from an interest
in preserving the 'mystery' of the text or in retaining the older
procedures, but from the conviction that interpretation is
inescapable. A poor thing but our own. For there is no 'text *as
it is*' or '*l'œuvre telle qu'elle est*' to be refused or accepted.[13] Here
again something like the old new-critical idealization of the
text as having some absolute and unchanging essence, a kind
of Platonic form, has quietly re-entered through the back door
of this marxist criticism after having been ceremoniously
banished through the front. The text, as we are becoming
aware, is always *the product of interpretation*, inasmuch as its
articulated sounds or marks on stone or paper—its system of
differences—have to be deciphered and construed before they
can mean anything at all. And they must be construed by
someone, which is to say, filtered through a subject, even if the
subject is redefined as the point of intersection or field of
interaction of material and historical forces and relations, or
as the mouthpiece of a wider 'interpretive community' or
'discursive formation.'[14] Such a play of forces and relations is
itself so complex, so problematic in their proportions and
pressures, as *itself to require 'explanation'* before that subject's
explanation can be explained or demystified. And who is to
explain the explanation of the explaining subject except yet

[13] ibid.

[14] Althusser's articulation of the subject with and within the ideological
'apparatuses' and material structures of society in *Lenin and Philosophy and Other Essays*,
tr. Ben Brewster (London: New Left Books, 1971) and elsewhere shares many of the
aims and difficulties of other, non-marxist attempts to decentre or deconstruct the
autonomous subject as the determining 'source' and reconstruct him/her as
determined by discourse. In this connection, see Jacques Lacan, *Écrits*, tr. Alan
Sheridan (London: Tavistock, 1977); Michel Foucault, *The Order of Things*, tr. Alan
Sheridan (London: Tavistock, 1970); and Stanley Fish, *Is There a Text in This Class?*
(Cambridge, Mass.: Harvard University Press, 1980).

another equally and necessarily explicable explainer? There would seem to be no escape from the infinite regress of such 'explanation', no emergence into the pure serene of an unmediated 'text as it is'.

The scientific 'explanation' of the 'text-as-it-is' begins to acquire an uncanny resemblance to the unscientific interpretation of the text as it might be, unless Macherey and Eagleton mean by the 'text as it is' nothing more than the material embodiment of the language of the text, the acoustic or graphic traces that constitute it as mere signifier. That would be a literary materialism all right, a materialism with a vengeance, and utterly irrelevant to the concerns of any conceivable literary criticism. For what has structural linguistics taught us, if not that the material sign as such is entirely arbitrary, albeit conventional, within a given language; its signifying power and interest lies on the other side of its materiality. What value or interest can there be in Homer's breath as breath, or Shakespeare's ink as ink? Such a linguistic materialism would be the merest technology of the text, comparable to the fetish of practical critics with the 'words on the page', as if those words solved our problems rather than created them. It would also be the most trivializing taxonomic formalism yet invented, hardly different from the interest of philatelists and numismatists in stamps and banknotes for their engraving, or coins for their art of relief.

It is only fair to say that neither Macherey nor Eagleton fall into so fetishistic a materialism. On the contrary, nothing could be further than the new 'explanation' from the fetishization of the text, of the words on the page, that characterizes the older fundamentalisms of 'new' and practical criticism. Seeking out, as they do, the gaps, silences, fissures of the text, Macherey and Eagleton are virtually unconstrained by the older, familiar conventions of textual attentiveness and fidelity. In this respect, their 'explanations' represent nothing other than interpretation at its freest or most licentious. If that which *is* said in literary texts is a matter of continual interpretive debate, that which is *not* said might seem more a promising ground for definitive, scientific criticism. But how can the unspoken be more determinate than the spoken, if it is by its nature open to interpolation? Only, it would seem, if that interpolation is already accepted as 'true'. In their explanation of texts, this is the procedure that Macherey and Eagleton follow:

This dilemma [of how to meet the disparate demands of bourgeois empiricism and 'a more intensively incorporating ideology' in mid-nineteenth-century England] is figured in *Middlemarch* in one of its key images: that of the *web* as image of the social formation. The web is ... a mid-point between the animal imagery of *Adam Bede* and some more developed theoretical concept of structure .... But ... the web's symmetry, its 'spatial' dehistoricising of the social process, its exclusion of levels of contradiction, preserve the essential unity of the organic mode .... The problem of totality within the novel is effectively displaced to the question of aesthetic form itself .... The novel, in other words, formally answers the problem it thematically poses. Only the novelist can be the centred subject of her own decentred fiction, the privileged consciousness which at once supervenes on the whole as its source, and enters into empathetic relation with each part. *Middlemarch*, one might say, is an historical novel in form with little substantive historical content. The Reform Bill, the railways, cholera, machine-breaking: these 'real' historical forces do no more than impinge on the novel's margins. The mediation between the text and the 'real' history to which it alludes is notably dense; and the effect of this is to transplant the novel from the 'historical' to the 'ethical'. *Middlemarch* works in terms of egoism and sympathy, 'head' and 'heart', self-fulfilment and self-surrender; and this predominance of the ethical at once points to an historical impasse and provides the means of ideologically overcoming it. History in the novel is officially in a state of transition; yet to read the text is to conclude that 'suspension' is the more appropriate term. What is officially offered as an ambivalent, intermediate era leading eventually to the 'growing good of the world' is in fact more of an historical vacuum .... [15]

The 'gap' in the novel's dealings with history reveals a corresponding 'gap' in evolving bourgois ideology—i.e. between the organic and the systemic conception of society—a gap filled by Eagleton with his own account of nineteenth-century British history. 'The Reform Bill, the railways, cholera,

[15] *Criticism and Ideology*, pp. 119–21.

machine-breaking: these "real" historical forces' that exist, to Eagleton's apparent regret, on 'the novel's margins' become the raw materials for an explanation of the novel, the finished form of which would be the official marxist history of Britain's industrialization, with its disintegrative and alienating effect on the emerging working-class—the historical account that led Marx to predict, scientifically, that the proletarian revolution would first break out there.

In filling the 'gaps' and 'silences' in his text with 'real' history, Eagleton can hardly be said to have avoided or transcended interpretation and achieved explanation. In the first place, how do we locate the fissures and silences in the apparently continuous fabric of the text except through interpretation, that is, through some form of educated guesswork at best or 'inspired divination' at worst, but based in either case on prior assumptions of the 'whole truth'. How can we know the fissure from the fiction, except by a process of wishful or willful thinking that promotes, in the service of special interests, one thing or one think over another. What counts as a gap? This procedure is nothing other, by Macherey's own account, than interpretation. I am not disputing his account of its nature, only his belief that it can be avoided, for it describes exactly what Eagleton has done. Eagleton, that is, has refused the text 'as it is' in order to revise or correct it in accordance with some ideal or norm of what it should be. A covert value-judgement has re-entered the discourse in contraband. Shades of Leavis again. He has located through interpretation what he deems the silence of his fictional text and filled that silence with what he takes to be the 'real' history the text cannot quite bring itself to tell. That there is at least a sneaking suspicion on Eagleton's part that this 'real' history may be, or may be thought to be, only another fiction is suggested by his repeated use of quotation marks around 'real'. His guilty conscience, however, does not quite prevent him from passing off interpretation as explanation, fiction as 'reality', marxist ideology as history, and criticism as science. Whether he proceeds in innocence or bad faith, Eagleton differs from the bourgeois interpreters he scorns not in the nature of his procedures but only in the magnitude of his claims. Despite the sneering self-confidence of its rhetoric, his criticism has fallen back into the very mystification it was supposed to have displaced.

III. THE RECALCITRANCE OF LANGUAGE

The error, that interpretation can be transcended and explanation achieved, arises in the first place from a gross miscalculation of the resistance and duplicity of language. It is not that these difficulties are wholly ignored but that they are seriously underestimated. For what is it but the suspected dangers of language, of literary language (if such a thing exists) *a fortiori*, that lead these critics to privilege the unstated, the '*non-dit*' above the stated in their texts, to seek out that which exists outside of and prior to any literary construction? It is the material relations of history behind the duplicities of textuality that they would make the object of study:

> Criticism, if it is to be a rational enterprise, must resolve the following problem. On the one hand it can only regard its object as empirically given, otherwise it risks confusing the rules of art with the laws of knowledge. The object of critical knowledge is not spontaneously available; it has first to be construed into a cognitive object—not replaced by an ideal and abstract model, but internally displaced so as to reveal its rationality. On the other hand, this knowledge, if it is to escape the normative fallacy, can only consider the work as it is, and must resist any temptation to alter it. To do otherwise would involve subjecting the work to a new set of rules (no longer technical rules of verisimilitude, but opportunist political or moral rules). Thus we must go beyond the work and explain it, must say what it does not and could not say: just as the triangle remains silent over the sum of its angles. But this manœuvre must be deliberate: we must not escape from empiricism only to fall into the normative fallacy (judgment and interpretive commentary are the two possible methods of *replacing* the work).[16]

Machery perceives that the root difficulty for a criticism that aspires to the status of a science, that is, a structuralism, is to define its object of inquiry. The problem is not squarely faced, however, in so far as the object of 'literary' criticism—like the

---

[16] *A Theory of Literary Production*, p. 77.

objects of the 'social' sciences—can never have the ontological stability that the natural objects of such 'hard' sciences as physics or even the organisms of biology do. The object of criticism, be it literature or even history is not an autonomous 'given', but has its existence primarily and ultimately *in language*, and therefore is not strictly speaking, an *object* at all.

For language, *a fortiori* literary language, is full of memories, traces, filiations, any of which are capable of being recalled to active service at any point. The relations between signifier and signified are subject to change without notice; they do not stand still to be studied. And even if an objective, a fixed status were somehow achieved for literary language, even if its shiftiness of signification were made to stand still and were studied like a crystal or a cell through some unprecedented consensus as to what constituted 'literature', and by extension 'history' and 'society', then the means of studying them—the microscope, as it were—would not be adequate to the purpose of scientific study, since *it too, as a metalanguage, is still nothing but language.* (Unless, of course, all critics agreed to be marxists, in which case they might be able to pretend, by agreeing on the nature of their method and their object, that a science of literature existed, though the history of marxism itself shows no such convergence toward happy consensus.)

This difficulty is suspected rather than confronted by both Macherey and Eagleton, and it continually returns to haunt them in the form, appropriately enough, of their own language:

Thus we must go beyond the work and explain it, must say what it does not and could not say: just as the triangle remains silent over the sum of its angles.

Only the novelist can be the centred subject of [his or] her own decentred fiction, the privileged consciousness which at once supervenes on the whole as its source, and enters into empathetic relation with each part.[17]

The repeated recourse of both critics to mathematical metaphors, to a pseudo-geometrical imagery—the image of

---

[17] Ibid., p. 77; *Criticism and Ideology*, p. 120.

the decentred circle is a central one for Macherey—reveals not
the scientific rigour of their discourse but, quite the opposite,
its longing for a language of scientific rigour. Their recourse to
metaphors borrowed from 'pure' or 'hard' science inadvertently
calls attention to itself as figurative rather than literal
language, as *literary rather than scientific discourse*, and no
sustained or formulaic repetition of them can succeed in
magically translating them from one domain of discourse into
the other, just as no sustained or aggressive repetition can
turn a marxist construction of history into a 'real' or 'true'
history.

It is not difficult, however, to understand why Macherey
and Eagleton would want to appropriate the discourse of
mathematics and science. What any science needs—and
scientists from Bacon onwards are explicit on this point—is a
system of notation free from ambiguity, a purely denotative
linguistic system in which each sign is clearly differentiated
from all other signs—no puns or figures of speech here, thank
you—and each signifier is matched with only its own signified.
Figuration must be avoided at all cost. There must be as little
slippage between signifier and signified as possible, in order
that the discourse can become a purely reflective and fully
adequate descriptive system. The *reductio ad absurdum* of this
procedure is represented in Swift's Laputa, where the
compulsion to avoid metaphor and figure is carried to the
point of avoiding language altogether through the desperate
expedient of carrying around the things one wishes to express.

It is almost possible for science and mathematics to achieve
such expressive adequacy only because of the specialized
training of its 'native speakers', the unique coherence of its
interpretive community. The language of science, that is, is
agreed and contractual, subject to rigid academic controls,
though even its conventions, historically determined as they
are, are open to contingency and change, and develop
multivocalities and ambiguities, the referential blurring or
dissonance or double exposure known to linguists as 'connotation'. Connotation, the ineradicable weed in the garden of
language, has always been carefully rooted out, or at least
controlled, by scientists. It has, with equal diligence, been
cultivated by poets. With such 'natural' languages as French

or English, and their heterogeneous communities of native speakers, the potential for mirror-like description is radically curtailed in a way it is not for such 'scientific' languages as geometry or calculus. Precisely because natural languages are riddled with the connotations of history and subjectivity, the *faits divers* of their speech communities, Humpty Dumpty's principle that 'words mean what I want them to mean' can never quite obtain—something that Dodgson, as a mathematician as well as a poet, would have been in a position to understand.

To be the scientists of literature they claim to be, the Althusserians would have to invent a wholly new language. Though this is a recurrent impulse in literary criticism, and precisely what Macherey and Eagleton try up to a point to do, it can never be done completely. If it could, such a language would not be understood outside its own community—one could preach only to the converted—another consequence common in contemporary criticism. This impulse to create a scientific critical discourse—a system of fixed signifiers adequate to denote the signified object of explanation without slippage—leads Eagleton not only to the specific adoption of a pseudo-mathematical terminology and an elaborate set of laws and formulas that supposedly 'govern' literary production, but to the more general stylistic trick of deploying a concrete vocabulary for the highly abstract concepts and processes he wants to describe. Such phrases as 'the *fissuring* of organic form' and 'an historical *vacuum*' are merely two of the numerous hard-edged nuggets that strew the surface of Eagleton's prose.

My point is not simply that terms from geology and physics have been enlisted for their specific suggestion of critical scientificity, but that they are deployed to underwrite a larger illusion of linguistic materialism. The pseudo-materiality of a highly concrete diction has been introduced into the language of criticism as if to make good the claim that the literary text under study is a material object or product, on which ideology has left its mark or inscription in a way that is concrete and can be measured. It is as though the fluctuations of differential signification were to be arrested and reified by recourse to hyper-concrete signifiers. But this Canute-like attempt to arrest interpretive flux is only another rhetorical gesture; the 'concrete' nouns and verbs Eagleton adopts are only metaphors, and as metaphors, cannot escape being interpreted figuratively, returned as it were to the domain of idealism, albeit an idealism of materialism. The play of signification that constitutes all texts, even that of history, cannot be so easily or wilfully made material; the materialist privileging of the 'concrete' in the binary opposition 'abstract/concrete' can itself be easily and wilfully deconstructed.[18]

Macherey and Eagleton, then, have done something very mischievous. They have denied literature and traditional literary criticism the privileged status of using language in such a way as to pretend exemption from historical process, as if literary language existed in some pure serene of the ideal and universal, but they have tried to retain that pretension for their own criticism by adopting a pseudo-mathematical or hyper-concrete discourse. They are guilty of attempting to dehistoricize their own discourse in precisely the way they will not permit the bourgeois writer/critic to do. If it was naughty for George Eliot (or her critics) to spatialize and so dehistoricize nineteenth-century social process by her recourse to the organic, and apparently transhistorical, imagery of a web, I cannot see why it is not, by the same token, equally naughty of Macherey and Eagleton to spatialize and so dehistoricize their own literary-critical discourse by recourse to the geometric, geological, and apparently transhistorical imagery of circles and triangles, fissures and vacuums. For geometrical and geological imagery is no less covertly historical than organic imagery. Personally, I have no objection to scientific imagery as such and have used some myself in this essay, but I have not made any claim on its behalf to a scientific status that escapes the historicity and rhetoricity of language.

In their attempt to replace critical interpretation with scientific explanation, these marxists have had to pretend that their language is nothing other than a system of signs adequate in its correspondence to literary history while remaining outside literary history in the same way that the

[18] For what I take to be a more productive approach to the problem of linguistic and literary materiality, see my final chapter.

language of mathematics and science is supposed to 'correspond' to the objective phenomena it describes while remaining outside them. Yet this implied identification of their historical explanations with science cannot help, by the nature of their language, but call attention to itself as metaphor, and metaphor is the traditional enemy of science. Indeed the particular metaphors they adopt silently assert the *historical* rather than the *scientific* status of their own discourse, place it, *in its very anxiety to be science*, at a certain point in European history, and thereby relativize and deprivilege it.

In sum, what Macherey and Eagleton have been attempting to do all along is to deprivilege 'literature' by assimilating it to 'history', then reprivilege 'history' in the name of science, and thereby their own discourse as 'scientific' historians. That their endeavour is undermined from within, however, is evident in the ambivalence of their own critical practice. Macherey seems, on the one hand, to hold it against Borges that his work seeks to dispense altogether with the referential content of history and to achieve something like the condition of pure structure, of contentless form, as represented in his favourite image of the labyrinth. On the other, he recognizes that this is also Borges's achievement, an original and considerable achievement. We have seen a similar self-division at work in Eagleton's desire to rewrite *Middlemarch* as a historical novel as part of his larger attempt to depedestal the great tradition. It is history that now assumes the dictatorship that literature held, the concept of literature having supposedly withered away, like the state in Marx's own residually Hegelian scheme of history.

Yet it is ultimately to no avail to replace the study of literature with that of history—even if we wished to do so—if history assumes the same privileged status formerly held by literature, since the same destiny of a deprivileging *coup d'état* lies in store for the newly reprivileged history. Here the deconstructive critique of linguistic determinacy comes into play. For history can always be turned back, through that critique, into literature. The firm and privileged ground of history, against which the literary text is now supposed to be explained (or explained away) turns out to be neither firm nor privileged. It begins to shift and slide beneath our metaphorical feet the instant its own textual character is recognized, its character 'as a plenum of documents that attest to the occurrence of events [and that] can be put together in a number of different and equally plausible narrative accounts of "what happened in the past", accounts from which the reader or the historian himself, may draw different conclusions about "what must be done" in the present.'[19] Whether these documents are oral or written, 'primary' or 'secondary', history—as distinct from the events it constructs—has no existence apart from texts and the language that constitutes them. Once the textual nature of history is recognized, the firm and privileged ground of marxist history as the basis for a scientific study of literature turns out to be not only not firm or privileged, but not even a ground at all; it is more like an abyss.

If a marxist critic were to recognize this, it would put him in exactly the position of those cartoon characters who remain blithely suspended in mid-air until they *realize* they are suspended in mid-air. Eagleton, at one point in his recent work, comes close to that self-deconstructive realization:

The present book, for example, is a text that . . . is intended as revolutionary rhetoric aimed at certain political effects, yet speaks a tropical language far removed from those in whose name it intervenes . . . . The rhetorical tropes and figures of my own discourse could be accused of undoing my rhetorical intentions, constructing a reading whose political clarity and resoluteness may be threatened by the very play of language that hopes to produce them. *What distinguishes the materialist from the deconstructionist* tout court *is that he or she understands such self-molesting discourse by referring it*

---

[19] Hayden White, *Metahistory: The Historical Imagination in Nineteenth-Century Europe* (Baltimore: Johns Hopkins University Press, 1973), p. 283. White continues: 'The best reasons for being a Marxist are moral ones, just as the best reasons for being a Liberal, Conservative, or Anarchist are moral ones . . . . The Marxist view of history is neither confirmable nor disconfirmable by appeal to 'historical evidence,' for what is at issue between a Marxist and a non-Marxist view of history is the question of precisely what counts as evidence and what does not' (p. 284). A similar view of science, scientific method, and scientific evidence is currently held by many philosophers and historians of science, and will be discussed in the next chapter. White, incidentally, is a marxist.

*back to a more fundamental realm, that of historical contradictions
themselves.*[20]

In acknowledging the dangers posed to the security of his
polemical position by a deconstructive philosophy of language,
Eagleton seems to think he can firm up his position by
appealing to the 'more fundamental realm of historical
contradictions themselves.' Yet what constitutes that 'more
fundamental realm' *tout court*, is only *more language* no less
precarious than his own, the *mise-en-abîme* down which he
would disappear if he were ever to realize fully the nature of
his imaginary perch. Marxism may be able to historicize
deconstruction, but that historicization is itself always subject
to a further deconstruction.

In the attempt to arbitrate the claims of the Althusserians
to a 'scientific knowledge of the literary past', we seem to have
reached an impasse from which marxist literary criticism
cannot seem to deliver us or itself. The privileging of history as
the means of explaining—scientifically no less—a now de-
privileged literature turns out to be itself wholly problematic.
The very historiography that is supposed to confer explanatory
power is, in the analysis, beset by the same difficulty as the
literature it was supposed to explain, namely its mode of
existence in the form of texts, the meaning of which remains
open to interpretation. Literary criticism can only become a
materialist science when historiography becomes a materialist
science, and there is no more agreement among marxist
historians, let alone historians at large, that the latter event
has taken place, than there is among literary critics at large
that the former has. Marxist criticism is prevented by the
necessary pretensions of its own discourse to the extra-
historical univocality of scientific discourse from fully recognizing the metaphorical nature, the rhetoricity or fictiveness,
of its own claim to having its referential resting-point in
history.

But because marxist historiography is only science by
metaphoric analogy, by a stretch of the imagination, its mock-
scientific language calls attention to itself as only another

---

[20] *Walter Benjamin, or Towards a Revolutionary Criticism* (London: New Left Books,
1981), p. 109. Italics mine.

equivocal language of figuration and fiction, which is to say a language of literature at best. In such phrases as 'the materialist conception of history' and 'the scientific knowledge of the literary past', let alone Althusser's 'concrete thought'—from the point of view of deconstruction, pure oxymoronic rhetoric—the full precariousness of the marxist critical project is implicit. Such a deconstruction of that project, in fact, is already foreshadowed in the ancient word 'historio*graphy*', a term marxist criticism seems systematically to avoid. With its quiet suggestion that 'history' is always 'history-as-written' or 'history-as-writing', history becomes something constituted by and inseparable from its textual mode of existence. The most poignant or piquant—depending on one's politics—illustration of history's dependence on the book, is the almost Borgesian image of Marx himself, surrounded by stacks of books, writing *Das Kapital* at a desk in the British Museum.

It is worth recalling that the difference between *historia* and *graphia*, which haunts the discourse of marxist criticism, had presented no difficulty at all for the broader 'scientific' movement, the expropriation of whose aims and methods had given it a new lease on life. For structuralism had already set itself the task of deriving from a variety of cultural 'texts' the conditions of their functioning, the rules that govern, on the analogy of language, their production and reception—but without seeing those rules as constituted by anything outside the discourse they constitute. In its 'grammar' of cultural texts, 'history' would remain a narrative structure (*récit*), in which what happens (*histoire*) is simply a sequence of events in chronological order, while 'historiography' (*discours*) becomes the formal relations in which those events are presented. The relationship between these two aspects of narrative, the told and the telling, corresponds to that which obtains between the signified and signifier within language in general, the former having no prior or privileged standing in determining the latter.

Quite the contrary, the signified (*histoire*) remains a function of the constitutive activity of the signifier (*discours*) to which it bears only an arbitrary relation. Meaning or content is systemic and conventional, i.e. discourse- and culture-specific, rather than constitutive and determining. What Althusserian

—later known as structuralist—Marxism attempted to do to structuralism was very much analogous to what Marx did to Hegel, or Trotsky tried to do to Shklovsky: to carry over its project of explaining the production of meaning while inverting the priority of the terms in which that explanation was to be carried out. Just as social being determines consciousness for Marx, and social content determines literary form for Trotsky—rather than the other way round—so for structuralist marxism the material relations of history determine the signifying forms of its textual constructs. These thus retain a trace, if only in the form of a negative or false impression, of the material relations that produce them. The purpose of this attempted re-materialization of the text was to account for what would otherwise have remained, as with its formal linguistic model, unaccounted for; to endow the text of history with a political motivation by situating the operations of that text, and our explanation of those operations, within a historical and ideological context that determines their form.

But this attempt to articulate the text with its material determinants puts, as we have seen, a new stress on the concept of 'ideology' as the mediating term between textual and material relations. As the complex of 'ideas, values, and feelings by which men experience their societies at various times', ideology is supposed to participate at once in the material relations that produce the text and in the language of which the text is made. Eagleton characteristically names this concept a 'tissue' and the term serves well to suggest both materiality and textuality; the original Latin sense of the word 'text', after all, means 'tissue'. Ideology thus serves a function similar to 'sensibility' within an older Leavisite criticism as that which links the writer and his writing with his age, or even to 'experience' within a still older biographical and historical criticism as that principle of coherence in the name of which the writer binds together or gathers into his own selective possession the *disjecta membra* of his life and time.

More recently, the term 'ideology' has begun to give way to 'discursive formations', Michel Foucault's term for the structure of the language in which a given historical *episteme* talks to itself, and which, like 'ideology', is co-opted to lend a sense of material concreteness to the apparently trans-material structures of language and textuality. But such concepts as ideology and discursive formations are only material by rhetorical transference, and as such are instinct with the metaphysical and idealist tendencies they were adopted to avoid. The need to articulate the structuralist perception of the linguistic nature of textuality with an older marxist understanding of history as material relations has led to the adoption of conceptual expedients which are themselves metaphoric, rhetorical functions; has led, that is, to a contradiction within the ideology of marxism itself.

The marxist need to accommodate a rival and idealist system of explanation of social constructs has not gone unquestioned from within marxism. 'Language as a model!' exclaimed the author of what is still one‘ of the most penetrating critiques of structuralism. 'To rethink everything through once again in terms of linguistics!'[21] That was the project of the late sixties and seventies, and Fredric Jameson's scepticism has turned out to be prophetic. The longed-for exit from the structuralist prison-house of language back into history was blocked in advance. Nor is the latest marxist endeavour to find a way out of the deconstructionist library of Babel by entering into its labyrinth of textuality likely to meet with greater success. To rethink everything through once again in terms of deconstruction! For that is precisely what Eagleton and others are now engaged in doing, as they seek that philosopher's stone of contemporary theory, a *materialist deconstruction.*

This latest oxymoronic project of a materialist deconstruction—perhaps it should be termed 'dysconstruction'—is surely as foredoomed to turn up, not a new theoretical ground, but more rhetorical figures—however brilliant the particular readings it produces—much as the earlier project of structuralist marxism did.[22] The need to counteract or co-opt the

---

[21] Fredric Jameson, *The Prison-House of Language* (Princeton: Princeton University Press, 1972), p. vii.

[22] The project of materialist deconstruction is developed in Eagleton's recent *The Rape of Clarissa* (Oxford: Basil Blackwell, 1982). The ultimate impossibility of his own problematic synthesis is unwittingly formulated by Eagleton himself, when he sees in Richardson's combination of textual productivity and bourgeois didacticism 'the pressing problem [of] how is a structural openness, the essential medium of transformed relations between producers and audiences, to be reconciled with a

weaponry of its most powerful rivals, to engage dialectically with their only too idealist theoretical systems, seems to be endemic to marxism as a demystifying—as distinct from deconstructive—counter-ideology. Its repeated attempts to shore up its historical foundations by expropriating the terminologies and methodologies of its rivals are futile in so far as they reveal only the metaphoricity of those 'foundations' and the residual idealism of its own terminologies and methodologies. But even if marxism's will to base itself on the materialist ground of real history remains a dream, it is a dream—or for some, a nightmare—arising from the guilty political unconscious of our over-privileged institutions, and one that thankfully shows no signs of going away. For marxism is the secular consience of our western liberal democracies; its appeal, as it is coming to see itself, is not theoretical or logical but moral and rhetorical, and no less powerful on that account.

necessary doctrinal closure?' (p. 22). An analogous project of reconciling Marx and Derrida is undertaken by Michael Ryan, *Marxism and Deconstruction: A Critical Articulation* (Baltimore: Johns Hopkins University Press, 1982): 'I am convinced that if marxists were . . . to carry the critique of capitalism and of bourgeois culture into the home turf of bourgeois philosophy and thought, the result would be something *like* a politicized version of deconstruction' (p. 44). As Ryan's italics suggest, the concepts of 'relation, difference, and antagonism' he studies in marxist and deconstructive thought can be *metaphorically* related. My own view is that the rigorous extension of deconstruction into politics would logically issue, not in socialism, but in anarchism. But cf. Christopher Norris, 'On Marxist Deconstruction: Problems and Prospects,' *Southern Review*, xvii. 2 (1984), pp. 203–11, for a more optimistic view of the project, and Terry Eagleton's contribution to 'The "Text in Itself": A Symposium,' ibid., pp. 115–46, for a recent defence of that 'hermeneutical violence' which I have variously termed in the foregoing pages 'systematic misconstruction,' 'textual harassment,' and 'dysconstruction.'

3

Structuralism in Retrospect

Le sémiologue est celui qui exprime sa mort future
dans les termes mêmes où il a nommé et compris le
monde.

Pour ma part, je ne me considère pas comme un
critique, mais plutôt comme un romancier, scrip-
teur, non du roman, il est vrai, mais du 'romanesque': *Mythologies, L'Empire des signes* sont des romans
sans histoire, *Sur Racine* et *S/Z* sont des romans *sur*
histoires ... Je pourrais dire que ma propre
position ... est d'être à l'arrière-garde de l'avant-
garde: être d'avant-garde, c'est savoir ce qui est
mort; être d'arrière-garde, c'est l'aimer encore:
j'aime le romanesque mais je sais que le roman est
mort: voilà, je crois, le lieu exact de ce que j'écris.

Roland Barthes

I. A SPECIFIC SCIENCE OF LITERATURE

Within the history of literary criticism, the year 1966 may well
come to be regarded, if not as miraculous or apocalyptic, at
least as auspicious of that crisis from which the institution has
not yet emerged, the transition from its interpretive or
hermeneutic to its theoretical phase of development. Not only
was 1966 the year in which Pierre Macherey published *Pour
une théorie de la production littéraire*, inaugurating the recent
vogue of 'structuralist' marxist criticism, but it was arguably
also the year in which structuralism itself came of age as a
literary-critical school and movement with the publication by
Roland Barthes of *Critique et vérité*.

As recently and publicly as 1963 in the *TLS*, Barthes had
denied it was yet either, at least in its specifically literary

manifestation.[1] But three years later, owing no doubt to the catalytic effect of Professor Raymond Picard's attack upon it, *la nouvelle critique* envisioned its programme in the sharpest self-definition to date:

We enjoy the benefit of a history of literature, but not of a science of literature, doubtless because we have not yet been able to identify fully the literary *object*, which is a written object. From the moment one grants that the work is the product of writing (and draws the implications of this), a *specific* science of literature (*une* certaine *science de la littérature*] is possible. Its object (if it exists one day) could never be to impose on the work a meaning, in the name of which it would claim the right to reject other meanings. Such a 'science' would undermine itself by so doing, in the way it has always done up till now. It could not be a science of content (to which only the strictest historical science could lay claim), but a science of the *conditions* of content, that is, of form. This will be its concern, the variety of meanings produced, indeed, *producible* by works. Such a science will not interpret symbols, but rather their multi-valence. In a word, its object will not be the 'full' meanings [*sens pleins*] of the work, but on the contrary the 'empty' meaning [*sens vide*] that supports them all.

Its model will of course be linguistic. Faced with the impossibility of commanding all the sentences of a language, linguists agree to establish a *hypothetical descriptive model*, from which they can explain how the infinite sentences of a language are generated . . . . There is no reason not to try to apply such a method to works of literature. These works are themselves comparable to immense sentences, derived from a general language of symbols through a specific [*certain*] number of regulated transformations, or, in a more general way, through a specific logic of signification which remains to be described. To put it another way, linguistics can give literature that generative model which is the basis [*principe*] of all science, since it is always a matter of having specific [*certaines*] rules at one's disposal in order to explain certain results.[2]

---

[1] 'The Structuralist Activity', reprinted in *Critical Essays*, tr. Richard Howard (Evanston: Northwestern University Press, 1972), pp. 207–20.

[2] *Critique et vérité* (Paris: Éditions du Seuil, 1966), pp. 56–8. Italics Barthes'. Translation mine. In this passage, the rendering of Barthes' phrase '*une* certaine *science de la littérature*' is doubly crucial. Rather than 'a kind of science' or 'some sort of science', I have translated '*une* certaine *science*' as 'a *specific* science', because Barthes' use of 'certaine', repeated three times in the passage is, as linguists would say, referentially specific. He has something definite in mind. 'Positive' is an alternative, but that has unfortunate connotations, particularly in the context of his attack on the outmoded pseudo-scientificity of Picard and Lanson.

The passage is worth quoting at some length, since it foreshadows the concerns that have since become familiar in structuralist poetics: the rejection of traditional interpretation and particular meanings in favour of the conditions of meaning, of the work's statement in favour of its grammar; the adoption of Saussurean *langue* or Chomskian 'competence' as analogies for that literariness within which particular works (like the *paroles* or 'performance' which are their linguistic counterparts) have their only meaningful existence; the cultivation of *system*, of a structure of rules enabling and governing the production and interpretation of a literary work in the first place, as the system of a language enables it to be produced and understood by its speakers; and above all, the emphasis on science and specificity as the desired and definitive, if not yet achieved, goal of literary study.

Lest this explicit commitment to a science of literature be ascribed—as it often has been, thereby preventing serious philosophical discussion—to some such Gallic foible as a passion for logic or a penchant for fashion, it will be instructive at this point to shift the scene from France in the sixties to America in the seventies. In introducing Tzvetan Todorov's *Poétique de la prose* to an Anglo-American audience, Jonathan Culler, in his role as cultural impresario, finds it necessary to supplement Richard Howard's purely linguistic efforts with some cultural translation of his own:

We [Anglo-American critics] have been accustomed to assume that the purpose of theory is to enrich and illuminate critical practice, to make possible subtler and more accurate interpretations of particular literary works. But poetics asserts that interpretation is not the goal of literary study. Though the interpretation of works may be fascinating and personally fulfilling, the goal of literary study is to understand literature as a human institution, a mode of signification.

The other problem is 'science' itself. While the French 'science', like the German '*Wissenschaft*', may have a less hard-edged meaning than the English 'science', and refer to a body of knowledge that is systematic but not so strictly rigorous as physics or chemistry, it still seems to me to carry in the context the methodological emphasis of our 'social *science*' or 'political *science*', the closest English counterparts I know to the French sense of '*sciences humaines*'.

The radical ambiguity of this key phrase, as will become apparent in this chapter, is only what might be expected from a critic whose own writerly ambivalence toward the scientificity of structuralism was to emerge in the course of his work.

When poetics studies individual works it seeks not to interpret them but to discover the structures and conventions of literary discourse which enable them to have the meanings they do.[3]

In stating the case for a structuralist poetics, Culler plays down the scientific, in favour of the systematic aspect of the new discipline, even to the point of suggesting—questionably —its consistency with the native, North-American system-making of Northrop Frye. Culler restates in softer tones than those of Paris the insistent structuralist distinction between poetics and interpretation—the one systematic and principled; the other subjective and ideological—and attempts to invert their relative standing within a climate of Anglo-American empiricism. The aspiration toward a totalizing and systematic understanding of literature at the expense of interpretation, of the direct pursuit and seizure of particular meanings, still emerges clearly. Yet even in this bland, plausible retailing of Barthes' luminous polemic, we may already glimpse disconcertingly the shape of things to come.

My purpose in returning to the scientific, or at least systematic, rationale of structuralist poetics is not to attempt to arbitrate once and for all the question of whether a structuralist science of literature, whatever that might be, can or does exist—though this is one of the few issues relating to literary study on which I personally have no doubts—but to raise the anterior question of why so many and such gifted critics wished at a certain time to think it could or does. (For the quotation I have taken from Barthes' *Critique et vérité* could be replicated many times over from the work of Todorov or Genette.) Why has the scientization of literary studies become a pressing issue, among both marxists and structuralists, on both sides of the Atlantic, during the past two decades? Let us remain for the moment in America. Here is Robert Scholes in 1974, on Gérard Genette's *Discours du récit*:

It would not be correct, and not even flattering, to suggest that Genette has enlarged the possibilities of criticism. *Criticism is plagued by an excess of possibilities as it is. What we need in criticism are limits, guidelines, ways of focusing our work so that we can avoid duplication* and enlarge

---

[3] *The Poetics of Prose*, trans. Richard Howard (Oxford: Basil Blackwell, 1977), p. 8.

our knowledge of the whole system of literature. Like Todorov, Genette offers us just that possibility. And I should like to think that in the present survey and discussion of structuralist activity in literature, that invitation is being accepted *and the possibilities of critical progress* are being enhanced.[4]

The movement, that is, seems to be negatively as well as positively motivated. It wants to avoid, as well as to achieve, something. The possibilities of critical progress' seem to be predicated on a settling of accounts, on a setting of 'limits, guide-lines, ways of focusing our work so that we can avoid duplication'. Criticism 'as it is', that is, in its familiar form of interpretation, has somehow got out of control, broken its confines, become a 'plague', an 'excess', a cancer. At last it is out: that interpretive activity which Culler concedes 'may be fascinating and personally fulfilling' has become, in Scholes's more anxious view, a nightmare of repetition and excess.

'Structure', 'system'—how firm these concepts feel against the flux, the superflux, of interpretation! At least a momentary stay against confusion, something to shore against the ruin, the rampage, of new and practical criticism. This state of affairs was particularly dire by the late sixties in America, where the individualism endemic in new criticism as a protestant and democratic institution—every man his own interpreter standing in sacred, unmediated relation to the words on the page—had been cultivated. In combination with the corporate structure—call it the rotarianism—of American academic life, with its routine of conference papers, publication, and promotion, it issued in a welter of journals, each offering a welter of 'readings' of everything, as we say, from *Beowulf* to Virginia Woolf. In England too, the delayed but inevitable success of practical criticism, also a puritan, petit-bourgeois movement which had issued in a new academic middle class, was precisely the problem. Practical criticism exhibited less and less of the old aristocratic reluctance to risk the questionable taste of expressing one's personal view of this or that book. After all, the old historical scholarship and older philology were impersonal; there was no way that research

---

[4] *Structuralism in Literature: An Introduction* (New Haven: Yale University Press, 1974), p. 167. My italics.

into the history of a language or a culture could be mistaken for self-expression or personal belief. And that was the lovely thing about it. Unless, of course, one read between the lines, but in that case personal expression was at least discreet and therefore permissible. So there was certainly reason for anxiety over the actual or potential multiplication of interpretations to the point where it was or soon would be impossible to 'know the literature' in the field.

We have encountered a paradox, however, that demands some explanation: the *nouvelle critique* seems to be capable of being perceived as both a *cause* of critical anarchy (by Raymond Picard, *et al.*) and as a *control* upon critical anarchy (by Robert Scholes, Jonathan Culler, *et al.*) at the same time. Indeed, Barthes' sort of criticism was capable, according to Picard, of '*n'importe quoi*', of '*généralisations abusives*' and '*extrapolations aberrantes*', and culpable for its disregard of '*les règles élémentaires de la pensée scientifique*'.[5] This paradox is explicable, up to a point, in terms of the different institutional contexts of French and Anglo-American literary study during the preceding decades. In France, where institutional control of interpretation has been more conservative, not to say repressive, something like a classic revolutionary situation may be said to have existed. The closest the *ancienne critique* in both its journalistic and academic forms had come to even the casual empiricism of Anglo-American 'new' and 'practical' criticism had been the *critique d'interprétation* of Sartre, Goldmann, and others. Yet this *engagée* marxist or existentialist criticism corresponds in certain ways more closely to the older historical scholarship that 'new' criticism had all but replaced in America by the late fifties, than to the formal renaissance of new criticism itself. An avant-garde critic like Barthes, unlike his structuralist followers in America, was trying to transform academic literary study from its *ancienne* to its *nouvelle* forms without passing through any interim stage. Hence, he had to do two things at once: to *free* criticism from the limitations and constraints of 'mimetic criticism' (*la critique vraisemblable*), which in marxist fashion he identifies with 'bourgeois' criticism; but also to establish, under the pressure of bourgeois

[5] *Critique et vérité*, pp. 12, 64, 66.

reaction, a new system of constraints that would save it from the charge and actuality of anarchism, of 'anything goes'. The programme of a 'science of literature' met both revolutionary requirements at once, of liberation and discipline, whereas in America, by contrast, the war of independence from the old philology occurred by stages, a longer and quieter revolution consisting of a period of exuberant self-expression (that of new criticism proper) and a period of ascetic self-scrutiny (that of the methodological reappraisal of the past decade).

In certain ways, however, the 'mimetic criticism' that Barthes sets out to subvert does correspond, in its bourgeois complacency, circularity, and unself-consciousness, to new and practical criticism. The conventions of mimetic criticism in 1965 (*'les règles de la vraisemblable critique en 1965'*) are, according to Barthes, *l'objectivité, le goût*, and *la clarté*.[6] Because this mode of criticism, like its Anglo-American counterparts, had been methodologically and ideologically unself-conscious —its practice far outran its theory—each of these features is actually a pretext for something else. Under cover of 'objectivity' masquerade highly questionable and outmoded notions of 'evidence', such as biography, history, laws of genre, psychology. 'Good taste' corresponds to the presuppositions of bourgeois morality and manners; 'clarity' is the mark of works that observe the habits of the realistic tradition. The conventions of mimetic criticism represent a set of covert value-judgements based on nothing more than convention and ideology, linked as they are to the study of classic literature and largely useless before contemporary works which transgress or transform the rules of the representational game. As a search for *the meaning* of a work, mimetic criticism is really helpless before the multivocality of literary language, whether it occurs in modern or classic texts. What seems a direct response to the words on the page is actually coded and mediated; the apparently innocent reading highly ideological. The project of dismantling this bourgeois ideology of literature had already been implicit in *Le Degré Zéro de l'écriture* (1953), in which *Barthes* calls for a kind of writing unbiased by convention or ideology. Such a hypothetical model (*écriture*

---

[6] ibid., pp. 17–35.

degré zéro, écriture blanche, écriture neutre) is of course as impossible in creative writing as in literary criticism. But by stripping away the illusions of bourgeois criticism, *Critique et vérité* clears a discursive space, makes imaginative room for the manœuvres of *la nouvelle critique* in something of the way that *Écriture degré zéro* had tried to do for *le nouveau roman*.

Even from so over-simplified an account of the academic context in which structuralist poetics emerged during the sixties, it becomes clear how it could be taken as either a new freedom or a new constraint, and how each of these aspects of the movement could be taken as either a welcome or unwelcome development. In fact, we seem to have been led back, from this brief historical sketch, to a fundamental structuralist principle: to wit, that myths perform a mediating role between the claims of profound cultural oppositions. Such a role or function is implicit in Barthes' oft-repeated definition of literature as 'institutionalized subjectivity', and it should not be surprising to find criticism (conceived as existing either within or outside the institution of literature) working in much the same way: 'The goal of all structuralist activity, whether reflective or poetic, is to reconstruct an "object" in such a way as to manifest thereby the rules of its functioning (the "functions") of this object. Structure is therefore actually a simulacrum of the object, but a directed (*dirigé*), interested (*interessé*) simulacrum, since the imitated object makes something appear which remained invisible or, if one prefers, unintelligible in the natural object'.[7] What better way, then, to seek the 'empty sense' of structuralism as a science of literature than to essay the structuralist protocol upon Barthes' own *œuvre*, that is, to reconstitute his work in such a way as to make manifest the rules of its functioning, to cause the *langue* of his various *paroles* to appear in the ultimate hope of revealing the 'structurality' of structuralism itself? For even if there is no longer any institutional pressure on us to perfect the techniques of a mode of criticism it once seemed we might all one day be practising, the exercise may at least reveal why its chief exponent came eventually to put it behind him.

---

[7] 'The Structuralist Activity', *Critical Essays*, pp. 208–9.

II. THE SYSTEMATICITY OF SYSTEMS

In order to plot the system, better still the 'systematicity', of Barthes' long effort of system-making, we shall have to perform a number of by now classic structuralist moves. To wit, we shall treat Barthes' *œuvre* as Lévi-Strauss treats myth, that is, as a synchronic totality, of which the matrix represents a kind of cross-section. That matrix is made up of what Lévi-Strauss terms 'constituent units', or 'functions' which bear the same relation to the total system as phonemes do to the phonetic system of a language. His schematization of the Oedipus myth provides a useful precedent. There he points out that there is no need to include either all versions of a myth or all the units of any one version in order to reveal its laws, but only enough to form 'bundles of relations' among them. 'The true constituent units of a myth are not the isolated relations (or "mythemes") but bundles of such relations, and it is only as bundles that these relations can be put to use and combined so as to produce a meaning.'[8] Thus, we can proceed to identify the constituent functions (to use Propp's term) or relations (to use Lévi-Strauss') in Barthes' work as a whole, noting that each function will be at a given time linked to a given subject. Lest my selection of works and functions seem too arbitrary or exclusive, I am only applying Propp's principle of excluding particular species in his account of the morphology of the folk-tale. In formulating Function XIV, for example, 'The Hero Acquires the Use of a Magical Agent', it is understood that the magical agent may be a horse, a ring, a gusla, or something else.[9] Since it is a body of critical writing we are dealing with in Barthes' case—as distinct from language, myth, cuisine, or fashion—we will need a term for its gross constituent units analogous to the linguists' 'phoneme', Lévi-Strauss' 'mytheme' and 'gusteme', and Barthes' own 'vesteme'. Let us call the gross constituent unit of a literary-critical system, then, a 'scripteme'. The total system of Barthes' work can now be projected

---

[8] Claude Lévi-Strauss, *Structural Anthropology*, trans. Claire Jacobson and Brooke Grundfest Schoepf (London: Allen Lane, 1969), p. 211.

[9] Vladimir Propp, *Morphology of the Folktale*, trans. Laurence Scott (Austin: University of Texas Press, 1975), p. 43.

in the matrix of its constituent scriptemes (see pp. 84–5).

What emerges from this matrix is of course a distinct pattern. 'All the relations belonging to the same column', as in our Lévi-Straussian prototype, 'should exhibit one common feature which it is our task to discover.'[10] Note that in the first column all the relations have to do with a condition of constraint, stasis, or frustration, while all the relations in the second column represent acts of liberation from that condition by means of an almost magical methodological efficacy. Let us say, then, that the first column has as its common denominator a literary-critical status quo of received ideas, tradition, conventional wisdom. It is obvious, still paraphrasing Lévi-Strauss, that the second column expresses the same thing only inverted: a deliverance from this listless and constrained state by means of a methodological breakthrough or innovation, a new knowledge glowing with explanatory power. The function of the third and fourth columns may not be immediately apparent. There, in the third, we find essentially a repetition of the state of affairs obtaining in the first, but a repetition in terms of the new 'liberation'. What was a liberation in column two may once again become frustration or constraint in three. The fourth column expresses the scriptor's recognition of this potential contradiction, together with the claim or hope of its transcendence. Thus, it becomes clear within our matrix that the early opposition of *l'écriture classique* and *l'écriture degré zéro* represents the same scripteme or 'bundle-concept' within Barthes' total system as does the mid-career opposition of *la critique vraisemblable* and *la nouvelle critique*, as does the late opposition of *texte de plaisir* and *texte de jouissance*. Similarly, the fourth-column 'liberations' of marxist, anthropological, freudian, semiological, and 'erotic' structures, whatever their individual differences, all belong to what is essentially the same position in a system of oppositions between what might be termed, at the most general level, *the routine text* and *the charismatic text*. The fifth column is present only in the form of the present analysis.

Given such a structural matrix of Barthes' own structuration, how much better placed are we to recognize the role of

---

[10] *Structural Anthropology*, p. 215.

Le Degré zéro de l'écriture (1953)	The bourgeois writer sees his world reflected in the enchanted glass of literary language (*l'écriture classique*).	In 1848, political events break the enchanted glass of language. The writer painfully reassembles the pieces (*la flaubertisation de l'écriture*).
Mythologies (1957)	The magicians of bourgeois commercial culture have disguised their artificial world as natural.	The marxist critic gives voice to the objects of culture, which proclaim their real identities.
Sur Racine (1963)	Racine is held captive by academic giants and theatrical dwarfs in the cave of convention.	The Freudian anthropologist frees Racine with a wave of the Oedipus legend.
Éléments de sémiologie (1964)	The knight sets out for the fairyland of semiology prophesied by the old Swiss hermit.	The knight enters the garden of semiology, claims it in the name of science, and names its creatures.
Critique et vérité (1966)	The giant Racinian scholar challenges the youthful new critic to combat.	The young knight unhorses the giant with the bright new lance of structuralism and slays him with the sword of system.
Système de la mode (1967)	The town is under the charm of fashion-language.	The clear-sighted semioclast points out that fashion-language has no clothes but many rules.
S/Z (1970)	The realist writer holds the bourgeois reader under the spell of the readerly (*lisible*) text.	The (post-)structuralist critic hews the readerly text into five 'codes' and 561 'lexias' with the magic sword of system.
Le Plaisir du texte (1973)	The reader dwells in a pleasure-garden of texts (*textes de plaisir*), a 'sanctioned Babel'.	The reader launches out into the 'atopic' landscape of blissful texts (*textes de jouissance*), and is promptly transformed into an author.
Fragments d'un discours amoureux (1977)	The lover languishes, abject and passive, under the spell of love.	The (post-)structuralist transforms the lover into an amorous subject by assimilating him to writing.

The socialist realist fails to see the cracks in the glass, and remains spellbound.

The modern writer and marxist critic see a vision of a new literary language (*l'écriture blanche, neutre, degré zéro*).

The Marxist anthropologist demystifies modern bourgeois culture, revealing its structure of myth.

The critic uncovers the structural anthropology of Racinian drama, and releases all its imprisoned types.

The semiologist projects a study of society as a system of sign-systems.

The knight reveals to the onlookers the principles of his lance-wielding and the secrets of his sword-play.

The knight of the empty sense (*sens vide*) embarks on his quest for the grail of structuralist poetics.

The semioclast breaks charm of fashion-language strips off its magic robe, and and dissects its anatomy.

The magic sword of system, out of control, hews literature into an infinity of categories, then transforms itself into an issue of *Poetics Today*.

The readerly text turns into a writerly (*scriptible*) text, the critic into a writer (*écrivain*), the sword of system into the pen of writerliness.

The beasts of law and custom bar access to the bower of textual bliss.

The reader/author slays the beasts of law and custom, enters the bower of textual bliss, and builds a temple of bliss in the form of a library of Babel.

The (post-)structuralist reveals the fragmented structure of amorous subjectivity as an ABC of love.

'science' within it? Science, in the successive methodological guises of marxist, anthropological, freudian, and semiological analysis—each of which lays claim to scientific status—seems to be the agency by means of which an older or routinized knowledge is replaced by a new and charismatic one within each of his books, as well as from book to book. It seems to carry with it in Barthes' system the catalytic or talismanic value of an *enabling* or *liberating* power. Science at once dispels the mystification of a previous mode of writing (or that of his own previous work), conventional wisdom, superstitution, dominant ideology—what he terms elsewhere the *doxa* or what-goes-without-saying—and galvanizes writing into movement. Yet science, in each of its successive forms, seems to turn at some point into yet another routine. The enabling, liberating power of science seems inextricable from its simultaneous potential to become a constraining, frustrating order. What frees and inspires becomes routinized as institutionalized mediocrity, as marxism does in the hands of the socialist realists or neutral writing does in the hands of the imitators of Hemingway and Camus, and, of course, as Barthes' own criticism does in the hands of his disciples or even in his retrospective view of his own work. The science of the day itself becomes convention, *doxa*, repetition, routine, in sum, an imprisoning superstitution requiring a further liberation. Hence the necessity within Barthes' total system for repeated change from one version of 'science' to another, with each new version holding the same promise and the same disappointment, i.e. the same ambivalence, at any given point in our cross-section of the system as a whole. Thus, Barthes himself, speaking of the period in which he wrote his most strenuously 'scientific' (some would say his most arid) books, *Elements of Semiology* and *Système de la mode*, refers to his '*rêve euphorique de scientificité*'.[11] Science, the enlightenment mode of rational liberation, seems to cast, as its shadow-side, a kind of nineteenth-century superstitution, that asks in turn to be dispelled or exorcised by a newer, more potent science.

This systematization of Barthes' system-making has given

---

[11] *Le Magazine littéraire*, no. 97, p. 20. Quoted by Philip Thody, *Roland Barthes: A Conservative Estimate* (London: Macmillan, 1977), p. 107.

rise to a number of problems, not the least of which—let it be admitted at last—is that of systematization itself. How can Barthes' work maintain a claim to being systematic when its procedures continually change? If the methods, as well as the objects, of a science change so freely, does it remain science? This raises the more basic question of where these structures or systems are finally located? In the 'object' or in the observing subject? In literature? In the Barthes who observes it? In the observer of Barthes observing literature? The system of Barthes' work I have offered, with its scheme of functions, relations, and 'scriptemes', might well have come out differently, if different procedures had been followed or if someone else had constructed it—but these two conditions, in the human as distinct from the physical sciences mean practically the same thing, since the way the object is conceived determines the procedures used to understand it.[12] Would our

[12] The succession of 'scientific' paradigms within Barthes' work suggests the influential account of the development of science itself offered by Thomas S. Kuhn, *The Structure of Scientific Revolutions* (Chicago: University of Chicago Press, 1962). According to Kuhn, the paradigm that has governed physical and biological science for the past three centuries, within which research is defined as a disinterested quest for 'objective knowledge' is now in question: 'Research in parts of philosophy, psychology, linguistics, and even art history, all converge to suggest that the traditional paradigm is somehow askew' (p. 121). The notion of an objective 'truth', to which science brings us ever closer, is giving way to that of a shared communal description of phenomena commanding only provisional assent: 'We have to relinquish the notion, explicit or implicit, that changes of paradigm carry scientists and those who learn from them closer and closer to the truth' (p. 170). This view that scientific paradigms do not investigate a given or prior 'object' but *constitute* it in a way more closely akin to the arts, historiography, and the humanities is variously developed by C. H. Waddington, *Behind Appearance* (Cambridge, Mass.: Harvard University Press, 1970); Paul K. Feyerabend, *Philosophical Papers* (Cambridge: Cambridge University Press, 1981, 2 vols.); Richard Rorty, *Philosophy and the Mirror of Nature* (Princeton: Princeton University Press, 1979); and David Bleich, *Subjective Criticism* (Baltimore: Johns Hopkins University Press, 1978). More directly concerned with the development of the institutions of the social sciences, but sharing the same general scepticism toward the objective validity of a given paradigm or episteme, is of course the massive *œuvre* of Michel Foucault.

In the light of this growing and persuasive body of thought, it is difficult to argue that alchemy, for example, does not have exactly the same epistemological status as chemistry, however surprising such a view might be to a professional chemist engaged in research. The chemist might well contend that chemistry is different from alchemy in that it works. To which the philosopher or historian of science might respond, that the pragmatic distinction between a scientific paradigm that 'works' and one that does not 'work' is itself constituted and defined by the assumptions and purposes of the paradigm. It 'works' if it produces the kind of results those employing it desire

matrix have changed if more of Barthes' works had been included? Or if his functional relations had been represented, not in the form of fairy-tale functions but in a more algebraic mode? And what would have happened to the matrix if I had tried to include the system of other structuralists—Todorov perhaps, or Genette, or Souriau, or Greimas—in order to make it more truly a meta-system in which the system of each critic's work became itself a 'systeme', a constituent unit within a meta-structure, or structure of structures, even if only at a given point of development, say, in 1966. And why limit ourselves to France? Should structuralism not be conceived at this point in the history of criticism as an international problematic, at the very least a Franco-American can of worms?

Clearly there is no limit on our ability to question the objectivity of our own structuration. Indeed, the master system-maker who could satisfy all demands of inclusiveness, justify the necessity of every exclusion, and achieve consensus, let alone agreement, that everything was in its proper place and there was a place for everything appropriate—such a master-builder would have performed a feat worthy, if not of a god, at least of Orpheus or Amphion, at the second of whose lyre stones took their places in the wall of Thebes. We have reached that point in our reflection on system-making where it begins to take on the characteristics of those activities to which it had been initially opposed. The more closely we examine our systems, indeed the minute we attempt to make one of our own, the more clearly we become aware of how wilful or arbitrary or expedient our choices and relations really are. Our system-making, undertaken in a spirit of science, changes back before our eyes, first into that dreaded and vilified thing, interpretation, and finally into a kind of, dare I say it, fiction or poetry!

and expect. Alchemists and chemists desire and expect different kinds of results from their activity, and would thus mutually deny the effectiveness of each other's practice.

The epistemological implications for those recent literary-critical movements which have claimed 'scientific' and 'objective' status are (1) they are operating upon an older, not to say outmoded, paradigm of scientific objectivity, and (2) their rhetorical self-justifications in terms of that older paradigm are misguided and unnecessary at a time when science itself is recognizing that its own methods are ultimately no more objective than those of the arts.

The scientific subject has not been able to maintain that distance in relation to the object which is necessary to maintain his role of scientist; rather, a merging or greeting of the perceiving subject with the perceived object has taken place, willy-nilly, which we associate with imagination. Our effort to construct the Barthesian system by turning his more or less expository prose into functional relations *à la* Propp and Lévi-Strauss—and how justified was that initial sleight-of-hand, after all?—only mirrors Barthes' own efforts to construct a system of literature. The exercise has proved highly instructive, however, not because it has been successful, but because it has been so spectacularly unsuccessful. If nothing else, it has revealed how difficult it is to distinguish Barthes the shaman or singer (or perhaps pied-piper) from Barthes the would-be scientist. Having translated his work into its constituent 'scriptemes,' can we ever rescue it from the never-never-land of folktale and myth back to the 'firm' ground of science?

III. THE DREAM OF SCIENTIFICITY

Would Barthes himself have even wished it to be rescued? By the time of *S/Z* (1970), arguably even earlier, Barthes had awakened from his self-styled 'euphoric dream of scientificity':

There are said to be certain Buddhists whose ascetic practices enable them to see a whole landscape in a bean. Precisely what the first analysts of narrative were attempting: to see all the world's stories (and there have been ever so many) within a single structure: we shall, they thought, extract from each tale its model, then out of these models we shall make a great narrative structure, which we shall reapply (for verification) to any one narrative: a task as exhausting (ninety-nine percent perspiration, as the saying goes) as it is ultimately undesirable, for the text thereby loses its difference. This difference is not obviously, some complete, irreducible quality (according to a mythic view of literary creation), it is not what designates the individuality of each text, what names, signs, finishes off each work with a flourish; on the contrary, it is a difference which does not stop and which is articulated upon the infinity of texts, of languages, of systems: a difference of which each text is the return.[13]

[13] *S/Z*, trans. Richard Miller (New York: Hill and Wang, 1974), p. 3.

Robert Scholes reads this passage as Barthes' repudiation of 'one important aspect of structuralist poetics . . . . This is not exactly a fair representation', he goes on, 'of the work of Greimas, Bremond, and Todorov, which Barthes had proudly introduced in *Communications 8* but it is close enough to be painful, and it indicates, though perhaps too starkly, too dramatically, a certain shift of emphasis within structuralism.' That shift, according to Scholes, has been toward the method's 'applicability to individual texts, and this has been a healthy phenomenon.' Scholes takes it as 'a sign of vitality that interpretative works as rich and satisfying as *S/Z* and Genette's *Figures III* have emerged from the structuralist matrix.'[14]

Has Scholes, not to mention Barthes, forgotten or mispoken himself? How can interpretation, that perverse child of bourgeois individualism, be so casually welcomed home, like a returned prodigal? Has interpretation really been reformed, its delinquent, even anarchic, tendencies chastened or purged? In fact, if we wish to be accurate about our kinship structures, we should have to call interpretation the locked-away grandparent rather than the prodigal child of structuralism, since its own prolific structuration has always already been engendered by a prior act of interpretation, with all its undeclared wilfulness or arbitrariness. This has often been remarked with reference to the structures of Propp, Lévi-Strauss, and Jakobson, all of which are *constructed*—the word itself is telling—according to a prior, if silent, act of interpretation, as to which categories and what data are relevant, before they are then applied to further data. This is exactly the procedure that Barthes parodies in the opening vignette of *S/Z*, and that I confess to using in my own mock-up of Barthes' system. Scholes is, in fact, under no illusion that Barthes has managed to avoid the pitfalls of traditional interpretation in his reconstructed version of it in *S/Z*. Barthes is criticized for being 'too arbitrary, too personal, and too idiosyncratic' in his choice and characterization of the 'codes' he finds at work—or is it at play?—in 'Sarrasine'. 'The system operating here is not systematic enough to be applied easily by

[14] *Structuralism in Literature*, pp. 148–9.

other analysts to other texts,' Scholes inconclusively concludes, 'yet there is a great emphasis on the process of systematization.'[15]

The problem was more serious than Scholes made it sound. The reason why structuralism/semiology always involves interpretation (and the ideological distortion that goes with it) is that in Saussurean linguistics there can be no signs without meanings, and meanings are culturally, i.e. ideologically, determined.[16] *Signifiant* and *signifié*, signifier and signified, are inseparable, as Saussure graphically put it, as the sides of a sheet of paper, so that any set of signs must have at least one meaning. What Saussurean linguistics does do away with is not signified meaning but direct, unmediated reference or denotation, since the linguistic signified stands between the linguistic signifier and any non- or extra-linguistic referent we might wish to denote. While the signified has been demoted, in so far as it can no longer be easily and directly identified with the referent, it cannot be done away with altogether. The structuralist temptation to discredit the signified is none the less very strong, since the signified-as-referent is the traditional and illusory counter of bourgeois, mimetic criticism, the

---

[15] ibid., p. 155.

[16] The desire to empty literary study of its ideological contraband informs the polemic of Susan Sontag, *Against Interpretation* (New York: Farrar, Strauss, and Giroux, 1967). For Sontag, an early fellow-traveller of *la nouvelle critique* and *le nouveau roman*, the object of giving over interpretation is to arrive not at a science of literature but an 'erotics of art'. To illustrate the ideological vagaries of interpretation, Sontag cites Elia Kazan's notes on his production of *A Streetcar Named Desire*: 'In order to direct the play, Kazan had to discover that Stanley Kowalski represented the sensual and vengeful barbarian that was engulfing our culture, while Blanche Du Bois was Western civilization, poetry, delicate appeal, dim lighting, refined feelings and all, though a little the worse for wear to be sure. Tennessee Williams' forceful psychological melodrama now became intelligible: it was about something, about the decline of Western civilization. Apparently, were it to go on being *a play about a handsome brute named Stanley Kowalski and a faded mangy belle named Blanche Du Bois*, it would not be manageable.' (Italics mine.) Here we have it: the *sens vide*, the empty structure of the play, its reduction to hardly more than a folk-tale function. Of course her version of the *sens vide* is very much another *sens plein*, one overflowing its spare confines with much the same neo-romantic ideology of savage nobility or proletarian energy overturning a decadent social order as that which informs Kazan's, only with an inverse valorization. No doubt Williams has activated in his play a semiotic code or system familiar to students of southern gothic writing, but how that system is 'constructed' is very much a function of the ideology of the semiologist/interpreter. For semiology implies ideology, and the semiologist is always an interpreter, whether or not he or she is aware of it.

reviled *critique vraisemblable*. Indeed, the ease with which mimetic—not to mention marxist—criticism has confused what belongs to language (the signified) with what does not belong to language (the referent), has been a minor scandal, and it is therefore hardly surprising that the signified became a neglected or enfeebled category in the strucaturalist account of literary language. 'Literature had been regarded long enough as a message without a code', as Genette wittily describes the excesses (*outrances*) of the Russian formalists, 'that it became necessary to consider it for a moment as a code without a message.'[17] To do so in the Russia of 1920 was a highly ideological, even counter-revolutionary act, and this aspect of Russian formalism did not, of course, go unnoticed by the political authorities.

But there can be no codes without messages, no signifiers without signifieds, in the Saussurean model of language, so a signified had to be posited if literature was to be considered afresh as a sign-system operating on that model. There were two possible ways of conceiving the literary signified available to structuralism, each taking a different point of departure and leading in a different direction. The first is termed by Barthes, following Louis Hjelmslev, 'scientific semiotics', or what came to be known in Anglo-America as 'structuralist poetics'; the second, 'connotative semiotics', or cultural semiology. In scientific semiotics or structuralist poetics, 'a first language (or language-object)' of the literary text becomes 'the system under scrutiny; and this system-object is *signified* through the metalanguage of semiology.'[18] In this way, structuralist poetics takes as its object the text as given and reconstitutes it into the laws of its functioning, the system or 'grammar' of its operation. The signified meaning of the text is thus always in effect a function of the metalanguage of structuralist poetics, an abstracted simulacrum or 'empty sense' of the text. In this way, any temptation to identify the signified meaning of the text with a non- or extra-linguistic referent—one characteristic and illicit move of mimetic

---

[17] Gérard Genette, *Figures I* (Paris: Seuil, 1966), p. 150. Trans. mine.
[18] *Elements of Semiology*, trans. Annette Lavers and Colin Smith (New York: Hill and Wang, 1968), pp. 89–92.

criticism—is ruled out. For example, the signified meaning of Boccaccio's *Decameron* is not to be found in fourteenth-century Italy or in its author's biography or psychology, but in Todorov's *Grammaire du Décaméron*, or perhaps in the revised grammars of that text proposed by Bremond, Scholes, or most recently, John Holloway.[19] But here a serious problem arises. For any such signified into which the text can be decoded through the operations of a structuralist metalanguage, can be seen as an incomplete decoding or unpacking of the text, as merely an interim or partial transcoding of it. Its 'real' structure or grammar may still underlie the partial structure or grammar just derived from it, which then becomes not a signified but another signifier to be decoded in its turn, an occasion for further structuration. The grammar of the *Decameron* arrived at by Todorov as its empty sense or signified is in fact regarded by John Holloway as the mere signifier of a still deeper meaning with which that grammar cannot be identified. For Holloway, the ultimate signified meaning of the text consists in a humour and pathos that is unreachable, perhaps even unthinkable, in the technical operations of Todorov's metalanguage. The liberal humanist ideology of meaning that Todorov's poetics had been designed to exclude from the text can thus be smuggled only too easily back into it.

The other approach to the literary signified, that which Barthes terms 'connotative' or cultural semiotics, and which he certainly favours in his own early and middle practice, might seem more promising, since it explicitly recognizes the cultural and inescapably ideological context within which signification occurs, and can therefore explain what Holloway does with Todorov's metalinguistic grammar of the *Decameron*. On this view, the signified of literature is to be sought and found, not in the system of the text's internal relations—for this now becomes the signifier of a second- or third- order system—but on the higher and wider plane of its cultural connotations: 'As for the signified of connotation, its character is at once general, global and diffuse; it is, if you like, a fragment of ideology; the sum of the messages in French

[19] See Tzvetan Todorov, *Grammaire du Décaméron* (The Hague: Mouton, 1969). John Holloway, *Narrative and Structure* (Cambridge: Cambridge University Press, 1979), pp. 1–19.

refers, for instance, to the signified "French"; a book can refer to the signified "Literature." These signifieds have a very close communication with culture, knowledge, history, and it is through them, so to speak, that the environmental world invades the system. We might say that *ideology* is the *form* (in Hjelmslev's sense of the word) of the signifieds of connotation, while *rhetoric* is the form of the connotators'.[20] The advantage of a connotative semiotics (or in Barthes' own case 'semioclasm') is richly illustrated in Barthes' practice of it in *Mythologies, Système de la mode, S/Z,* and elsewhere. By relocating the signified of literature on the higher plane of cultural system, the meaning of the text can no longer be identified with an unself-conscious ideological reading of it—the other characteristic and illicit move of bourgeois mimetic criticism—since the ideology informing such a reading is itself part of a cultural system that can in turn be decoded on its own plane of expression and thereby demystified. At the time of *Elements of Semiology* (1964), and even by the time of 'Myth Today', included in the 1970 edition of *Mythologies,* Barthes was sanguine that 'the future probably belongs to a linguistics of connotation, for society continually develops, from the first system which human language supplies to it, second-order significant systems, and this elaboration, now proclaimed and now disguised, is very close to a real historical anthropology.'[21]

In this tentative and qualified prophecy, Barthes was at least half right. Only half right, because even as he predicts the course that semiology/semioclasm, including his own for a time, was to take, he also foreshadows the logic of its demise, and of his own disillusionment with it:

---

[20] *Elements of Semiology,* pp. 91–2. See also 'Myth Today' in *Mythologies,* trans. Annette Lavers (London: Cape, 1972), pp. 109–59; and *S/Z,* pp. 6–9. Barthes' importnt distinction between metalanguage and connotation is incisively discussed by Fredric Jameson, *The Prison-House of Language* (Princeton: Princeton University Press, 1972), pp. 159–60: 'Barthean commentary is metalanguage in that it abstracts the structure of another more primary language, such as that of Michelet or that of Racine, and makes it available in a new and different form . . . In the phenomenon of connotation, on the other hand . . . it is the whole body of one language system which stands as a signifier for some more basic signified. The primary language system really thus has two signifieds: its regular content, which we receive consecutively as the text continues, and a second overall message sent us by the form as a whole.'

[21] *Elements of Semiology,* p. 91.

Each new science would then appear as a new language which would have as its object the metalanguage which precedes it, while being directed towards the reality-object which is at the root of these 'descriptions'; the history of the social sciences would thus be, in a sense, a diachrony of metalanguages, and each science, including of course semiology, would contain the seeds of its own death, in the shape of the language destined to speak it. This relativity . . . allows us to qualify the image which we might at first form, of a semiologist over-confident in the face of connotation. . . . We might say that society, which holds the plane of connotation, speaks the signifiers of the system considered, while the semiologist speaks its signifieds. . . . But his objectivity is made provisional by the very history which renews metalanguages.[22]

Whether the signified of literature is sought and located within the operations of the text or in those of its cultural context, the metalanguage in which those operations are expressed will itself be subjected, as another *signifying* system, to a further 'scientific' metalanguage, or 'meta-metalanguage', over which the former has no control—since society *'holds the plane of connotation'*—and to which it is foredoomed to yield its claim to an achieved, objective, fully *signified* status.

Each text, whether literary, cultural, or meta-linguistic, begets a structure as its signfied which comes to be regarded as another signifier, the occasion and material for further 'objective' structuration. This latest 'objective' structure, however, turns out to be only provisional; it can be taken, in turn, as the signifier of yet another, 'ultimate' signified. That signified, though offered, in effect, in the guise of the referent, the 'real', objective structure of the text or cultural context, can always be turned into only another signifier by the next poetician or semiotician who comes to it with a different idea *or ideology* of its 'real' signification. The fact that the linguistic signified, as part of the process of language, and the objective referent, as something beneath or beyond language, can never coincide, means that the structures of literature and culture are endlessly re-interpretable, that is, 'transcodable' from the status of signifieds into that of signifiers, back again into signifieds, and so on *ad infinitum*. The implication is that endless semiosis is inevitable.

[22] ibid., pp. 93–4.

If this is sadly true of the structure extrapolated for any given text (or *parole*), it is that much more sadly true of the master-structure (or *langue*) which is supposed to support all of literature. The effort of a given structuralist to reach that ultimate, stubborn, unself-yielding structure underlying literature, or even any of its supposedly more accessible, intermediate structures will resemble, depending on the strenuousness of his style, that of either the tortoise or Achilles in Zeno's paradox. With this poignant difference: that this unwinnable because interminable race will be joined by every semiologist/interpreter/ideologue who attempts to correct or reconcile the various structures proposed. The scandal of endlessly proliferating interpretation, which structuralist poetics was invented to tidy up, has re-emerged in the remedy. The Saussurean sequestration of the signified has thus opened the possibility of a 'science' of literature that is infinitely regressive, and of texts that are infinitely plural in meaning. Indeed, if one pursues the point with philosophical rigour, as Jacques Derrida did in the late sixties in a series of droll soliloquies on 'difference', this possibility turns into a logical necessity.

At that moment, the structuralist projection of a science or system of literature reduces itself to absurdity, an event noted with rueful irony in the opening paragraph of *S/Z*. If there can be no system of signs which is not also a system of meanings, and if that system of meanings turns into yet another system of signs which begets, in turn, another system of meanings, then no matrix or model or structure or system can ever stand alone without adumbrating further matrices, models, structures, systems and so on *ad infinitum*. None of these would have any more claim to privilege, to replacing all others, than did any single interpretation in the mode of the much reviled *critique vraisemblable*. There is now neither beginning nor end to structuration, no foundation for a free-standing structure of structures which would be the definitive object and limiting objective of the enterprise. The demystification of univocal meaning, necessary as it was for displacing traditional interpretation, has not cleared the ground for an objective science of literature, but uncovered an abyss of writerly multivocality and interpretive plurality in the very place where that science was supposed to have stood. The structures of structuralism are thus rendered doubly precarious by its own premises and processes; they are both the product of nothing other than interpretation, and are themselves endlessly reinterpretable into other structures.

IV. THE TORTOISE OR ACHILLES?

The possible consequences of this predicament for literary study are foreseen by Barthes in 1970 with an acuity akin to clairvoyance: 'A choice must then be made: either to place all texts . . . under the scrutiny of an indifferent science, forcing them to rejoin, inductively, the copy from which we will then make them derive; or else to restore each text to its function, making it cohere, even before we talk about it, by the infinite paradigm of difference, subjecting it from the outset to a basic typology, to an evaluation . . . . Our evaluation can be linked only to a practice, and this practice is that of writing'.[23] *S/Z*, then, is Barthes' Achillean attempt to pursue the second alternative. If interpretive multiplicity cannot be avoided, it can at least be pursued in the full swiftness of writerly self-consciousness. This he calls the 'second operation' to which he subjects writing: 'interpretation (in the Nietzschean sense of the word). 'To interpret a text is not to give it a (more or less justified, more or less free) meaning, but on the contrary to appreciate what *plural* constitutes it.'[24] The reconstitution of interpretation as writing in effect closes the gap between subject and object, criticism and literature by openly acknowledging and participating in the plurality of difference, the full panoply of *writerliness* latent in all writing.

It is not surprising that even Barthes' apologists have found bones to pick with *S/Z*: a by now familiar arbitrariness in the choice of its five codes; the absence of a code relating specifically to narration; a lack of specificity in the final, 'cultural' code; a certain inexplicitness concerning Balzac's intentionality or self-consciousness; a need to 'castrate' Balzac's text in the interest of its own 'writerliness'.[25] This list

---

[23] *S/Z*, pp. 3–4.   [24] ibid., p. 5.
[25] See respectively Robert Scholes, *Structuralism in Literature*, p. 155; Jonathan Culler, *Structuralist Poetics* (London: Routledge and Kegan Paul, 1975), pp. 202–3;

of objections could even be extended. It is not clear, for example, whether 'Sarrasine' finally emerges as a classic or modern, readerly or writerly, text, or for that matter, whether Barthes finally deplores Balzac's complicity in the conventional ideology of realism shared with his audience, or admires Balzac's consummate skill in manipulating it. Finally, is Balzac's pluralism limited or unlimited? Or are such objections really beside the point, arising as they do out of expectations that may well be misplaced from the outset or displaced in the end. Such questions, that is, reflect uncertainty over whether *S/Z* is to be taken as interpretation as we have known it—after all, it does reaffirm a commitment to interpretation in some sense and is inward with its twenty-page text to the point of devoting 200 pages to it—or as structuralist poetics as we have come to know it. It does, after all, trade in the 'structures' of five 'codes', 561 'lexias', and ninety-three 'digressions'; it uses Greek terms to name its categories as if it were some new medical science diagnosing diseases of the body, then abbreviates them in the acronymic newspeak of computer-science; it offers an impressive array of diagrams, schemas, and matrices. The concentration of analytical energy upon the work, to the point of shattering it in the way of 'a minor earthquake' is certainly not what we have come to expect of poetics, with its serene, sweeping, aerial mapping of the large contours of the literary landscape. At the same time, its show of system, its display of technical terminology and apparatus is not what we expect of interpretation. In the face of the strenuous, self-conscious, even self-parodic performance of *S/Z*, the literary 'competence' presumed by structuralist poetics does not seem to serve us as well as the structuralists themselves might have hoped.

'The narrative competence of the reader,' writes Genette with reference to Proust, 'this very competence is what the author relies on to fool the reader by sometimes offering him false advance mentions, or *snares*—well known to connoisseurs of detective stories. Once the reader has acquired this second-degree competence of being able to detect and thus to

Terence Hawkes, *Structuralism and Semiotics* (London: Methuen, 1977), pp. 118–19; Philip Thody, *Roland Barthes*, p. 115; and Barbara Johnson, 'The Critical Difference', *Diacritics*, viii. 2 (June 1978), pp. 2–9.

outmaneuver the snare, the author is then free to offer him *false snares* (that are genuine advance mentions), and so on.'[26] This is a just description of Barthes' own working method in *S/Z*, and an adoption of his own term. The work, in presenting us with some characteristic features of poetics and some characteristic features of interpretation—but not a complete set of either—has led us to bring false generic expectations to bear on his text, to fall for the misleading snares of quantification on the one hand, and immanence on the other. The show of system turns out mainly to quantify arbitrariness, and the appearance of interpretive immanence leads not to a unified 'reading' but toward a barely controlled fragmentation or multivocality. The work turns out to be poised not between the old interpretation and the new poetics but rather between the new poetics and a still newer interpretation. This process of self-repudiation and self-transcendence is already familiar from our attempt to systematize Barthes' earlier works, each one of which in some sense repudiates or transgresses the category of the previous one. The 'difference' in the case of *S/Z* seems to be that Barthes' characteristic self-repudiation and self-transcendence occurs not diachronically or dialectically from one work to another, but simultaneously and structurally within the same work. *S/Z* is at one and the same time a structuralist and mock-structuralist text.

If there is any truth in this view of *S/Z*, it need not pose a problem, at least not a problem unfamiliar or insoluble to formalist and structuralist poetics. 'Every great book', writes Tzvetan Todorov, structuralism's chief theorist of genre, 'establishes the existence of two genres': 'the genre it transgresses' and the 'genre it creates'.[27] But these genres are never simply given. The problem is in deciding into which genre, if any, a given work fits, which, that is, it transgresses and which it creates. This is always a matter of interpretation, and one on which there can never be certainty, no matter how many categories there are. For example, are the 'codes' and 'lexias' of *S/Z* 'snares' or 'false snares'? The generic status of the work, and the concomitant expectations we bring to a

---

[26] Gérard Genette, *Narrative Discourse*, trans. Jane E. Lewin (Oxford: Basil Blackwell, 1980), p. 77.

[27] *The Poetics of Prose*. p. 43.

reading of it, turn on this decision. If they are 'snares', the work is at least mock-structuralist, and a new genre will have to be invented for it. If they are 'false snares', then the work remains structuralist, if imperfectly so, since the writer does not see the arbitrariness which we have seen to attach to them, but which is not tolerated in structuralist poetics. So to read Barthes' 'codes' as 'false snares' is rather a drastic alternative, since it presupposes that the writer does not know, or at most knows less well than his critics, what he is about. This is an unsettling conclusion to reach about a work explicitly conceived as an endorsement, even celebration, of writerly self-consciousness. And if this indeterminacy haunts a work of mere criticism, how much more doggedly it must bedevil works of 'literature'.

At this point it seems like a good idea to retrace the steps that have led us to this point, and return to the vignette of ascetic bean-gazing with which Barthes opens *S/Z*. That exemplary instance of visionary—or hallucinatory—myopia had been offered as a model of the activity of 'the first analysts of narrative', by which we assumed (along with Robert Scholes) Barthes was repudiating the work of his structuralist colleagues, including perhaps his own earlier work. But there are other possible meanings. The first analysts of narrative could refer to the Russian formalists, on whose work that of the structuralists could be seen as a refinement. Nor would it be entirely fanciful to identify Barthes' image with *S/Z* itself, which is a no less rapt meditation on a narrative of bean-like proportions, and a no less exemplary model of critical method than anything previously published by the structuralists. But to read *S/Z* as a prolonged indulgence in the exercise it initially ridicules, is to assign the work to a new genre we can only term mock-mock-structuralist, and recuperate it thereby as a work of structuralist, if not straightfaced, poetics.

Of making many genres—within either the diachrony of literary history or the synchrony of a given text's plurality—there seems to be no end, once the processes of writerly self-consciousness have been activated. Perhaps the master-trope for those processes is to be found—speaking of fairy-tales—in the motif of the sorcerer's apprentice. Faced with the multiplication of formal possibilities that writerliness releases, the vast embarrassment of actual and potential texts, the student of writing has two courses open to him. He can multiply the terms in his lexicon and the categories in his taxonomy in the vain hope of fixing the flux of the world's textuality ('there have been ever so many . . .')—or that of a single text!—with the wave of a newly devised model. Or he can acknowledge that a given text may always be assimilated to different models and thereby eludes definitive classification. The former course will result, as the past decade has made abundantly clear, in a flesh-wearying proliferation of categories, matrices, and neologisms, in the spectacle of a progress of positivism masquerading as science. The latter course will result in the abandonment, on the part of the student of writing, of any ambition or pretension to scientific objectivity, and the acquisition of a new ambition or pretension to writerly status. The tortoise or Achilles? One must choose.

How could it be otherwise, when the critical text has achieved or acquired the same sort of ambiguous or free status as the literary text it studies? Just as it is ultimately undecidable whether 'Sarrasine' is a 'readerly' or a 'writerly' text, so is it equally undecidable whether *S/Z* is a work of structuralism or mock-structuralism or mock-mock-structuralism. No presumed or actual literary competence can help us out of these dilemmas. So complete is the mockery that has been made of our carefully constructed categories by the texts they are designed to name and comprehend, that it cannot be recuperated by a tortoise-like persistence in taxonomy to the very vanishing point of scientificity. The more categories we construct, in fact, the more we *miss* the object we seek to classify, since writerliness certainly delights in, may even be defined by, its capacity to elude or boggle our best-laid classifications. By its aspiration to full writerly status, its recognition and exploitation of 'the infinite paradigm of difference', *S/Z* has raised problems well and truly beyond the resources of structuralist poetics to resolve. If it employs the tactics of connotative semiotics to defamiliarize realism, to reveal it as convention rather than nature, *S/Z* also employs the still less familiar strategies of writerly difference to defamiliarize semiotics, to reveal the arbitrariness its ideology of objectivity conceals.

What, then, are we finally to make of this structuralism with a difference, this text that dismantles system in acting out its revisionist fidelity to system, that dreams of objectivity being awake? Its subtle disturbance of structuralist method certainly did not halt the 'progress' of the latter, which carried on for some time in precisely the manner Barthes foresaw. The hypertrophication of structures and taxonomies produced by the new poetics in the decade of the seventies bears an uncanny resemblance not only to the Byzantine scholasticism of the old historicist positivism, but to the burgeoning impressionism of the old *critique d'interprétation* they were designed to check and replace. Perhaps the self-criticism or self-irony implicit in *S/Z* was too subtle to have been noticed by so busy and extroverted a band of disciples. It is, in any event, only a logical development of the restless self-revision that characterizes Barthes' work from the beginning, a self-revision now carried to the flash-point of self-deconstruction. If every charismatic, liberating text or movement subsides, sooner or later, into routinization, why should structuralism have been any different?

Yet the 'difference' of *S/Z* is precisely its dizzying recognition of difference, of inescapable displacement. If each charismatic, liberating method will require a new liberation from the routine it will soon become, this round of repetition can be broken only by anticipating routinization, by building the liberation of difference and displacement into the charismatic text *at the very instant of its enunciation*, before it can become familiarized, naturalized, and routinized. For such a text to be fully plural and writerly, it would have to be always already displaced from the signposts and landmarks of its own conventionality. It must, in fine, be forever different from itself. Such a recognition of inbuilt structural difference, with its simultaneous invitation to, and frustration of, diverse construction, I have already termed 'mock-structuralist'. It is also, of course, poststructuralist. With *S/Z*, Barthes bids farewell to the dream of systematic sweetness and light in which structuralism was born, and to the role of poetician/semiologue as a scientist standing in the sun and observing the world's textuality yield up its structures beneath his god-like gaze. Now the poetician becomes indistinguishable from the poet, no longer seeking to 'cover' the text and explain its operations from outside it,[28] but to enter fully into the dark places, the differences and displacements of the text, to inhabit, operate, and rewrite it from within. What is discovered in the process is not a chain of signification traceable to a goal or resting-point, but something more like a chain-reaction producing an energy out of all reasonable proportion to the mass of its source, and begetting as its by-product a strange new particle of powerful negative charge. Always 'there', though never quite 'present', that particle has left its trace within the criticism of the past decade and come to be identified with the name of deconstruction.

[28] Barthes' description of the structuralist objective in 1963 in 'What is Criticism?', *Critical Essays*, p. 259.

4

Deconstruction Reconstructed

> Perhaps these laws that we are trying to unravel do
> not exist at all. There is a small party who are
> actually of this opinion and who try to show that, if
> any law exists, it can only be this: the Law is
> whatever the nobles do.
>
> Franz ·Kafka

I. THE POWER OF NEGATIVE THINKING

In the unlikely event that some Nobel Prize committee of the
future decides to honour the discoverers of so anti-humanistic
a concept as deconstruction, it will be faced with more than
the usual difficulties in determining where to bestow the
award. The search for the founder or originator of the
discourse of deconstruction, flagrantly post-modernist and
avant-garde as it is, would discover, upon examination of its
major texts, a number of earlier candidates already nominated
as worthy of the honour. The short-list of nominees might well
have to stretch back behind the deconstructors of the present
to include those relatively recent inquisitors of language who
underwrite their work—such acknowleged precursors as
Heidegger, Nietzsche, and Freud—or even well behind them
to Gorgias and the pre-Socratics,[1] who did their *ur*-deconstruc-
tive philosophizing before writing had fully become its

---

[1] The first work of thoroughgoing (what I shall later term 'hard-core') deconstruction to come down to us, so striking in its wholesale anticipation of the contemporary
project as to demand reconsideration of the cultural and philosophical context that
could have conditioned it, is the fifth-century BC treatise *On Not Being, or On Nature* by
Gorgias, the argument of which was summarized by Sextus Empiricus: 'Firstly . . .
nothing exists; secondly . . . even if anything exists, it is inapprehensible by man;
thirdly . . . even if anything is apprehensible, yet of a surety it is inexpressible and
incommunicable to one's neighbour.' 'Against the Logicians', I. 65, in *Sextus
Empiricus*, trans. R. G. Bury, ii (London: Heinemann, Loeb Classical Library,
1935), p. 35.

medium, and who would themselves have had to have, within the logic of deconstructive or differential textualism, their own, ever more remote, precursors. While Nobel Prizes are often awarded belatedly or retrospectively, such an infinite regress or *mise-en-abîme* of likely candidates for the dubious title of 'founding father of deconstruction' would make something of a mockery or a nonsense of the committee's august deliberations.

But even if our hypothetical selection committee, like all such actual committees, were to persist, adopting some more or less arbitrary expedient of exclusion to make its work easier—like confining its short-list to candidates of the past twenty years—there would still be difficulties in the way of making an individual award. For the formulation of the special theory of deconstruction now being applied to literary and philosophical texts, while traceable to two or three institutions, cannot be identified definitively with the work of any one or two or three of their members. Rather, the award would have to be made jointly, as it often is in the sciences, to the concerted activities of at least two research teams working more or less independently but arriving at similarly momentous results at around the same time. And it would be hard to identify the 'primary author' or 'chief investigator' of each 'team'. In the absence of a 'citation-index', who could say which of our deconstructors was the most active influence on his colleagues?

Then too, there would still be the anterior problem of the discourse of deconstruction itself. Where did it come from? Why was it necessary or even possible to think deconstructively —allowing for the individual brilliance of the minds involved —in Paris, New Haven, and Baltimore during the late sixties and early seventies? Why deconstruction there and then? For perhaps these were mere local manifestations of a process of dislocation that had begun in the individuals concerned long before and elsewhere. Why, for that matter, deconstruction here and now? For the larger institutional and cultural question also remains to be addressed: why did, and still does, deconstruction gain and retain such a grip on us? These are doubtless questions of the future, and whether or not a Nobel Prize committee takes them up, the increasing self-reflective-ness of the institution of literary and philosophical study is not likely to leave them aside. The biographies, however deconstructible that form may be, of our recent deconstructors remain to be written, and the displacements of a more inward and personal kind within their present institutional centrality, explored.

The task of historicizing deconstruction along these lines, lines not necessarily or exclusively marxist or freudian, will be a demanding project in its own right. Our more immediate and modest purpose is to sketch the outward role of deconstruction within the drama of contemporary literary theory, for even that, despite the increasing number of books on the subject, is still widely misunderstood. Let it be stated at the outset, especially in the light of our dealings with recent marxist and structuralist poetics and our fantasy of a frustrated Nobel Prize committee, that the aim of deconstruction is not, never has been, and could never be to scientize or objectify the study of texts. If the structuralist 'dream of scientificity', in Barthes' phrase, was a reaction to, or overcorrection of, the 'engaged' critique d'interprétation, marxist and existentialist, and bourgeois critique vraisemblable, that preceded it, then deconstruction, in its French form at least, may be seen as a reaction to that reaction and an overcorrection of that overcorrection. While deconstruction has not fully engaged with the scientific and philosophical 'rigours' of the latest marxism in the way it has with those of structuralism and phenomenology, it is none the less fair to say that the claim or aspiration of the Althusserians to a specific scientific knowledge, not of literariness or poeticity, but of ideology, would be found equally misguided.

The irony of both movements, structuralist and marxist, from the viewpoint of deconstruction, is that the effort to establish a specific science of textuality or ideology is baffled from the outset by their own accounts of the nature of language, accounts which have the unforeseen effect of abolishing their own specific objects of investigation. Whereas marxist criticism loses sight of the textual object—if it was ever really aiming at it—on the far side of signification, where the object–text merges as a signified into the surrounding text of history or ideology, structuralist poetics, in turn, misses its target on the near side of signification, where the literary text, as a signifier, is lost among the forest of signs and sign-systems within which human experience lies encoded. While nothing like agreement exists among either structuralists or marxists concerning the status or even the existence of a specifically 'literary' (as distinct from 'ordinary') language, there is, as we have seen, a tendency within the peculiar logic of each of these disciplines to deny in the name of methodological rigour or ideological purity, the claim to privilege (or, in the extreme case, existence) once enjoyed by literature in the palmy days of bourgeois individualism and idealism. Literary language (whatever such a thing might be) is to be returned to the egalitarian ground of history itself or to the enveloping element of language and sign-systems in general, and thus disappear as an object of study in its own right.

While French deconstruction, by which I refer primarily to the work of Derrida and late Barthes, also merges literary language into *écriture*, or writing and textuality in general, it fully accepts the consequences of doing so and does not seem at all alarmed at the disappearance of the specifically literary object as such. Its American counterpart, while similarly putting into question the objective status of the literary text conferred on it by its own chief predecessor—the new criticism—has not been content to abandon the category of literary language as a privileged or distinctive mode of utterance. For like the *nouvelle critique*, the new criticism too had posited a certain objective or 'hypostatized' status for the literary text, and brought to bear upon it a critical method for processing its rhetorical texture of irony, paradox, and ambiguity. That method, if it never claimed to be—and sometimes disclaimed being—a 'science', was nothing if not a specialist technology. At the same time, the new criticism was reluctant to dispense with its traditional humanist self-justification in terms of the supposed moral and cultural value of literature and its study: hence its retention of the notion of a canon, its residual practice of evaluation, and its long-term practical and theoretical effort to work out a ticklish *détente* between the rival claims of a value-laden tradition and those of a value-free technique.

What the Yale deconstructionists, institutional heirs

apparent to new criticism, did, was to reveal the formal project of their predecessors as having barely scratched the surface of the rhetorical multiplicity it had set out to explore, and its historical and humanistic project, dependent on the recuperated unity and coherence of text with tradition, as fundamentally incompatible with that formal project. A much closer, more strenuous and dangerous encounter with the literary text than was ever dreamed of by the new criticism was on the agenda, along with a new literary history, now reconceived 'from the point of view of the poets'. Both projects were to be underwritten by a far more thoroughgoing investment in literary theory than the occasional speculations of the new criticism, nothing less than a reconsideration of writing and textuality *'jusqu'en l'origine'*, from the ground up.[2] The one agenda item carried over from the new criticism was the search for a distinctive and privileged literary language, the existence of which was presumed, however radically the category would have to be redefined or expanded beyond such anachronistic conceptions of it as a well-wrought repository of moral value and formal intricacy.

Given such differences in historical and institutional provenance and the diverse turns they have since taken, it could be questioned whether French and American deconstruction have enough in common to be viewed as aspects of a single movement, and whether the various critical practices even on one or the other side of the Atlantic are compatible enough to be designated by a shared label, however suggestive of a sceptical minimalism it may be. We shall come to grips directly with the question of what common denominators deconstructive practice, for all its apparent variety, may hold; for the moment, let us approach it indirectly, by way of the

---

[2] See respectively Geoffrey Hartman, 'Toward Literary History', *Beyond Formalism* (New Haven: Yale University Press, 1970), p. 356; and Paul de Man, 'Criticism and Crisis', *Blindness and Insight: Essays in the Rhetoric of Contemporary Criticism* (New York: Oxford University Press, 1971), p. 7. The most penetrating and balanced account of Yale deconstruction's complex relations with new criticism, phenomenology, structuralism, and Derrida is offered in Wallace Martin's 'Introduction' to *The Yale Critics*, eds. Jonathan Arac, Wlad Godzich, and Wallace Martin (Minneapolis: University of Minnesota Press, 1982), pp. xviii–xxxvii. See also Christopher Norris, *Deconstruction* (London: Methuen, 1982), and Vincent Leitch, *Deconstructive Criticism* (New York: Columbia University Press, 1983).

common effect it has produced in the institution of literary, and to a lesser extent so far, philosophical study. For that effect has been undeniably single and strong, and can only be characterized as one of intense anxiety. Indeed, in looking back at the institution's early reaction to deconstruction when it emerged in the late sixties and early seventies, it is not difficult to identify the source and account for the strength of that anxiety. Deconstruction was, well, different. 'Difference' or *différance* was, after all, its philosophical watchword and principle, and the new terminologies and methodologies with which it intervened in the institutional discourse were certainly different from those the institution, particularly the Anglo-American institution, was used to.

Not only was deconstruction different from the critical and pedagogical practices in place in the sense of being alien and unfamiliar—that, after all, was true of structuralism as well—but deconstruction appeared to be disturbingly different from itself, maddeningly elusive in the unpredictable repertoire of terms and procedures then being mounted in rapid succession under its name: '*différance*', 'misprision', 'aporia', 'undecidability', '*mise-en-abîme*'. . . . What would they think of next? Not quite or yet a school or a movement, its reluctance or inability to routinize itself—as distinct from structuralism's eagerness to do so—rendered it uniquely threatening to any institutional mentality. This potential enemy was doubly dangerous for being at once different and protean, not fully or clearly one thing or the other, indistinctly different. At a time when the older orthodoxies of new and practical criticism were under challenge from several theoretical quarters, deconstruction was sometimes conflated in the general alarm with other heretical movements, mistaken for a version of structuralism or confused with a kind of marxism, as often by the heretics themselves, anxious for avant-garde reinforcement, as by the defenders of the old faith, undiscriminating in the acuteness of their sense of present danger. Only at a later stage in the ongoing triumph of theory, could it begin to be recognized that deconstruction stands against not only the old new criticism but the methodological novelties of marxism and semiotics as well in mighty and binary opposition.

II. THE LEOPARDS IN THE TEMPLE

As its oxymoronic self-appellation suggested from the beginning, deconstruction was always, given its negative understanding of the differential and deferential nature of language and textuality, a practice oppositional to all philosophies of representation and construction, the newer as well as the older, an anti-methodical method. Operating from the margins, it exposed and released the anxiety of reference and representation at the only too metaphorical heart of more conventional methods, the anxiety necessarily repressed in the interest of any claim to a positive or systematic knowledge of literary texts on which our academic institutions have traditionally been based. As a form of oppositional practice, deconstruction gained considerable strategic and tactical advantage of its marginal or liminal status—comparable to that of such other liminal phenomena as ghosts, guerillas, or viruses—over its more cleary defined, predictable, indeed institutionalized, and therefore vulnerable opponents and would-be allies. With the linguistic resourcefulness and mobility accruing from an extreme language-scepticism, deconstruction had the capacity to come in under existing or emerging critical systems at their weakest point, the linguistic bad faith on which they were built.

We have already alluded to the deconstructive subversion, or more accurately, sublation of new criticism itself, in so far as American (as distinct from French) deconstruction carried to an unforeseen flash-point some of new criticism's most cherished principles. By scrutinizing the words on the page harder than new criticism ever had, deconstruction discovered not their translucent and free-standing autonomy but, in a radical defamiliarization, their dark, even opaque, character as writing, black marks on white paper; not the organic unity that binds together irony, paradox, and ambiguity in a privileged, indeed redeemed and redeeming, language, but unrecuperable rhetorical discontinuity. Both French and American deconstruction have demonstrated their capacity to undermine the extroverted structuration of semiotics with mole-like persistence, worrying away at its linguistic underpinnings until its Babel-like towers teetered vertiginously before collapsing into the groundlessness of their own pseudo-scientific discourse. And both are fully capable of taking, at any point they choose, the rhetorical 'ground', the historio-*graphic* soap-box as it were, out from under the solemn hectoring of Althusserian marxism, leaving it with a lost sense of direction, the fuddlement of acute aporia. Little wonder, then, that of the several schools of criticism vying for institutional dominance, deconstruction was, in its difference, the most feared, vilified, and misprized.

Nor is there need to document in any great detail the political and psychological conflicts that no doubt lent added piquancy, even at times acrimony, to what might have been quite amicable philosophical differences. We are dealing, after all, with recent institutional history to which most of us have borne witness, and it does not take a Michel Foucault to remind us of the will-to-power that inheres in any will-to-knowledge and its institutional discourse. Suffice it to say that considerable power was and still is at stake, nothing less than that latent in the pedagogical discourse and practice of literary study at all levels, from post-graduate programmes down to the school curriculum (more on this shortly), so the anxiety has run high in proportion to the stakes at risk. While the agitation has so far been felt mainly at the top of the pyramid, it is clear to all concerned that the repercussions could be massive and long-term. For those critics concerned not with maintaining the continuity of institutionalized literary study in something like its present historical formal-ism, but with transforming it into a revolutionary political practice, deconstruction has come to be identified as an élitist cult and a reactionary force. More or less explicit in the work of such marxist or leftward commentators as Hayden White, Frank Lentricchia, Fredric Jameson and Terry Eagleton, is the view of deconstruction as regressive, a throwback not to the Russian formalism of the teens and twenties, as was structuralist poetics, but if anything, to the dandyist aesthetic-ism of the nineties, a displaced religion of art.[3]

---

[3] See Hayden White, 'The Absurdist Moment in Contemporary Literary Theory', *Contemporary Literature*, xvii. 3 (Summer 1976), pp. 378–403; Frank Lentricchia, *After the New Criticism* (London: Athlone Press, 1980); Terry Eagleton, *Walter Benjamin* (London: Verso, 1981), pp. 108–9, 134–6, and *Literary Theory: An Introduction* (Oxford: Basil Blackwell, 1983), pp. 127–50.

The ultra-high formalism of deconstruction, arising from its obsession with linguistic difference and duplicity, returns criticism in such a view, to the idealist metaphysics from which it was supposed to deliver it, while the practitioners of deconstruction become the chiefs of a hermeneutic mafia or the high priests of a new mystery cult. The mark of such a cabal is its style—a frequent target for all opponent sides—or rather its styles. For even after allowing that deconstruction has many styles, what they have in common is the challenge of difficulty and danger. So much so that charges of a deliberate obscurantism designed to exclude all but an élite—only those who already know will understand and so be saved—are not infrequent.

But the strongest reaction by far to deconstruction, no less allergic but much more alarmist than that of the marxists, has come from the upper reaches of the literary critical establishment across the English-speaking world. This is not really surprising, since it has the most to lose. For such figures as René Wellek, M. H. Abrams, and E. D. Hirsch—to confine ourselves for the moment to America—deconstruction poses a fundamental threat to the institutional and pedagogical practices of a long dominant critical and historical humanism going back to the Renaissance.[4] Despite their conscientious pastoral care, that orthodoxy is breaking up, and deconstruction offers no help in holding it together. Quite the opposite: as a theory of language and literary language subversive of the notion that the meanings of literary texts are determinate or determinable, much less, in M. H. Abrams's unfortunate phrase, 'obvious and univocal', and hence the notion that the study, not to mention the practice, of literature is a socially meaningful and valuable activity, deconstruction has been rejected as 'apocalyptic irrationalism', 'cognitive atheism', and 'dogmatic relativism'.

The fine excess of these phrases, the woundingness or woundedness of these words, should not be underestimated.

---

[4] See respectively René Wellek, 'The New Criticism: Pro and Contra', in *The Attack on Literature* (Brighton: Harvester, 1981), p. 99; M. H. Abrams, 'The Limits of Pluralism: The Deconstructive Angel', *Critical Inquiry*, iii. 3 (Spring 1977), pp. 425–38; and 'How to Do Things With Texts', *Partisan Review*, xliv. 4 (1979), pp. 566–88; and E. D. Hirsch, *Aims of Interpretation* (Chicago: University of Chicago Press, 1976), pp. 11–13, 146–58.

The self-avowed language scepticism that deconstruction cultivates, indeed flaunts, as its philosophical programme (or counter-programme), its self-proclaimed resistance to the imperialistic or totalitarian tendencies toward 'positive and exploitative truth' built into any critical system[5]—be it marxist or semiological, historical or new-critical—obviously have grave institutional consequences. In this respect, deconstruction is a voice (or as we shall see, several distinct voices) crying out not in the desert but amid the superabundance of our over-nourished institutions. Or perhaps more precisely, crying out within the desert of that superabundance. How else should the established institution react to a school that must, by its own logic, oppose institutionalization, with its tendencies toward concensus and routine, as yet another manifestation of the original philosophical sins of logocentricity, positivism, and reification? What, after all, is an 'establishment' or an 'institution' if not something only too pervasively and oppressively present? Worse yet, the rebels who are making these defiant gestures toward existing institutional authority are, it might seem, rebels without a cause, some of the institution's own favourite sons. Harold Bloom is the former student of M. H. Abrams at Cornell; Geoffrey Hartman, of René Wellek at Yale. Even Paul de Man, as a teaching fellow at Harvard, served his time under Reuben Brower in one of the smaller but more fruitful vineyards of 'close reading'.

Yes, there seems to be an element of Oedipal re-enactment at work, with the overreaction on both sides, on the part of the fathers as well as the sons. When M. H. Abrams maintains the availability of literature's 'obvious and univocal sense', or René Wellek reaffirms the achievements of Yale formalism against the 'apocalyptic irrationalism' of its deconstructive successors, these academic patriarchs are insisting, like latter-day Lears, that in our dealings with language, something, even if it lacks the total conviction of ultimate certainty, is preferable to nothing: 'Nothing will come of nothing. Speak again.' Imagine their shock and dismay to hear their own beloved offspring reply that the something they cherish and affirm is based on and amounts to nothing more than

[5] Geoffrey Hartman, Preface to *Deconstruction and Criticism* (New York: The Seabury Press, 1979), p. viii.

philosophical nostalgia or wishful thinking. What else could the patriarchal reaction be when filiation itself, once conceived as a benign relation through which something precious is passed on—be it literary influence or real estate—is put into question. All the more disturbing when those who raise the question are themselves, again like Cordelia, the apples of the patriarchal eye.

From a sense of *lèse-majesté* on behalf of the institutional superstructure, it is a short step to offence on behalf of the affronted subject. What is the subject, after all, except what it is defined to be by those who are officially, i.e. institutionally, appointed to teach it. So that any critique of the institution, *a fortiori* a critique so radically sceptical, is necessarily construed as a critique, in this case virtually a dissolution or demolition, of the subject itself. In this respect, the reaction to deconstruction is analogous to an early and still persistent reaction to psychoanalysis: an irrational fear that, if this sort of analytical activity is pursued, the subject of it, be it literature, the personality, or even the person himself, will veritably disappear, be analysed, as it were, out of existence. The fear of self-annihilation in its extreme form may also be akin to the superstition among some primitive tribes that photography steals the souls of its subjects. From the doubtful standpoint of deconstruction, what both fears—that literature or human personality have their very existence imperilled by some ways of scrutinizing them—have in common is a superstitious or magical or sacramental view of language, within which the relation between signifier and signified is a sacred and inviolate given: words mean exactly what they say. Hence the primal terror aroused in some quarters by the very term 'deconstruction'—after all, the word has the same root-meaning as 'analysis', a 'loosening-up'—quite apart from the actual disintegrative thrust of deconstructionist, indeed all structuralist and post-structuralist thinking, in which that fundamental relation of language is seen to be problematic.

Whatever its causes, the anxiety of the institutional reaction to deconstruction is suggested not only by its rhetorical charge but by its logical contradictions. The view of deconstruction as a nihilist plot is incompatible with the view of it as an élitist cult. Why would the high priests of a religion of literature want to abolish the source of their status and power? Such a state of affairs would be akin to the mafia lobbying for the extirpation of opium networks in south-east Asia, or to the venerable comic routine of a man sawing off the bough on which he sits. Deconstruction cannot, within Aristotelian logic at least, be what each of its chief polemical opponents has claimed—a priestly cult and a nihilist plot—at one and the same time. Or can it? We could reply that within the current system of institutional politics, deconstruction may well seem élitist and conservative in relation to marxism, while in relation to our established formalism it may seem utterly radical. But to leave it at that would be to play into the hands of deconstruction by accepting its extension of the structural linguistic principle that that which has its existence within a system of differences with no positive terms, is in the nature of the case contradictory, perverse, multivocal, mind-boggling, thus leaving the scandalous undecidability of its institutional position intact, and letting it off the hook of its own potential anxiety. We shall have to return to the paradoxical position of deconstruction within the institution; but first we must decide whether it is really one thing that is causing all this trouble, and if so, what sort of thing it is.

III. FOUR WAYS OF GETTING ACQUAINTED WITH THE NIGHT

So far my argument has been that the more vocal reactions to deconstruction have been anxious misconstructions of it, that they are mutually contradictory, and that they reveal as much about their own motivating anxieties as they do about deconstruction. Moreover, it seems possible to argue further that, far from undermining the subject of literature to the point of annihilating it, deconstruction is the only mode of contemporary criticism attempting to maintain, by radically redefining, its distinctive status. In examining the case for deconstruction as a contemporary defence of poetry, we shall first have to establish that we are dealing with a theory coherent enough or at the very least, with a set of practices compatible enough to warrant a common sobriquet, however ironically self-denying. This is precisely what was denied a few years ago in a review–article by Denis Donoghue. Since then, he has divided the deconstructionists into 'epi-readers' and 'graphi-readers', the former maintaining a traditional view of literature as the vehicle of a prior authorial voice, and the latter concerned 'with writing as such', rather than 'as transcribing an event properly construed as vocal and audible'.[6]

Only the latter, for Donoghue, deserve the name of deconstructionists, and he illustrates what he takes to be their characteristic procedures by applying them to a simple poem by Robert Frost, 'Acquainted with the Night':

> I have been one acquainted with the night.
> I have walked out in rain—and back in rain.
> I have outwalked the furthest city light.
>
> I have looked down the saddest city lane.
> I have passed by the watchman on his beat
> And dropped my eyes, unwilling to explain.
>
> I have stood still and stopped the sound of feet
> When far away an interrupted cry
> Came over houses from another street,
>
> But not to call me back or say good-by;
> And further still at an unearthly height
> One luminary clock against the sky
>
> Proclaimed the time was neither wrong nor right.
> I have been one acquainted with the night.

'In an orthodox reading', Donoghue comments, 'you follow the speaker's feeling from the first word to last, taking account of the degree of assertiveness in "I," the precise degree of knowledge claimed in "acquainted," the relation between the apparent precision of "acquainted" and the vagueness of its object, "the night". . . , the tone of those repeated "I have" phrases.' 'Reading a poem', he concludes, 'is like meeting its speaker.'[7]

---

[6] *Ferocious Alphabets* (Boston: Little Brown, 1981), p. 151.

[7] 'Deconstructing Deconstruction', *New York Review of Books*, xxvii. 10 (June 12 1980), p. 37.

That, at least, is how reading a poem used to be, according to the assumptions and principles of the new criticism as set out in *Understanding Poetry* and rehearsed by Donoghue. 'What form', he goes on to ask, would a deconstructive reading of Frost's poem take?' That is not a rhetorical question:

It would start by suffusing the 'I' of the first line with doubt; questioning its neo-Cartesian assumption, and the blatant punctuality with which it implies a speaker. It would note that the printed words are given only as script, and that the reader is urged to convert them into acoustic signs: speech is supposed to be more fully present than print. The deconstructive critic would question the apparent assumption, in the first line, that someone—the speaker— exists, and has existed even before the 'I' of his self-assertion; and that this 'person' guarantees the authenticity of what he says by presiding over it as a controlling consciousness.

The critic would then question the confidence with which Frost's first line begins and ends; begins, in the assertive presentation of the 'I' who speaks; and ends, with the equally assertive presentation of whatever experience 'the night' is supposed to denote. He would ask himself whether the apparent slide from the dogmatic 'I' to the vague, third-pronoun 'one' is an evasion making possible the more extreme evasiveness of 'the night,' a phrase as sonorous as it is obscure; or merely a decent confession of misgiving about the assertiveness of 'I' in the first place. The critic would then go through the poem, diagnosing every example of blindness or naivete in Frost's relation to his language; the false confidence with which he proceeds; the uncritical assumption that by miming a voice he is verifying a personality.[8]

In fairness to Donoghue, he does state that he has not seen a deconstructive reading of Frost's poem, that it might surprise him, and that this is the form it would take if it did *not* surprise him. The reading he has offered, however, is precisely what a deconstructionist would *not* say about Frost's poem, at least no deconstructionist I know of in New Haven or Paris.

While Donoghue's act of critical ventriloquism echoes some of the widespread rumours concerning deconstruction within the academy—the dissolution of the subject, the death of the privileged authorial self, the primacy of writing over speech—

[8] ibid.

it does not reconstruct the dispositions of its original accurately enough to qualify even as good parody. The deconstructionist concentration on 'writing' rather than speech, for example, is never guided by the desire to 'question the apparent assumption . . . that someone—the speaker—exists, and has existed even before the "I" of his self-assertion.' Only the most naïve reader of poetry, certainly no astute reader of *Understanding Poetry* with its new-critical emphasis on the concept of the persona, would identify the speaker of a poem with its author or with any actual person, or the poem with an assertion of the author's beliefs. The deconstructionist concentration on the category of 'writing' is aimed rather at inverting the relative standing of writing, remote as it is from its author and, consequently mistrusted, according to Derrida, since Plato, for its insincerity, elusiveness, and unreliability, and speech, falsely identified with present, authoritative intent. In the Derridean view, writing provides the logical model for the working of all language (including speech), with its deferral, dispersion, and dissemination of present meaning beyond the author's power to control or even know. Thus, there can be no question of 'this person [guaranteeing] the authenticity of what he says by presiding over it as a controlling consciousness.' Yes, deconstructionists do sometimes point to writing as 'black marks on a white page' with something of the same exultant air that new and practical critics used to point to 'the words on the page'. While the former, like the latter, could easily become a catch-phrase, it is still employed in the effort not to dissolve or annihilate the text but to defamiliarize it, to refresh perception of it by redirecting attention to a process of signification that, however basic, had been overlooked or forgotten or repressed in previous critical practice. The endless deferral of definitive meaning that writing reveals and speech conceals but cannot prevent or stop, had been too easily or wishfully short-circuited by a 'logocentric' or 'phonocentric' interpretive tradition predisposed to seize, fix, and foreclose meaning (or the illusion of meaning) through the surreptitious return of writing to speech.

Nor is it quite just to envision our hypothetical deconstructionist going through the poem, 'diagnosing every example of blindness or naivete in Frost's relation to his language; the false confidence with which he proceeds; the uncritical assumption that by miming a voice he is verifying a personality.' On the contrary, it is not the poet who is culpable for blindness, naïvete, false confidence, or uncritical phonocentrism; it is a certain kind of interpreter. 'Poetry', in the words of one of the more austere and demanding masters of deconstruction, 'is the foreknowledge of criticism.'[9] Or again, 'Literature . . . is the only form of language free from the fallacy of unmediated expression.'[10] Hardly the sort of pronouncement we should expect from Donoghue's dyspeptic pedant, picking away at the poem until the poet, abashed at his own presumption, shrinks back into his place. The 'blindness' that the same deconstructionist posits as part of the inescapable destiny of interpretation is always an aspect of our *construction of the text*, rather than of some prior or primary 'text itself'. The text is only accessible, only exists through interpretation, and must thus always already hold the potential insight that enables recognition of the blindness of any of its constructions. Deconstruction, as the term suggests, is the shadow-side, the dark alter ego, the spectral conscience of construction. Hence its predisposition toward authors and texts of a critical, theoretical, or philosophical nature. Deconstructive criticism is not to be confused with 'destructive' criticism, the relation between them being roughly that of the neutron bomb to the hydrogen bomb. Both may devastate the texts on which they work—what critical method does not?—but the former, because it leaves all constituent parts undamaged, enables their reassembly on the more abstract plane of its own commentary, in the form of an 'aftertext' that survives the blast. So there may be life after deconstruction after all.

What, then, *would* a deconstructive critic have to say about Frost's poem, if he were to surprise Donoghue and not say what the latter says he would say? That of course depends very much on which deconstructionist is nominated as the spokesman for deconstruction. For, even though I am arguing for a 'core' activity deserving of the label—be it hard- or soft-core deconstruction—obviously there is considerable variation

---

[9] Paul de Man, *Blindness and Insight*, p. 31.   [10] ibid., p. 17.

in tactical emphasis among its practitioners. Who would be so audacious or foolhardy as to put oneself in the place of Jacques Derrida, *doyen* of hard-core deconstruction, reading Frost's 'Acquainted with the Night'? Faced with the task of reading Shelley's 'The Triumph of Life', Derrida seems to have had trouble enough putting himself in his own place.[11] Faced with Frost's poem, he might well concentrate on Rilke's *'Am Rande der Nacht'*, or perhaps on Stevens's 'An Ordinary Evening in New Haven', possibly printing these texts side by side, and casting his commentary in the margins or in footnotes. He might go on to perplex textuality further by teasing out the tantalizing echoes and overlapping senses of *soir* and *noir*, or *nox* and *vox*. Finally, bearing the burden of all these puns and traces, he might disappear down a deep intertextual crevasse between Hegel and Nietzsche, only to reappear on the far-out side of a passage from Husserl. He might even insinuate his commentary—this is not unlikely—between the lines of the poem, or cross it out even as it is written, place it *sous rature*, so that it states and unstates itself at the same time. You will understand why I am reluctant to write in the persona of Jacques Derrida; such an art of ghost-writing would be more like a cartoon or a caricature than an impersonation. Perhaps a cartoon drawn on a postcard?

If Derrida, as the hardest of the hard-core deconstructors, is for the moment too hard to crack for our purpose, perhaps the soft-core variety will prove more malleable. 'What Harold Bloom is doing in this book', writes Donoghue, 'I have no idea; he is not a deconstructor,' and Geoffrey Hartman, according to the same source, is 'one of the most vigorous opponents of Deconstruction.'[12] While there is general, as well as their personal, agreement that Bloom and Hartman are not of the same species of 'boa-deconstructor, merciless and consequent' as Derrida, de Man, and Hillis Miller, they are still in Hartman's own words, 'barely deconstructionists'.[13] What makes them so, and how would it condition their reading of Frost's poem? Hartman answers the first question by claiming that 'though they understand Nietzsche when he

---

[11] See his 'Living On' in *Deconstruction and Criticism*, pp. 75–176.
[12] 'Deconstructing Deconstruction', pp. 37–8.
[13] *Deconstruction and Criticism*, p. ix.

says "the deepest pathos is still aesthetic play," they have a
stake in that pathos: its persistence, its psychological provenance. For them the ethos of literature is not dissociable from
its pathos, whereas for deconstructionist criticism literature is
precisely that use of language which can purge pathos, which
can show that it too is figurative, ironic, or aesthetic.'[14] But
even if the wound inheres ineradicably, incurably in the word
for Bloom and Hartman, they have none the less found ways
of deferring the presence of that pain that are distinctly
deconstructive. I have in mind Bloom's saturnine master-
theory of the anxiety of influence, with its corollary of
compulsive misreading, and Hartman's more mercurial ex-
positions of literary–historical belatedness.

What maintains the right of Bloom and Hartman to
membership in good standing in the deconstructive fraternity
is the challenge their mature work poses, in different ways, to
those twin positivist fictions of literary history; the fiction, that
is, of an originary, authorial self, and its complement or
supplement (actually its unwitting contradiction) of a benign
and paternal poetic influence. Both of these concepts are
dispersed into intertextual relations, in Bloom's phrase, 'the
hidden roads that go from poem to poem', or into the ghostly
transactions of genius, Genius, and *genius loci*, in Hartman's
more conservative scheme.[15] Against the background of
Bloom's heroic tale of the anxiety of influence and Hartman's
impressionist sketches of the post-romantic afterglow, of the
westering of poetic imagination into the evening or autumnal
tones of the England and New England climate, it should not
be too hard to set Frost's poem. Within their distinctive
versions of a de- and reconstructed literary history—be it a
map of strong misreading or a progressive demystification of
romance, neither Bloom nor Hartman would have much
difficulty reading—or is it misreading?—Frost's 'Acquainted
with the Night'.

Far from 'suffusing the "I" of the poem with doubt', both
might begin by placing it in literary-historical relation to its
precursors, at least two of whom are more or less explicitly

[14] ibid.
[15] See Bloom, *The Anxiety of Influence* (New York: Oxford University Press, 1972),
p. 96; and Hartman, 'Toward Literary History', in *Beyond Formalism*, pp. 356–86.

recalled. One such precursor is the visionary 'I' of Dante's *Commedia* (whence Frost derives the *terza rima* of his poem), the 'I' who awoke in a *selva oscura* in the middle of life's journey. That speaker, too, was acquainted with the night, the dark night of the souls of the underworld city of Dis, full of cries, as well as that of his own soul. The other is the 'I' of another visionary poem, Blake's 'London', also a walker in a city of dreadful night, the darkness of whose 'midnight streets' is pierced only by the successive cries of infant, chimney-sweeper, hapless soldier, and youthful harlot. But those cries were in other national literatures, poetic traditions that tempt identification with 'the interrupted cry' that 'Came over houses from another street, / But not to call me back or say good-by.' The speaker of 'Acquainted with the Night', whatever else he may be, is well acquainted indeed with the nocturnal visions of Dante and Blake. He may also know Hopkins's 'terrible' sonnet, 'I wake and feel the fell of dark, not day', nor is Francis Thompson's 'City of Dreadful Night' very far away.

Yet Frost's poem, while in what Bloom (speaking of Yeats) calls 'the line of vision', is not of it, and Frost might well be seen, in such a reading, as a member not of a romantic visionary company but of the subvisionary company of post- or anti-romantic modernism. In the finely atonal triumphs of such poems as 'The Oven Bird', who knows 'in singing not to sing', or 'Acquainted with the Night', with its 'luminary clock' proclaiming 'the time was neither wrong nor right', Frost measures his literary-historical distance from the moral visions, from what Shelley terms the 'beautiful idealisms of moral excellence' of high romanticism, and masters the psychological consequences of that distance, the anxiety of his belatedness. The poem defines itself, that is, against a tradition only too monumentally in place. Whether 'Acquainted with the Night' is ultimately to be placed and discussed in relation to its precursors under the revisionary ratios of *clinamen* (swerving), *tessera* (completion and antithesis), or *apophrades* (the return of the dead)—more on this later—and whether genius, Genius, or *genius loci* plays the largest role in its making and working—these ghostlier demarcations I leave to Bloom and Hartman to determine, if they can, on an ordinary evening in New Haven. What I hope emerges from this exercise, however, is that, far from dying and disappearing as a result of the anxiety or belatedness they would be likely to diagnose in it, Frost's poem actually flourishes, proves itself truly a poem of their climate. Though *which* anxiety of revision the poem exemplifies may not be perfectly clear, it is precisely its anxiety that, far from annihilating the poem, gives it a new lease on life, or at least on the afterlife of interpretation. Poetry, at least modernist poetry, is an 'achieved anxiety'; for Bloom it is poetry because it *is* an anxiety.[16] Misprision is a mode of partial recuperation, a fortunate fall, an aurora of autumn.

But what is likely to become of the poem were it to fall into the clutches of the boa-deconstructors, who dwell with demoniacal delight in the slippery groundlessness of discourse, the dark backward and abysm of words? *Pace* Donoghue, once again, it is only indirectly that the speaker, the 'I' of the poem, would attract the deconstructive gaze of J. Hillis Miller. In Heideggerian fashion, Miller would wind himself around and strike directly at its language, would argue that *man spricht nicht*; *Sprache spricht*. Language does the talking, not the speaker, and what it says it simultaneously unsays. Take the word on which the poem turns: 'acquainted'. 'I have been one *acquainted* with the night'. The word is familiar, yet formal; indeed, it is very difficult to pin down its particular sense in this context. The *OED* defines it to mean 'personally known; mutually known; having personal or experimental knowledge of', and derives it through the Old French 'acoint', to the Latin 'a(d) cognitum' (past participle of *cognoscere*, 'to know'), formed, from *com* (together) plus *gnoscere* (to come to the knowledge of), which derives in turn from the Greek *gignoskein*. So even if the status of the *'cogito'* is not at issue in the poem, the status of its 'knowledge', of the *'cognosco'*, is.

But what kind or degree of knowledge does the speaker claim? The *OED* pinpoints, but cannot resolve, the problem when it defines the substantive form 'acquaintance' as 'knowledge of a person or thing gained by intercourse or experience, which is more than mere recognition, and less

---

[16] *The Anxiety of Influence*, p. 96.

than familarity or intimacy.' This might be my meaning if I were to say 'Yes, I am *acquainted with* Derrida's work, but I don't really *know* it all that well.' Just what kind or degree of knowledge do I have? Superficial or intimate? Of all the synonyms for the verb 'know', Frost seems to have settled on the one that most effectively keeps at bay the degree of inwardness that characterizes the speaker's knowledge of 'the night'—what Donoghue rightly terms a 'phrase as sonorous as it is obscure'—maintains it as an open question. The poem's enumerative or itemizing structure, its inventory of the objects of the speaker's 'acquaintance', would seem to suggest a thoroughgoing, personal intimacy with all aspects of 'the night', while the repeated action of his moving on, a mover apparently unmoved by what he knows, suggests an opposite sense of detached or purely cerebral knowledge, a sense usually conveyed, according to the *OED* by words derived not from *cognoscere* but from *scire* and the French *savoir*.

Then too, the indeterminacy of the time—it is 'neither wrong nor right'—and of the auxiliary verb as well—does the present perfect verb, 'have been', mean that he 'was' but 'is no longer' or that he still 'is'?—only reinforces our sense of the poem's unwillingness—or is it a matter of inability?—to explain itself. It could almost have been titled, with equal propriety, 'Unacquainted with the Night'. What emerges from such a deconstructive reading is not the absence of a presence in the speaker, as Donoghue expected, but something more like the presence of an absence in the speaker, a mind or a voice which is simultaneously there and not there, a kind of revenant or voyeur whose mode of existence, being posthumous or alienated, puts historical time and its own personal history into brackets or into abeyance. Needless to say, the aporia to which the poem leads in such a reading, its simultaneous offer and withdrawal of meaning, would be seen by Miller as the successful accomplishment of its literary and philosophical mission: to blow the cover on logocentricity, on the 'tradition of presence', with its epistemological and interpretive idealism.

For Paul de Man too, Frost's poem might well present a 'language-problem', but one that underlies—and undermines —not only 'traditional' mimetic and moral interpretation, but deconstructive interpretation as well. (Hence the awesome respect, reductively ascribed by Frank Lentricchia to rhetorical authoritarianism, in which de Man is held by his Yale colleagues.)[17] This language-problem is one of 'rhetoricity' or 'figurality'. How can we know, de Man generally asks, whether to take a given usage literally or figuratively? Consider 'the night' in 'Acquainted with the Night'. So far, all of our hypothetical readings—perhaps they are more like educative guesses or heuristic examples—have assigned a certain degree of figurativeness to 'the night', let alone to the 'interrupted cry', 'luminary clock', and 'the time' that is neither wrong nor right. Whether we assimilate 'the night' to such literary categories as 'the city of dreadful night' or 'the dark night of the soul' of religious and visionary tradition, or to such psychological or epistemological concepts as 'empathic suffering' or 'painful introspection', what we have done is tacitly assume the poem is *not* to be taken literally as an account of actual walks in and around a city. We have explored one or another figurative dimension in our reading of Frost's poem, proceeded, that is, on the assumption that the poem does not mean what it apparently says, or say what it actually means. We have jumped to the conclusion, perhaps without even realizing it, that sign and meaning do not coincide in the poem, so that a law, a logic, a system must be invoked or formulated to account for its putative deviations from literal or unproblematic referentiality. Such a law of deviation would render the poem's equivocations or multivalences intelligible as figurative language.

Were we not justified in doing so? A linguist might point out that we know whether to take a given speech-act literally or figuratively only by an appeal to context. The statement, 'My love is a rose', could be taken literally or metaphorically depending on whether it appears in the memoirs of a gardener, the confessions of a flower-fetishist, or an Elizabethan sonnet. If I say, 'Beautiful weather we are having here in Melbourne', you could decide whether I mean it literally or ironically only by looking out of the window, or perhaps at the expression on my face (though this is more doubtful, since

[17] Lentricchia, *After the New Criticism*, Ch. 8.

facial expressions, too, are a language requiring a 'reading'), or if it is a written statement read at a distance, the generic context in which it occurs. Similarly with literary interpretation, a context—be it linguistic or extra-linguistic—is invoked or constructed to enable us to make the most preliminary decision as to whether the language before us is to be taken literally or figuratively.

In the present case, however, such recourse to context is of little avail, since the various contexts one might bring to bear—the linguistic fabric of the poem in question, that of Frost's work as a whole, his biography, the critical tradition on his work—seem to be capable of supporting either choice. It is as if the statement 'My love is a rose' appeared in a sonnet by an Elizabethan gardener who was also a flower-fetishist! Such poems as 'Stopping by Woods' or 'The Road Not Taken' or 'Mending Wall' or 'After Apple-Picking' are notorious for the seamless simultaneity with which they fuse an apparent literalism with an equal and opposite potential for figurative meaning. Is Frost to be read as a straw-between-the-teeth regionalist, a laconic farmer-poet, or as a 'terrifying' seer of dark and uncanny imagination? As is usually the case in matters of interpretation, both traditions are available and could be cited in support of one choice or the other.[18] I know which reading of Frost's poetry I find more congenial, and I could document it by citing the heading under which this particular poem, with three others, was first printed in *West Running Brook*: 'Fiat Nox.' Is it possible to take 'literally' the scriptural paranomasia of this dark classicist? Is it possible to take any statement 'literally', or are there only varying shades of figurativeness or rhetoricality? As de Man himself has remarked of one of his own questions, is it possible to know whether the question I have just asked is rhetorical or not, and so know whether and how to answer it?[19]

Even if the 'literal' interpretation of a given text is not really possible, the figurative potential of language being what it is, there is still no limit on figuration. Frost makes explicit in

---

[18] An incisive critique of the assumptions underlying the conflicting interpretations of Frost's poetry is offered by Richard Poirier, *Robert Frost: The Work of Knowing* (New York: Oxford University Press, 1977), pp. 226–45.

[19] *Allegories of Reading* (New Haven: Yale University Press, 1979), p. 10.

'Mending Wall' for example, that he is speaking figuratively when he decribes the neighbor as moving 'in darkness, as it seems to me,/Not of woods only and the shade of trees'. Yet the precise shade of figurative meaning, the nature of the neighbor's atavism or enlightenment, remains, in Donoghue's phrase, as sonorous as it is obscure. Try as I might to support some version of the figurative against the more literal reading—surely our modern, secular version of the spiritual sense against the carnal in traditional scriptural hermeneutics —there is Paul de Man patiently and scrupulously taking us through text after text and showing how literal meaning unsays figurative, as figurative does literal, or figurative does figurative, without any definitive means of resolving the problem and returning the text back into univocality or unity, as new criticism would have tried to do. Literary language, identified in a later essay by de Man with the 'shape all light' of Shelley's 'Triumph of Life' (that is, with an ongoing, recuperative, and potentially endless capacity for disfiguration and refiguration), can thus never be reduced to fixed or definitive meaning, to some higher unity, or to 'positive or exploitative truth.'.[20]

The hermetically sealed structure of Frost's poem having been softened up by these preliminary manœuvres, the time may now be right for an all-out deconstruction of it *à la* Derrida himself. In working up to such an attempt, I mentioned earlier that Derrida might well see fit to insinuate his commentary between the lines of the poem, or cross it out even as it is written, place it *sous rature*, so that it states and unstates itself at the same time. But what if the poem has already done just that? What if the poem is always already the writerly foreknowledge—here I am enlisting the tactical and terminological support of Barthes and de Man—of all possible readerly or critical constructions or misprisions of it? What if the traces of other reconstructible poems can still be detected around the lines of this poem? These other poems are not, strictly speaking, 'readings' or interpretations that offer themselves to particular critics or poets in particular contexts at particular moments. Nor are they previous poems in the

[20] See Paul de Man, 'Shelley Disfigured', *Deconstruction and Criticism*, pp. 39–73.

canon that this poem misreads, represses, and thereby saves. They are other poems that this poem writes and erases in a single moment, writes and erases in a moment of fear and desire: fear of being what they are, and desire to be what they are. These other, alternative poems exist within earshot of the written poem, within its *aura* so to speak, and are heard simultaneously within and through it. These 'aural' poems are collaborations of text and reader, writing and speech; they are written and heard between the lines on the page, just as the central poem of which they are the aural alternatives may be said to be written between their lines.

So 'Acquainted with the Night' wants and does not want to be a poem called 'Acquainted with Delight' and a poem called 'Unacquainted with Delight'. And it both desires and fears to be terminal, to rule out these alternative subvocalizations. To rule them out, if it could be done, would be to achieve a free-standing monumentality to itself alone, but in so doing, to admit its own death. Not to rule them out would be to accept the condition of being undefinitive and incomplete, but also to underwrite its own perpetuation, its completion elsewhere. Hence the phrase 'one acquainted with' merges, under pressure of articulation, with 'unacquainted with', while remaining distinct from it; 'the night', with 'delight' and not with 'delight'. 'I have walked out in *pain*' and not in 'pain' but 'rain'. 'But not to call me back or say "you'll die."' In Freudian terms, the controlled, formal, fully socialized language of the poem is at once concealing and revealing the libidinous energy behind or beneath its care and caution, concealing and revealing its original lability: primary processes appear in the place of secondary processes. 'The night' hides and reveals, displaces and condenses, as in dream-work, the delight of gratified desire and the fear of death that inhere in it. The printed poem writes and erases the other, more outspoken and explicit poems that proceed from its overdetermined centre, the aural poems it fears and desires to be. What such a 'reading' ultimately deconstructs of course is any possible recuperation of the text as a unitary utterance. Unlike Harold Bloom, who sees strong poems as creative and repressive misreadings of poems already in place and recoverable, we can read Frost's poem as the creative and repressive misreading of poems it has itself written and not written. No conceivable application of a law of deviance or revisionary ratio or system of rhetoric can bring interpretive sense or consensus out of a text that is simultaneously 'there' and not 'there', that says and unsays itself in one and the same breath.[21]

IV. THE PROBLEM OF OUR LAWS

It is on this crucial issue that the deconstructionist defence of poetry takes its leave forever from structuralist poetics, and divides into its own soft- and hard-core versions: on the question of how much positive assertion, of active system-making, a given deconstructionist will allow in his own work or in that of others, while remaining sceptical and anti-systematic. Consider, first, deconstruction's inevitable parting of the ways with structuralist poetics. Here is Jonathan Culler coming to terms with what he takes to be the critical implications of the Derridean view of language:

The paradoxes and undecidables which this perspective [of Derridean *différance*] discloses as the unavoidable basis of language and thought are more familiar and more easily exemplified in the realm of literature than elsewhere. The very notion of rhetorical figures . . . captures a fundamental paradox. A rhetorical figure is a situation in which language means something other than what it says, a violation of the code. But *lest that violation introduce a radical undecidability to linguistic situations, leading us to wonder how we could ever know whether language means what it appears to be saying, these violations are codified, as a repertoire of highly artificial and conventional devices which writers can draw on to produce meaning.* What looks at first like an inaugural creative act, a violation of the code, is accounted for by the formulation of a code on which its meaning is said to depend.[22]

[21] The foregoing 'Derridean' reading is actually a rewriting of an inspired reading by my colleague Dr Simon During, itself written upon the occasion of his hearing the deconstructive readings that precede it. The result is very much a palimpsest of intertextuality within which it would be difficult, if not impossible, to discriminate the contributions of Derrida, During, and myself—not to mention the ghostly presence of the late Barthes, and who knows who else. The difficulty of sorting out such intertextual indebtednesses, even as they are acknowledged, is surely one of the points of the exercise.

[22] *The Pursuit of Signs* (London: Routledge and Kegan Paul, 1981), p. 41. My italics.

Faced with the 'radical undecidability' of language, *a fortiori* of literary language, the structuralist poetician seeks and finds a way out of his predicament: there are underlying laws, codes, grammars that turn out after all to govern what is apparently lawless, scrambled, ungrammatical in language. The perennial positivist in Culler has come to the aid of the ephebe deconstructionist, rescuing him from the dizzying aporia of the Derridean perspective he has for the moment adopted, returning him to the firm domain of law and order from the dizzying drop of the *mise-en-abîme* down which he very nearly disappeared. The 'canny critic' in Culler—to adopt Hillis Miller's by now notorious distinction—has saved the momentarily 'uncanny critic' in him from the deconstructive consequences of his own perception.[23] The US marshal of structuralist poetics has fought it out with Yale's hermeneutic mafia and emerged victorious, returned the town to its law-abiding critical citizens as a clean, well-lighted place.

It is unfortunate that Culler's psychomachia, the philosophical gunfight in the OK Corral of his consciousness, has ended so quickly and conventionally with the forces of law and order winning out. It is no doubt the case that laws and grammars of rhetorical figures can be—have been—formulated from Aristotle and Quintilian to John of Garland to George Puttenham to Fr. Walter Ong in order to re-codify and thereby render intelligible the transgressions of the grammatical code which those figures exemplify. But the very fact that there have been so many historical attempts at such taxonomies of tropes—perhaps as many such 'grammars' of rhetorical figures, as there have been interpretations of any single classic text—should in itself give us pause. Moreover, as Gerard Manley Hopkins once remarked (and Geoffrey Hartman often repeated), rhetoric is the *teachable* part of poetry, the part, that is, that lends itself to codification, to being recuperated back into the grammatical fold. But this re-grammatization of rhetoric is not to be identified or confused with the grammatization of poetry. As Paul de Man has shown, even the attempted grammatization of rhetoric is always already undone by the rhetorization of grammar with which it

<hr/>

[23] See J. Hillis Miller, 'Stevens' Rock and Criticism as Cure, II', *Georgia Review* (Summer 1976), p. 345.

coincides at every point, as an object moving in light cannot avoid casting its shadow.[24]

For the deconstructive defender of poetry, what characterizes 'poetic', as distinct from 'ordinary' or even 'rhetorical' language is an element of excess or surcharge, a saving remnant or precious residue that remains unexplained, indeed inexplicable, above and beyond the explanatory power of whatever historical interpretive system (in the name of which its study is institutionalized) we may bring to bear on it to capture and comprehend that residue. If rhetoric is the teachable part of poetry, poetry is the unteachable part of language, that which has not only violated the laws of conventional grammar but has anticipated all attempts to bring it back under the rule of law through the concessions of subsequent legal reforms. Poetry is, as it were, always already deviant, outside the law, at least never quite lawful enough to be predicted, and unruly enough to cause surprise, even shock, however often the law is reformed.

Once criticism realizes this, once it achieves an ironic or ludic recognition of the inadequacy of its own law-making, understands that its legal systems are already obsolete, riddled with loopholes, inapplicable even as they are codified, it turns into deconstruction, which is nothing other than language scepticism in the mode of play, an exacting and rigorous form of play, but play all the same. The only alternative to the ludic attitude, after such knowledge, would be morose silence. After all, if literature is the foreknowledge of criticism, if the literary text—and deconstruction must maintain that category; *its* question is not whether 'literature' exists, but how inclusive the category should be—always already knows in advance what the critic seeks to discover, then the legislative labours of the latter can never be completed. Logically speaking, the deconstructionist knows himself to be in the position of Sisyphus or Achilles in his race with the tortoise, and whether he performs his absurdist labour with *brio* or lapses into silence is entirely a matter of personal style or mood. Oscillating dizzily between high play and deep scepticism, according to the angle from which it is viewed, deconstruction is to criticism as mania-depression is to psychopathology. Or if not the mania-depression of hard-core deconstruction, at least the high anxiety of soft. For it is at this point of critical self-consciousness that the hard- and soft-core deconstructionist part company from one another as well as from the structuralists/semioticians, a band of extroverts for whom anxiety is altogether unknown and alien.

Consider the problematic case of Harold Bloom. While he cannot be counted among the hard-core deconstructionists, neither can he be counted among the structuralists, for all his system-making. In the proto-structuralist poetics of Bloom's strong precursor Northrop Frye, the six phases of each of his four modes neatly return on themselves to complete a circle, within which all the literary texts of that mode are contained. In the barely deconstructionist poetics of Frye's critical offspring, Harold Bloom, the six revisionary ratios form not a circle but a snake, a lacertine constrictor perhaps, which swallows its own tail, or perhaps squeezes a laugh out of itself, depending on the attitude of the interpreter: 'The hugely idiosyncratic Milton shows the influence, in places, of Wordsworth; Wordsworth and Keats both have a tinge of Stevens; the Shelley of *The Cenci* derives from Browning; Whitman appears at times too enraptured by Hart Crane'.[25] Thus the last of Bloom's revisionary ratios turns back on the first, and undoes the system as a positive, or pseudo-historical, construct. In the end, Bloom's is, in his own phrase, a negative exuberance, much as his delurian myth of creation is an implosion. As Geoffrey Hartman points out, 'the revisionist relation is basically a tricky attempt to establish commensurability between incommensurables. The "ratio" turns out to be a false and, ultimately, "fearful" attempt at "symmetry."'[26] In fairness to Bloom, his quasi- or pseudo-*Anatomy*, a positive construct if there ever was one, doubts itself just in time to become an *Anxiety*, which is also—remember?—Bloom's definition of a poem.

For it is at this point, too, that deconstruction, by doubting its own constructs and questioning its own rhetoric, would like to turn into poetry. Having dispensed with the fiction of

---

[25] *The Anxiety of Influence*, p. 154.
[26] *The Fate of Reading* (Chicago: University of Chicago Press, 1975), p. 55.

objectivity, of scientific distance or logical command in relation to literature, deconstruction relinquishes any claim to status as science, but only to make an equally ambitious or pretentious claim to status as literature. Criticism has always made this claim implicitly, furtively, embarrassedly. Which of us would deny the prestige of full literary status to the essays of Sidney, Johnson, Shelley, Arnold, or Eliot? Which of us has not thought, secretly and wishfully, his own essays their equal? In deconstructive criticism that claim comes out of hiding; the writer inside the critic comes out of his closet. The activity of criticism now justifies itself not by system or science—that justification has been tacitly given away—but by writerly values, turning as it does between the poles of linguistic play and rhetorical force. Hence the baroque vocabulary of Bloom, the babylonish dialect of Hartman, the compulsive paranomasia of them all. Are these not some of the oldest, most ingrained features of poetry? In this respect, deconstruction, for all its byzantine erudition, aspires to a rebarbarization or rejuvenation of an over-refined, routinized, or decadent form. Of all recent movements, deconstruction represents the closest approach yet made by criticism to literature itself. Is it any wonder then that it has been anxiously dismissed by more positive and logocentric schools, as literature itself has repeatedly been from Plato onwards, as a disturbing fantasy, an impolite or impolitic fiction, or just a tall story?

V. THE ANXIETY OF DECONSTRUCTION

We have already seen how, and up to a point why, deconstruction has manifested, over the past decade, such an uncanny power to arouse anxiety in the institutions of learning that house and host it. Indeed, each new attempt to come to grips with deconstruction—even recent sympathetic attempts to make sense of it by returning it to the conformations of our institutional discourse—may itself be regarded as the latest, admittedly mild, attack of that continuing anxiety. Having at last been accepted as a fact of institutional life, deconstruction now presents us with the problem of how best to live with and control it, like a recently discovered disease that has proved not to be fatal, as was first feared, but merely discomforting, and for which there is still no known cure, though research continues. If we have not yet learned how to stop worrying altogether and love deconstruction, we have at least passed beyond the initial shock of its recognition. There are even signs that deconstruction may prove, in the course of its progress, to be self-deconstructing, i.e. self-curing, so that those who come down with it may eventually find themselves diagnosed as normal once again, well and truly able to carry out the institution's business as usual. And if that turns out to be the case (so runs the argument of this chapter) it will be a new and serious occasion for anxiety. For what I want now to contend is that deconstruction is, or ought to be by its own logic, not only the cause that anxiety is in the institution, but institutionally anxious in itself.

This latter anxiety arises out of its own uncertain potential for institutionalization, the questionable capacity of a practice so profoundly oppositional, sceptical, and anti-systematic to turn into a transmissable, teachable programme in its own right. For there is great potential for anxiety in deconstruction's apparent desire to destabilize the interpretive structures and de-naturalize the conventions through which institutional authority is manifested and perpetuated, while remaining unwilling quite to relinquish any claim to institutional authority for its own practices. In institutional terms, what the new marxists and the old new critics—the schools that have reacted most intensely to deconstruction—have in common is the premiss that authority in interpretation is necessary and resides in communal, i.e. institutional, consensus; each is anti-authoritarian only with respect to the other's authority-conferring community. Both are threatened and scandalized by a deconstructive anti-authoritarianism so radically individualistic or solipsistic that it denies the interpretive authority and the communal basis for it, not only of other communities but of its own community as well—to the extent it can be said to form one—and then has the further audacity to insist on its own institutional pride of place. These conflicting impulses within deconstruction express themselves in the apparent insouciance with which deconstruction transgresses the communal rules of the language game known as literary criticism while continuing to play it, in repeatedly exceeding the rules of the game by introducing an element of free play deriving from a heightened and ever-present awareness that the rules of the game were arbitrary in the first place. Such a gambit might be tolerable even to other players who are playing more 'seriously', i.e. conventionally, that is, who are so caught up in the game, and have so internalized its rules, that they have forgotten or repressed their own awareness (if they ever were aware), of the original arbitrariness or groundlessness of those rules. But it becomes intolerable once it is clear to these honest souls that the deconstructive transgressors, the disintegrated consciousnesses at the table, are not just kibitzing, but playing to win, and have on eye firmly fixed on the institutional stakes. That is having it both ways, or as some would call it, cheating. In either case it is breaking the rules that the community has agreed to play by, the rules that by virtue of this agreement, may be said to constitute the community.

Deconstruction's desire to have it both ways, to be in the community, even in its mainstream or bloodstream, but not *of* it, is more than a matter of wanting institutional prestige and influence, while violating some of the institution's most honoured conventions and taboos, like making more puns than is thought seemly, or writing books without footnotes. It is a matter of putting into question the very constitutional and contractual basis, the rationale of social consent, on which the institutionalized interpretive community exists—what may be termed its major premiss that there is something which requires and justifies, in social and historical terms, the service it renders, and for the sake of which it structures its activities. That something, that *sine qua non* and *raison d'être*, is the presumed existence of literary or poetic, as distinct from ordinary, language. Here we encounter a further paradox that the one deconstructionist for whom, as far as I can tell, this distinctive category does not exist, is also the one who is least subject to, and least the object of, institutional anxiety. For Derrida, as for the late Barthes, the category of literary language has dissolved, through the powerful reagent of *différance*, into writing and textuality in general. The relative absence of anxiety over and in Derrida—this is admittedly hard to measure—may well have to do with the primarily philosophical context of his work. For the institution of philosophical, as distinct from literary, study has long since given away—at least in Anglo-American culture—any social or missionary rationale and is to that extent less predisposed, if not quite immune, to institutional anxiety. The idea has been around for some time now among philosophers, particularly Anglo-American philosophers, that theirs is a highly technical language-game of only marginal social and practical consequence, and whether or not they accept this view, the re-emergence under the name of deconstruction of extreme language-scepticism in the mode of play is not likely to carry much shock-value for those familiar with the work of Nietzsche, Heidegger, and Wittgenstein. We shall have to return to the marginal standing of philosophy as an institution; for literary deconstruction, as we shall see, continues to propose a dubious merger with it.

It is rather American—specifically Yale—deconstruction, proceeding as it does upon the humanist premiss of literariness, and aware of the increasingly imperilled centrality of its institutionalized study for culture at large, that occasions the anxieties I have been describing. Perhaps the richest irony of the situation is that the definitions of literary language it still feels compelled to produce, ought to be, as the only poststructuralist defence of poetry on offer, the shibboleth of institutional acceptance, indeed, respectability. But that defence is so uncanny and paradoxical that it does not feel to the institution like a defence at all. Rather, it seems more like a surrender of the power of literary language to engage with, let alone enhance, anything beyond itself that might, in turn, lend it privilege, validity, or in the language of the Supreme Court, 'redeeming social value', in particular the moral, mimetic, or expressive value conferred on it by traditional poetics:

For the statement about language, that sign and meaning can never coincide, is what is precisely taken for granted in the kind of language we call literary. Literature, unlike everyday language, begins on the far side of this knowledge. . . . The self-reflecting mirror-effect by means of which a work of fiction asserts, by its very existence, its separation from empirical reality, its divergence, as a sign, from a meaning that depends for its existence on the constitutive activity of this sign, characterizes the work of literature in its essence. It is always against the explicit assertion of the writer that readers degrade the fiction by confusing it with a reality from which it has forever taken leave.[27]

I have selected this definition of literary language from the work of Paul de Man, not because his definition is singularly fugitive or teasing. Definitions comparably threatening to the institution's sense of cultral mission could be culled from the work of Geoffrey Hartman, for whom art is characterized by the 'generic impurity' of being 'ambiguously involved with sacred and profane' and 'always inauthentic vis-à-vis the purity of ritual and vis-à-vis a thoroughgoing realism,' or even from the work of Harold Bloom, for whom a poem is not a relief or release from, or a resolution or expression of, an anxiety, but itself 'an anxiety'.[28] I single out de Man's definition because it states in terms more unrecuperable and uncompromising, more austere and demanding if you will, than the others, the deconstructive defence of poetry as a denial of precisely what the institution of literary study has traditionally thought of itself as being about. Literature, for de Man, remains an enlightened mode of language, 'the only form of language' he calls it in the same passage, 'free from the fallacy of unmediated expression'; but its enlightenment consists precisely in its disclaimer of what is normally claimed for it—its special immediacy or at least its special power to mediate something outside itself and something important to us. The revelation literature offers is that it can never be what the institution of its study blindly takes it to be.

Having brought out into the open, in luminous essay after essay, the anxiety of reference that blinds and vitiates the

----

[27] *Blindness and Insight*, p. 17.

[28] Geoffrey Hartman, *Beyond Formalism*, pp. 20–3; Harold Bloom, *the Anxiety of Influence*, pp. 93–6. Compare J. Hillis Miller, 'The Fiction of Realism: *Sketches by Boz, Oliver Twist, and* Cruikshank's Illustrations', in *Dickens Centennial Essays*, eds. Ada Nisbet and Blake Nevius (Berkeley: University of California Press, 1971), p. 85: 'No language is purely mimetic or referential, not even the most utilitarian speech. The specifically literary form of language, however, may be defined as a structure of words which in one way or another calls attention to this fact, while at the same time allowing for its own inevitable misreading as a "mirroring of reality".

constructive labours of the normal humanists who compose the institution, de Man might reasonably be expected to be urging that we write paid to those labours and dismantle the existing institutional support-system that sustains them. Or at least that we radically change the departmental and curricular structures that promote in their *wissenschaftlich*, systematic way the misunderstanding of literature as something whose relation to and meaning for society can be ascertained by the historicist and/or formalist methods in place in the academy. It is just such a need for sweeping institutional change, after all, that the marxists, given their own materialist demystification of bourgeois literary study, incessantly proclaim. They openly aspire to reconstitute the institution anew from the ground up, the ground being a not-so-new version of history and the study of literary forms giving way to the study of ideological formations. That may be, from the deconstructive viewpoint, only another and more intense manifestation of the old anxiety of reference, but at least it has the courage and candour of its conviction or fantasy. Indeed, some younger, self-styled deconstructionists of my acquaintance, none of them at Yale, would like to see the institutional structures that the old historicist and formalist anxiety of reference shores against its ruin give way to more expansive and flexible institutional structures that would bend with what they take to be the new bliss of difference that deconstruction, in its French forms at least, promises. They envision a carnivalization of the institution in which the old divisions between departments of national literature, between departments generally, disappears, and a new free play reigns, where students are given high marks for making puns and dispensing with footnotes.

The logical outcome, in institutional terms, of deconstruction would surely have to be some kind of anti-institution, where the full writerly fluidity of differential intertextuality could flourish without the guilt or anxiety induced and controlled by the oppressive superstructures and restrictive routines of departments, canons, methodologies, and footnotes. Perhaps it was some such academy without walls that the late Roland Barthes had in mind when he answered an interviewer's question about the place of literary study in the

university to the effect that 'it should be the only subject'.[29]
After all, if deconstruction stands, as Richard Rorty suggests,
in the same relation to 'normal' criticism and philosophy as
'abnormal' sexuality or science do to their 'normal' counterparts—'each lives the other's death and dies the other's
life'[30]—should not its chief practitioners outspokenly advocate
the legal and constitutional reform of the institution, if not
actively attempt to found a new anti-institution of an
unabashedly utopian kind?

In fairness to the Yale deconstructionists, they have braved
considerable communal opprobrium by proclaiming, up to a
point, the unnegotiability of their differences with the institutional definition of the subject. 'A critic must choose', wrote
J. Hillis Miller, 'either the tradition of presence or the
tradition of difference, for their assumptions about language,
about literature, about history, and about the mind cannot be
made compatible.'[31] Yet the cry for large-scale institutional
reform that such incompatibility ought logically to issue in has
not been forthcoming. However different the deconstructive
definition and defence of literature, it seeks neither blissfully
to abolish a canon, nor radically to alter it, nor even to rewrite
afresh the institutional style-sheet of our dealings with it. Yale
deconstruction may argue for, may even exemplify, the play of
difference in its approach to literature, but there can be no
mistaking that in so doing it is *hard* at play. No bliss, no
jouissance, not even much *plaisir*, here in puritan New Haven,
thank you; we prefer 'rigour', 'strenuousness', 'ruthlessness',
anxiety, and old-fashioned 'hard work'. For all its puns and
abandonment of footnotes, this free play turns out to be very
hard work after all. The highest compliment Geoffrey
Hartman can pay to the work of Paul de Man is to call it 'a
kind of generalized conscience of the act of reading',[32] and
conscience, as students of medieval allegory well know, is no
figure of fun, at least not in working hours. What prevents

---

[29] In an interview in *France Nouvelle*, 5 May 1975. Quoted by Philip Thody, *Roland Barthes: A Conservative Estimate* (London: Macmillan, 1977), p. 107.
[30] 'Philosophy as a Kind of Writing', in *Consequences of Pragmatism* (Minneapolis: University of Minnesota Press, 1982), p. 107.
[31] 'Georges Poulet's "Criticism of Identification"' in *The Quest for Imagination*, ed O. B. Hardison, Jr. (Cleveland: Case Western Reserve University Press, 1971, p. 216.
[32] 'Signs of the Times', in *The Fate of Reading*, p. 311.

Yale deconstruction, unlike its Parisian cousin, from giving itself up to an abandonment of the institutional controls of method and system, and embracing a complete *laissez-faire* regarding the object of that method and system, is the distinctly puritan work-anxiety it continues to share with the older institution, whose forms it largely accepts despite its declared differences with the traditional rationale for those forms.

But what, then, is the point of all this sweat and strain? Having relinquished all claim that the strenuous study of literature will confer on its students any positive benefit of cultural or historical identity, moral goodness, psychological wholeness, or even philosophical wisdom—the traditional humanist justifications for the institutionalized study of the canon—Yale deconstruction seems content that the institution continue to exist for the sake of work alone, in so far as its *Aufhebung* of work is also an emptying out of work's former purposes and justifications: 'The whole of literature would respond in similar fashion [i.e. as Proust responds to de Man's deconstruction of his rhetoric], although the techniques and the patterns would have to vary considerably, of course, from author to author. But there is absolutely no reason why analyses of the kind here suggested for Proust would not be applicable, with proper modifications of technique, to Milton or to Dante or to Hölderlin. This will in fact be the task of literary criticism in the coming years.'[33] What is at issue here is not the logic or accuracy of de Man's prediction—his prophecy, uttered more than five years ago, is coming only too true—but its tone of equanimity. Deconstruction is indeed proving thoroughly amenable to routinization at the hands of the institution to whose authority it once seemed to pose such a challenge of incompatibility. More than that, it has all but become the institution, as its life and activity rapidly become indistinguishable from the life and activity of the institution at large, as one classic text after another is subjected to moves and reflexes increasingly predictable and programmatic, and the aporias and undecidabilities, the *mises-en-abîme* and impasses, the absences and deferrals and misprisions in the

---

[33] Paul de Man, *Allegories of Reading*, pp. 16–17.

canonical literature are relentlessly unfolded. Deconstruction has made so much work for us all, it hardly seems to matter that, not only do the traditional justifications for that work no longer apply, but no justification, certainly no *cultural* justification, other than the technical challenge of the work itself, seems to be offered.

It is at this point that the full anxiety of deconstruction begins to appear. The last thing deconstruction wants to be, or be seen to be, is an empty technology of the text, like its old rival, structuralist poetics. So it now emerges that the traditional humanist justifications of hermeneutics and history, according to de Man himself, may even *reappear*, if the institution only goes one step further in meeting the challenge:

It would involve a change by which literature, instead of being taught as a historical and humanistic subject, should be taught as a rhetoric and a poetics prior to being taught as a hermeneutics and a history. The institutional resistances to such a move, however, are probably insurmountable. . . . Yet, with the critical cat now so far out of bag [*sic*] that one can no longer ignore its existence, those who refuse the crime of theoretical ruthlessness can no longer hope to gain a good conscience. Neither, or [*sic*] course, can the terrorists— but then, they never laid claim to it in the first place.[34]

De Man's professed scepticism about the full institutionaliz-ation of deconstruction is at this point surely rhetorical. The institutional 'change' he recommends is minimal and moderate —still no call for a full-blooded utopia of differential bliss, but only for more 'theoretical ruthlessness'. Such a change, in fact, has either already taken place, or soon will, as courses in, conferences on, and centres for the study of methodology and theory not only proliferate, but move from the periphery to the longed-for metaphorical 'centre' of the discipline.

But even if this change has already occurred, or is about to occur, why would de Man be content to see it happen? Why would deconstruction acquiesce in what, on its own terms, would be a form of self-destruction? How can it accept its own

[34] 'Professing Literature: A Symposium on the Study of English', *Times Literary Supplement* (Dec. 10 1982), pp. 1355–6. A more closely argued exposition of this view is advanced by de Man in his 'Foreword' to Carol Jacobs's *The Dissimulating Harmony* (Baltimore: Johns Hopkins University Press, 1978), pp. vii–xiii.

institutional routinization with the same insouciance it once displayed in transgressing the institutional routines by which literature was supposed, by being reduced to law and order, to yield up its truth? If the diverse academic formalizations and normalizations, grammatizations and rhetorizations, have been revealed, by de Man's own highly principled practice, *not* to be capable of negotiating the transition from the semiotic to the hermeneutic and historical, that is, from sign to meaning, how is studying them *first*, logically or chronologically, going to help? That nostalgic or desired transition can *never*, by de Man's definition of literary language, be methodically made, no matter what new priority is given to the study of rhetoric and poetics, or with whatever 'theoretical ruthlessness' that study of method is pursued.

The 'critical cat' is indeed so far out of the bag that its existence cannot be ignored, but why should de Man think, or wish to think, it will find any ground, old or new, to stand on by seeking out departments of philosophy or theory? While the proposed merger of deconstructive criticism with philosophy and theory no doubt identifies an area of hard work shared by deconstruction and the traditional institution, that area would have to be, by de Man's own lights, one of continuing contention rather than new-found accord. For the interests at stake are opposed and incompatible. What has deconstruction taught us if not that there is no theoretical 'ground' so long dreamed of by philosophy outside of writerly practice, from which epistemology, ethics, and now writerly practice itself can be positively described? What has Derrida taught us but that the philosophical tradition, including deconstruction, *is* writerly practice. De Man's proposed institutional merger with philosophy and theory—if he means by it the Kantian kind, and what else has poetics proved itself to be?—would be at once regressive and counter-productive. It would be like the managing director of a growing company recommending to its shareholders an equal merger with an all but bankrupt competitor, whose imminent collapse will give the company a complete monopoly of the market. As Richard Rorty describes those 'weak textualists' who think they are adding the prestige of philosophy to their criticism when they discuss a writer's epistemology: 'Thus conquering warriors might mistakenly think to impress the populace by wrapping themselves in shabby togas stripped from the local senators.'[35] On the other hand, if de Man is recommending merger with what Rorty terms the 'abnormal' philosophical tradition, culminating in Derrida and de Man himself, that variously denies the real or potential groundedness of discourse, he is recommending only what has already taken place. Whatever his Yale colleagues may mean by philosophy and theory when they recommend it, de Man is certainly no 'weak textualist', and we must give him the benefit of the doubt by assuming it is the latter kind of merger he has in mind, which is to say, more of the same.

But in the very ambiguity of de Man's proposals, we sense the impasse confronting deconstruction itself as it ponders the possibilities of its institutional future and the full anxiety it quite properly feels in the situation. Too puritan and conscientious to abandon itself to the textual hedonism of its French counterpart, which in its utopianism could never be institutionalized anyway, Yale deconstruction has only two courses open to it, neither of which it can pursue without anxiety. Either it can continue to mount its project of opposition, which would now mean to oppose the routinization of its own earlier practice by resisting the co-option of its techniques by the institution, now composed of its own graduate students and disciples, by withholding its blessing from the impending deconstruction of the canon by textual techniques now only too familiar and repetitive. It is, of course, an open question whether and how long even such resourceful critical minds as we are dealing with could maintain the deconstructive edge of such an adversary role, could continue to devise new ways of rescuing difference from the authoritative presence they have become in the work of their epigones. Even if they could so maintain the energy of deconstruction, the puritan dissidence of their dissent, they would have to abandon all hope of institutional *détente*. That eventuality must be a cause for anxiety. The alternative would be to acquiesce fully in their present institutionalization, to give their blessing to the wholesale routinization of deconstruction now under way. For deconstruction to do that would

---

[35] 'Idealism and Textualism', in *Consequences of Pragmatism*, p. 156.

be for it to cease to be deconstruction, for it to pass into institutional history. That thought too must cause considerable anxiety.

Whether the conscience of deconstruction is good or bad, it certainly exists and is powerful enough to bring upon itself in its current dilemma an acute *malconfort*, an aporia with a vengeance. For Paul de Man was never more clairvoyant than when, more than a decade ago, he foresaw his own present situation: 'All true criticism occurs in the mode of crisis . . . In periods that are not periods of crisis, or in individuals bent on avoiding crisis at all cost, there can be all kinds of approaches to literature: historical, philological, psychological, etc., but there can be no criticism . . . Whether authentic criticism is a liability or an asset to literary studies as a whole remains an open question'.[36] This account of the nature of criticism as difference from institutional norm is of course perfectly consistent with de Man's account of the nature of literature, and indeed underwrites deconstruction's own aspiration to literary status. Were deconstruction now to avoid crisis by acquiescing in the assimilation of its critical difference, its questionable status as a liability or an asset, by settling down under institutional auspices to the no longer hard but now empty labour of processing the entire literary canon, it would no longer be 'true criticism' but just another 'approach to literature'. For deconstruction will be 'true criticism', by its own lights, only as long as whether it can be done at all, and what it means institutionally to do it, remain open questions. Just as a number of critics in the mid-sixties, among them the present charismocrats of deconstruction, were writing against formalist and historical interpretation and calling, from within the institutional routine that new and practical

---

[36] *Blindness and Insight*, p. 8. Compare Derrida: '*Form* fascinates when one no longer has the force to understand force from within itself. That is, to create. This is why literary criticism is structuralist in every age, in its essence and destiny. Criticism has not always known this, but understands it now, and thus is in the process of thinking itself in its own concept, system and method. Criticism henceforth, knows itself separated from force, occasionally avenging itself on force by gravely and profoundly proving that separation is the condition of the work, and not only of the discourse on the work. Thus is explained the low note, the melancholy pathos that can be perceived behind the triumphant cries of technical ingenuity or mathematical subtlety that sometimes accompany certain so-called "structural" analyses.' *Writing and Difference*, trans. Alan Bass (Chicago: University of Chicago Press, 1978), pp. 4–5.

criticism had become, for different styles of reading, so critics are now beginning to write *from within theory*—the present book is just one example—*against the institutionization of theory*, including that of deconstructive theory.

Having all but prevailed within the academy and secured its institutional line of succession through the process described long ago by Max Weber as the routinization of charisma,[37] some exponents of deconstructive theory now envision its expansion beyond the walls of departments of English, French, philosophy, and comparative literature. Hillis Miller, for example, sees the time as right for colonizing the pedagogy of the schools.[38] So it was always written. And despite his caveats concerning theory, Geoffrey Hartman aims at nothing less than the repossession in the name of literary theory of the wider cultural discourse by an adventurous band of well-trained, versatile hermeneuts for hire, offering their skills for the decipherment of textuality in law, medicine, and commerce.[39] One cannot help wondering whether they are to be deconstructive textualists, and if so, imagining the sober justices of the Supreme Court listening to their briefs!

Yet it was de Man himself who once cautioned that 'a literal-minded disciple of . . . Frye is given license to order and classify the whole of literature into one single thing which, even though circular, would nevertheless be a gigantic cadaver.'[40] With its positive and positivist capability, its massive potential for reductive reification, Frye's protostructuralism once seemed the methodological antitype of deconstruction, with its insistence on negative capability, its inbuilt recalcitrance to being turned into 'positive and exploitative truth'. It was difficult indeed not to concur with Hartman that 'to imagine children of the future performing little Anatomies as easily as they now do basic operations in mathematics may

---

[37] See *The Theory of Social and Economic Organization*, trans. A. M. Henderson and Talcott Parsons (New York: The Free Press, 1964), pp. 363–73.

[38] 'On Edge: The Crossways of Contemporary Criticism', *Bulletin of the American Academy of Arts and Sciences*, xxxii. 4 (Jan. 1979), pp. 13–32.

[39] See 'A Short History of Practical Criticism', in *Criticism in the Wilderness* (New Haven: Yale University Press, 1980), pp. 293–5. Hartman does, however, go on to express self-deconstructive reservations in the same essay (p. 299): 'I remain skeptical . . . about the possibility of a truly comprehensive literary theory or literary history.'

[40] *Blindness and Insight*, p. 26.

not be everyone's Utopia.'[41] Fortunately for us all, Frye's utopia of 'sweet science' did not quite come off. Perhaps that means there is still hope we may yet be spared all the potential utopias of deconstructive theory, where little aporias and *mises-en-abîme* are extrapolated from the world's textuality as easily, normally, and literal-mindedly as 'close readings' once were.

[41] 'Ghostlier Demarcations: The Sweet Science of Northrop Frye', in *Beyond Formalism*, p. 25.

5

Toward A Poststructuralist Practice: A Reading of Shakespeare's *Sonnets*

> About anyone so great as Shakespeare, it is
> probable that we can never be right; and if we can
> never be right, it is better that we should from time
> to time change our way of being wrong.
>
> T. S. Eliot

I. EXEMPLARY TEXTS

Having argued that the institution of criticism should stop trying to do what it cannot do, i.e. seek out some monist or foundationalist rationale for its existence and activity—and continue to do what it can do, i.e. read and re-read an ever negotiable canon of texts with all the resourcefulness available to it—I am duty-bound to set an example by putting that argument into practice. And since one of the resources currently available to criticism is that snowballing body of theoretical discussion which is the subject of this book, we can hardly do other than try its exegetical power by bringing it to bear upon a classic text. After all, if it has become a new institutional convention to theorize our practice, the least those of us can do who contest the pure good of theory from within it is to put to the test whatever value it holds for our practice, to read our canonical texts with one eye on them and the other on the theoretical journals. Or to put the matter the other way round, if one distinguishing feature of a classic text is its capacity, by virtue of the long interpretive tradition that has grown up around it, to read us even as we read it, to register the press-marks of our changing institutional discourse, then our classic texts should be able to tell us something about our theorizing, to refine it to a new level of self-consciousness, if not altogether out of existence.

No classic text illustrates this two-way traffic, or as we say nowadays, this intertextuality of our reading better than Shakespeare's *Sonnets*. In their unrivalled power to attract exemplary readers, the *Sonnets* have offered just such a window on criticism throughout their modern interpretive history. The richness of their rhetorical texture, loaded as it is with irony, paradox, and especially ambiguity, has provided grist for the processing—or overprocessing—of new-critical formalism, as exemplified by William Empson's reading of *94* ('They that have power to hurt . . .'). Northrop Frye, operating from a 'critical middle-distance' where texture gives place to structure, has mapped the contours of the renaissance 'topocosm' they archetypify and the conventions of the sonnet they extend and culminate. More recently, one of their number has been co-opted to fill out the paradigm of the structuralist analysis of poetic language developed by Roman Jakobson and Claude Lévi-Strauss. Has any of the poems chosen over the years by Jakobson for linguistic analysis demonstrated better than Sonnet 129 how poetic language is characterized by 'the projection of the principle of equivalence from the axis of selection onto the axis of combination,' or the 'introverted nature of the poetic function', its concentration upon a 'message', in which 'everything becomes *significatif, réciproque, converse, corréspondant*, and . . . a perpetual interplay of sound and meaning establishes an analogy between the two facets, a relationship either paranomastic and anagrammatic, or figurative (occasionally onomatopoeic)'?[1]

I cite these readings of the *Sonnets* from among many others of the recent past, for the clarity with which they reveal the crystalline structure of the critical prisms that refract them. And as criticism now turns from its long preoccupation with such positive features of poetic language as form and genre, is there any text, or group of texts, in the literary canon that so readily lends itself to exploration of the negativities, absences,

---

[1] See William Empson, *Some Versions of Pastoral* (London: Chatto and Windus, 1935), pp. 89–115; Northrop Frye, 'How True a Twain', in *Fables of Identity* (New York: Harcourt, Brace, 1963), pp. 88–106; Roman Jacobson and Lawrence G. Jones, *Shakespeare's Verbal Art in* 'Th'Expence of Spirit' (The Hague: Mouton, 1970). Jacobson's discussion of poetic language in general is further elaborated, with various critiques of it addressed, in 'A Postscript to the Discussion on Grammar of Poetry', *Diacritics* (Spring 1980), pp. 22–35, from which the above quotations are taken.

and indeterminacies of textuality itself? More specifically, is there any pre-modern text better suited to serve as a test-case for the universalizing claims of deconstruction, as a general theory of poetic or literary language (albeit a negative one) that has so far confined its hermeneutic practice largely to post-romantic literature? For despite the vast body of positivist scholarship on the *Sonnets*, with its restless reaching in a spirit of *Literaturwissenschaft* after the biographical and historical identifications that supposedly explain them—in fact, as an unintended consequence of all that busy and contradictory scholarship—the *Sonnets* might well seem on the face of it to have been constructed, Shakespeare's prophetic soul dreaming on things to come, with the idea of deconstruction in mind.

Consider their most obvious features as poetic narrative, features that remain striking and tantalizing in their undecidability or over-determination in spite of all the scholarship they have occasioned. The *Sonnets* present to us a cast of characters—an ageing poet, a fair and noble youth, a successful rival poet, an untrustworthy dark lady—characters whose density and definition fluctuate unpredictably as the sequence progresses between the mimetic modes of allegorical abstraction and autobiographical concreteness. These characters make fitful appearances in a more or less triangular action as variously vivid and shadowy as their own characterizations. We hear of absences, betrayals, recriminations, and reconciliations counterpointed against the poet's continuing and self-conscious preoccupation with his art. We hear enough to persuade us that actual people and events in Shakespeare's life are here implicated, enough even to tempt us to try and reconstruct the intimate relations of the *ronde*, some acquaintance with which was presumably shared by that group among whom Shakespeare's 'sugared sonnets' were circulating in manuscript by 1598. But what we hear is too little or to ambiguous to identify the players in this *drame à clef* with any assurance, or to interpret in detail the action it spasmodically advances, so much of its apparent burden of reference remains obscured between the poems and between the lines of the poems. Who, for example, had the power to hurt and did not use it?

But the invitation to a deconstructive re-reading of the

Sonnets proceeds from a congeniality anterior to the inbuilt discontinuities of the genre or the failure of an older historical scholarship to reach consensus on how to fill their gaps by identifying their protagonists and construing the relations among them. It arises rather from the peculiar nature of Shakespeare's *Sonnets*, as distinct from Sidney's or Spenser's, as a text that calls attention to its own literal textuality, its teasing and frustrating mode of existence as a printed book remote, distinct, orphaned from whatever authorial intentions, biographical retentions, and mimetic pretensions it might have been expected, in the light of conventional practice, to carry. The title-page of the 1609 quarto bears no acronymic sublimations, unlike most Elizabethan sequences, of its protagonists or theme, merely the cryptic glorification of its 'onlie begetter'. The absent presence of this dedicatee has tempted and frustrated identification with the fair youth of the sequence, among a host of other candidates. Moreover, certain bibliographical and textual anomalies have led scholars, despite the fact that the poems are on the whole well printed, to propose numerous reorderings of the sequence to force its supposed plot to yield up its secrets. Yet after all these attempts at identification and rearrangement, only A. L. Rowse has arrived at confidence, a scholarly consensus of one.[2] The positivist yearnings of an older historical scholarship to pin down the personal experience of an originary author are thus bound up with the dream of reconstructing a stable, authoritative text of the *Sonnets*. Both projects were baffled from the outset by the unco-operative aloofness of their free-standing textual autonomy.

Given the positivist incapability of an older biographical and bibliographical scholarship to fill the gaps in its own construction of the *Sonnets*, what followed was not a new negative capability in subsequent dealings with them. For such a labour of the negative was not always, and certainly not yet, thinkable in our institutional discourse. What followed was rather the displaced positivism of the new-critical and proto-structuralist analyses already mentioned, content to make due with the text as it stands but not quite

[2] For his 'solution', see *Shakespeare's Sonnets: The Problems Solved* (London: Macmillan, 1973), and *Shakespeare the Man* (London: Macmillan, 1973).

content to relinquish the quest for unified and ascertainable meaning. For Northrop Frye, such problems as what actual people and events in Shakespeare's life his sonnets record, or whether the love professed in the earlier half of the sequence is homosexual were effectively dissolved, if never quite resolved, when the poems were regarded as expressions of a distinctively literary language. To the vexed question of whether some of the sonnets celebrate homosexual love, for example, Frye advances a uniquely modern answer: it doesn't matter. When read in terms of the conventions of Elizabethan sonneteering, within which mistresses are invariably female and fair, Shakespeare's sonnets offer no less than two masterly variations, two unprecedented moves in the game, by introducing two presiding mistress-muses, a 'lovely boy' and 'a woman coloured ill'. They have less to say, that is, about 'experience', particularly Shakespeare's own, than about poetry and its conventional and archetypical, ever-ready and ever-recyclable subject-matter. We find in the *Sonnets*, 'the authority of Shakespeare behind the conception of poetry as a marriage of Eros and Psyche, an identity of a genius that outlives time and a soul that feeds on death.'[3] In his elegant appropriation of the leading motifs of the *Sonnets*, Frye redefines the source of their power over generations of readers as their paradoxically authorless authority, their equipoise between personal attitude and impersonal structure, their oscillation, as it were, between voice, with its individual 'grain', and language or discourse, with its homogenizing conventionality. 'The authority of Shakespeare', which Frye uncompromisingly refuses to locate in the biographical experience of the poet is none the less finally invoked in the more disembodied form of a reconstituted poetic tradition. A similar process of re-establishing the authority of the *Sonnets* on the basis, not of Shakespeare's supposed possession of his experience, but of his relation to his language, is at work in different ways in the notable studies of Sigurd Burckhardt and Roman Jakobson.[4]

Yet such formalist or structuralist readings of the *Sonnets*, while they may foreclose certain traditional problems of

---

[3] Frye, 'How true a twain', p. 106.
[4] See Sigurd Burckhardt, 'The Poet as Fool and Priest', in *Shakespearean Meanings* (Princeton: Princeton University Press, 1968), pp. 22–46.

interpretation, also create new ones. Is it sufficient any longer to locate the poetic authority of the *Sonnets*, their claim to being read as something like a type or definition of poetry itself, in Shakespeare's mastery of his literary or linguistic resources as distinct from the possession of his personal experience? Even if it were possible to do so at a time when the very existence of a distinctive and privileged poetic language is in question, would not the nature and conditions of such mastery have to be specified rather than merely assumed or asserted? The notion of authority seems to be inseparable from the notion of a personal author, of a literary will-to-power, yet the notions of genre, tradition, and language are all im- or trans-personal, and a *persona* is not a person. Thus Michel Foucault, addressing the question of authorship and echoing Roland Barthes' structuralist manifesto that 'it is about time that criticism and philosophy acknowledged the disappearance or the death of the author,' goes on to wonder 'if this notion [of writing as having "freed itself of the theme of expression", as referring "only to itself", as "opening up a space where the subject continually disappears"] does not transpose the empirical character of the author into a transcendental anonymity?' 'Does not the representation of writing as an absence', he goes on, 'simply repeat in transcendental terms the religious principle that tradition is at once unalterable and never complete, and the aesthetic principle of the survival of the work, its endurance despite death?' In illustration of the lingering inadequacy of the post-modernist deconstruction of authorship, Foucault asks: 'If I discover that Shakespeare was not born in the house which one visits today, this obviously is not going to alter the function of the author's name; but if someone proves that Shakespeare did not write the sonnets which pass as his, that is a change of another kind, one that affects the function of the author's name.'[5] And in the latter hypothetical case, it need hardly be added, the way we would read the *Sonnets*, our sense of a distinctive will—pun intended—to expression (whatever may be expressed) and design on our response (however

---

[5] 'What is an Author?', *Partisan Review*, xlii. 4 (1975), pp. 603–14. Reprinted in *Textual Strategies: Perspectives in Poststructuralist Criticism*, ed. Josué V. Harari (Ithaca: Cornell University Press, 1979).

various that may be) at work within the linguistic machinery of the text. Neither the structuralist displacement of authorship into the transcendent authority of linguistic system, or of genre and tradition, nor the poststructuralist disappearance of the author into the transcendent anonymity of differential textuality seems quite able to obliterate our doubtless naïve, superstitious, and romantic sense of the poet, in Wordsworth's words, as 'a man speaking to men'.

This rehabilitation of the residual subject, of the ghost in the machine of language, is already implicit not only in the contextualist poststructuralism of Foucault, but in textualist poststructuralism as well. For like Foucault, Paul de Man is sceptical of the capacity of structuralist and poststructuralist analysis of writing ever to do away with the need for an authorial subject, and expresses this scepticism in terms of the ancient—some would say anachronistic—concept of 'voice':

But even if we free ourselves of all false questions of intent and rightfully reduce the narrator to the status of a mere grammatical pronoun, without which the narrative could not come into being, this subject remains endowed with a function that is not grammatical but rhetorical, in that it gives voice, so to speak, to a grammatical syntagm. The term *voice*, even when used in a grammatical terminology as when we speak of the passive or interrogative voice, is, of course, a metaphor inferring by analogy the intent of the subject from the structure of the predicate.[6]

The proscription of the intentional fallacy, devised by new criticism to rule out the too easy confusion of the literary and the empirical or biographical aspects of authorship, turns out to be very difficult to enforce. When it is strictly enforced, the authorial voice as will-to-expression is either transcendentalized into the authority of literary tradition itself, as in Frye's reading, or trivialized into the mechanistic anonymity of grammatical and linguistic forms, as in Jakobson's. From the

[6] *Allegories of Reading* (New Haven: Yale University Press, 1979), p. 18. See also Geoffrey Hartman's recuperative reflections on 'voice' in *Saving the Text* (Baltimore: Johns Hopkins University Press, 1981), pp. 4–8: 'The personification of "Sprache" shows that those who put author or ego down are still potentially mastered by the idea of presence itself, which persists even without the concept of a sovereign subject because of the privilege accorded to voice ("Die Sprache *spricht*") as the foundation of the written word.'

poststructuralist perspectives of Foucault and de Man, the former operation delivers up a presence that, like godhead, is not really a presence but merely a resting-point for readerly anxiety in quest of presence (since the supposedly authoritative presence of literary tradition is constituted only by so many authors each as individually absent as the one in question); and the latter operation, an absence that is not really an absence, in so far as the apparently anonymous impersonality of linguistic manipulations, as in programmed computation, always implies someone, an intentional if not biographical subject, doing the manipulating.

Each of these poststructuralist reflections, different as they are in their contextual and textual emphases, reintroduces into the discussion of poetic authority an element that was notoriously absent from the diversely structuralist readings of Frye and Jakobson; namely, the historical and rhetorical dimensions, which are not simply assimilable to tradition or language. For Foucault, the idea of the author remains a meaningful but not metaphysical concept, a 'strong moment of individualization in the history of ideas' and 'a founder of discursivity'.[7] For de Man, literary or poetic language consists precisely in its rhetorical elusiveness, in its irreducibility either to the personal presence associated with voice or the impersonal constructions of language. What remains to be seen is how far these formulations can help to define the peremptory authority of Shakespeare's *Sonnets* over generations of readers, their special power as mighty begetters of readings. In what does that poetic authority consist, and by what is it conditioned? What is the nature of their Shakespearean rhetoricity and their Elizabethan discursivity, and what is the relation of the two?

II. POETIC MONUMENTS

Obviously these questions can be engaged only through another reading of the *Sonnets*, one that would take account not only of their declared rhetorical ambitions, but of the undeclared discursive formations that condition them. In the

---

[7] 'What is an Author?', pp. 604, 611.

interest of economy, we might do well to focus initially on a single sonnet, one that raises explicitly the question of poetic authority. Such sonnets are of course not hard to find in Shakespeare's sequence, and I have settled on 55 for my point of departure. As one of the poetic 'highs' of the *Sonnets*, asserting as it does in the most unequivocal terms its power to confer a special status on its author, its object, and itself, 55 has always attracted critical attention. It has also been quite recently discussed as deriving directly from a sonnet by Spenser published in *The Ruines of Rome* (1591), itself a translation of one of Joachim du Bellay's *Antiquitez de Rome*. So 55 plunges us, conveniently for our purposes, into that nexus of renaissance intertextuality which might be termed the 'ruins poem', contemporary examples of which occur in at least three European languages. Let us confine ourselves, however, to Spenser and Shakespeare:

> Hope ye my verses that *posterity*
> Of age ensuing shall you ever read?
> Hope ye that ever immortality
> So mean harp's work may challenge for her meed?
>   If under heaven any endurance were,
> These *moniments*, which not in paper writ?
> But in porphyr and *marble* do appear,
> Might well have hoped to have obtained it.
>   Nath'les my lute, whom Phoebus deignd to give,
> Cease not to sound these olde antiquities:
> For if that time doo let thy glorie live,
> Well maist thou boast, how ever base thou bee,
> That thou art first, which of thy Nation song
> Th'olde honour of the' people gowned long. (*RR*, 32)

> Not *marble* nor the gilded *monuments*
> Of princes shall outlive this pow'rful rhyme,
> But you shall shine more bright in these contents
> Than unswept stone, besmeared with sluttish time.
>   When wasteful war shall statues overturn,
> And broils root out the work of masonry
> Nor Mars his sword nor war's quick fire shall burn
> The living record of your memory.

'Gainst death and all oblivious enmity
Shall you pace forth; your praise shall still find room
Even in the eyes of all *posterity*
That wear this world out to the ending doom.
So, till the judgment that yourself arise,
You live in this, and dwell in lovers' eyes.[8]

Whether Spenser's sonnet is a 'source' for, or 'influence' on, Shakespeare's, and what such terms might mean within such a context of renaissance intertextuality, are not of immediate concern. For our present purposes, it suffices that the two sonnets share a number of topics, tropes, and terms, and taken together, form a kind of meditation on renaissance authorship. We may think of the relation between them as antiphonal or dialectical, whereby Spenser's sonnet frames, in the most tentative, even querulous, terms, a question to which Shakespeare's offers a supremely self-confident answer.

That question is not merely the literary one of how poetic authority, and the immortality consequent upon it, is to be achieved in contemporary practice, but the literary-historical one of what conditions and underwrites it. How, in a belated age and barbarous northern vernacular, can the classics of insolent Greece and haughty Rome be equalled or surpassed? For both poems take as their point of departure the ringing claims of Horace and Ovid to a poetic survival beyond physical death and material decay, the word 'monument', common to both sonnets, explicitly echoing Horace's *'exegi monumentum aere perennius'*.[9] Both Horace and Ovid had based their poetic claims on Rome's imperial domination, and the insurance it provided for the universal literary hegemony of Latin. The problem facing the sixteenth-century English or

[8] *The Works of Edmund Spenser: A Variorum Edition*, eds. Greenlaw, Osgood, Padelford, Heffner, vii 8 (Baltimore: Johns Hopkins Press, 1947), p. 153; *Shakespeare's Sonnets*, ed. Stephen Booth (New Haven: Yale University Press, 1977), pp. 48–51. All subsequent quotations from Shakespeare's *Sonnets* are to this edition. The argument for Spenser/du Bellay as Shakespeare's source was advanced by A. Kent Hieatt, 'The Genesis of Shakespeare's *Sonnets*: Spenser's *Ruines of Rome: by Bellay*', *PMLA* vol. 98, no. 5 (October 1983), 800–814. italics in the quotation above are Hieatt's.

[9] *Odes* III.xxx.1. Compare Ovid, *Metamorphoses, XV*. 871–9. Booth (p. 227) cites other renaissance versions of the commonplace.

French poet, as the Spenser/du Bellay sonnet makes painfully explicit, is whether a poem written in a belated vernacular can also aspire to immortality when it is not underwritten by the guarantee of imperial greatness, particularly when the very monuments that bear witness to Rome's and Egypt's grandeur have themselves crumbled. In projecting, tentatively in Spenser and confidently in Shakespeare, the power of poetry to transcend the power of empire, both poems are precursors of Shelley's 'Ozymandias'. While they hold no hint of the latter's romantic irony toward the aspirations of imperial conquest itself, both Spenser/du Bellay and Shakespeare anticipate something of Shelley's scepticism towards the imperial self-projections of monumental sculpture that go with it. So much so in Shakespeare's case, as to elaborate in terms even more explicit and extravagant than Horace's, the paradox that poetry, at least his own, will outlast—despite the apparent perishability of its graphic or vocal medium—the monumental art and architecture of royal conquest—despite the apparent durability of their harder media of marble and stone.

On what, then, is Shakespeare's poetic self-confidence grounded, if not on something like the imperial theme of his Roman precursors? Had Shakespeare taken a more Shelleyan approach to the Ozymandian situation he sketches, his confidence might well have been underwritten by a neo-platonic poetic, certainly available to an Elizabethan poet and often invoked by Spenser, that asserts the eternality of spiritual form over its mutable material embodiments, and hence the superior potential of poetry as 'airy nothing' to body forth 'the forms of things unknown' over those plastic arts which still participate in the corruption of matter. Though Shakespeare might have appealed to neo-platonic poetics, explicitly or implicitly, to support his claims, and seems to do so elsewhere, he does not do so in 55. Given the extravagance of those claims, in fact, such an apeal would not really have lent much support. For even if poetry, by virtue of its linguistic medium, can be considered less material than the plastic arts, and hence suitable for the representation of a transcendent ideal of beauty, nobility, glory, or whatever, its claim to transcendence is still only relative, since manuscript, printed pages, and even the articulated breath of speech are still matter, and therefore subject to expiration and decay. But Shakespeare's claim, like Horace's and Ovid's, but unlike Spenser/du Bellay's, is absolute. It is made without neo-platonic support, in defiance of conventional logic, and against historical precedent. After all, even if Shakespeare could not know of the fire in the Cotton library that was to decimate much of his own earlier national literature in 1731, he could not have failed to know of the calamitous burning of the Alexandrian library in 47 BC, which consumed many a deathless classic among the 40,000 manuscripts destroyed.

Nor does Shakespeare's sonnet open an appeal, as several of his plays do, to any realist, as distinct from idealist, mimetic programme in staking its claim to poetic perdurability. The object that the poem promises to deliver up for all time is notoriously obscure. It is hard to say just what 'these contents' even refer to, that are supposed to 'shine bright'. The youth's beauty? His nobility or achievements? His corpse? For the context of marble and stone monuments, the constricting form of the sonnet, and the closing anticipations of resurrection and judgement have suggested this last reference to some readers. We cannot even be sure that the 'you' the poem addresses itself to representing is the youth. Northrop Frye registers Shakespeare's cavalier unconcern with exactitude or verisimilitude of reference and representation when he notes, with throwaway wit, that 'although the poet promises the youth immortality, and clearly has the power to confer it, he does not lift a metrical foot to make the youth a credible or interesting person.'[10] The power of immortality which Shakespeare ascribes to his rhyme, and which his readers, with Frye, freely concede to him, does not seem to be based on or sustained by any *a priori* relation, any close or detailed resemblance, explicit or implicit, between poetry and material or empirical reality whatever. The claim of power is based on nothing other than its own assertion of power. It is entirely tautological, self-referential, and rhetorical. The power of poetic survival seems to consist solely in the poem's presumed rhetorical power to compel future readings: 'As long as men

[10] Frye, p. 89.

can breathe, and eyes can see,' Shakespeare writes in an analogous vein in *18*, 'So long lives this, and this gives life to thee.' Perhaps what is most remarkable about the claim is that it has proved to be entirely self-fulfilling.

In pointing to the rhetorical nature of Shakespeare's enunciation of poetic authority and perdurability in *55*, I am not suggesting that its force can be wholly explained in terms of a renaissance rhetorical programme then in place, or that adherence to such a programme is what insures its poetic success. In fact, Shakespeare's poem, with its initial restatement and subsequent elaboration of a Horatian and Ovidian *topos*, does illustrate a principle fundamental to renaissance rhetorical theory, namely that of *copia*, of virtuoso elaboration on a received theme. This widespread rhetorical practice may well be regarded as the renaissance counterpart or forerunner of the post-romantic phenomenon of creative misprision, a means of engaging and overgoing classical models and thereby extending a potentially tongue-tying tradition by reweaving it.

Such commonplace rhetorical tactics as hyperbole and negative comparison, both employed in the opening line of *55*, are in the service of this larger rhetorical strategy. The frequent and characteristic recourse to hyperbole, often combined with classical allusion, is familiar enough as a chief constituent of Marlowe's mighty line, from which Shakespeare doubtless learned much, and negative comparison is one of the chief means by which Milton aspires to overgo classical epic, 'to soar above th'Aonian mount': '*Not* that fair field of Enna . . .' The extravagant variation on a received topic characterizes Shakespeare's own earliest efforts in epyllion, comedy, and tragedy; his *Venus and Adonis* and *Rape of Lucrece* multiply the metamorphoses of their Ovidian sources, and his *Comedy of Errors* and *Titus Andronicus*, the mistaken identities and vindictive atrocities of Plautus' *Menaechmi* and Seneca's *Thyestes* respectively. This rhetorical gambit is no doubt also at work in the bold paradoxes with which he develops the traditional poetic claims of Horatian and Ovidian sources in *55*, so as to revivify and redouble their old force through the surcharge of a new rhetorical *energia*.

It would be grossly reductive, however, to think that *55*—or the *Sonnets* generally, since this is their persistent under-theme—authorize themselves simply through the single-minded following out of a renaissance rhetorical programme. After all, the strategy of *copia*, with its panoply of particular rhetorical tactics, is itself only a norm or model that by its own logic would itself have to be exceeded for a true authority to emerge. Great numbers of Elizabethan sonnets, including that of Spenser/du Bellay, make some of the same moves as Shakespeare's 55 in rhetorically invoking and extending classical precedent to legitimate themselves, yet fail to make good their poetic aspirations in the only way they can be made good: by compelling future readings. Shakespeare himself complains half way through his sequence that the imitation of his own rhetoric by rival poets has left him barren and tongue-tied, 'enforced to seek anew / Some fresher stamp of the time-bett'ring days' (*82*.7–8). To achieve the kind of poetic authority Shakespeare envisions, he would have to tap some 'source' deeper and more powerful than any set of classic examples or programme of rhetorical variation, thereby anticipating and pre-empting his own potential imitation and obsolescence at the hands of others. His poetry would have to be different from its own potential rhetorical reduction or anatomization.

This does not mean that the authority Shakespeare envisions and claims has nothing to do with rhetoric, only that it is not rhetorical in any simple sense, i.e. that it is not logical, or has empirical designs on its putative object and potential readers, or uses a repertory of devices for effecting those designs. The project so confidently proclaimed in 55 seems closer to the rhetorical mode described by Paul de Man and Roland Barthes, as 'performative'. Barthes defines a 'performative' utterance, adopting the term from J. L. Austin, as 'a rare verbal form (exclusively given in the first person and in the present tense) in which the enunciation has no other content (contains no other proposition) than the act by which it is uttered—something like the *I declare* of kings or the *I sing* of very ancient poets.'[11]

---

[11] 'The Death of the Author', in *Image-Music-Text*, tr. Stephen Heath (New York: Hill and Wang, 1977), pp. 145–6.

Though not exactly cast in present tense, and without giving up all empirical designs on its object and audience, Sonnet 55 seems very close to this performative mode in its aspiration to a royal or bardic bringing into being of its object, to making itself good and itself flesh in something like the eternal present of its utterance. So it might well seem tempting at this point to try to account for the triumphant poetic authority of Sonnet 55—as opposed to the more limited authority of any number of its Elizabethan congeners—as a function of this performative quality, that is, in terms of the consistency and integrity with which it maintains the self-subsistence of its performative mode. Such an approach would at least have the advantage of re-inscribing the poem within the modernist, post-authorial, performative poetic advanced by Barthes, among others, within which '*writing* can no longer designate an operation of recording, notation, representation, "depiction" (as the Classics would say) and every text is eternally written *here* and *now*.'[12]

But there are some obvious difficulties in the way of such an approach. One is that it begs the question of value-judgement. The success or failure of performative utterance, like any other poetic mode, doubtless has something to do with its quality in the evaluative sense. Shakespeare, in fact, implies as much, that the immortality of his poem depends on just such a historical judgement, when he alludes to the Christian judgement that will ultimately determine the fate of the youth himself. It is only such a saving judgement of quality, after all, that could persuade posterity to take the necessary pains to preserve the paper on which his sonnets are written or printed—the paper we are repeatedly reminded, in this sonnet and elsewhere, is as subject to combustion, oxidation, and decay as 'yellow leaves' themselves—in order to read and re-read them in times to come, to give them breath and voice, and hence, their own 'life' or 'afterlife' by analogy with that of the youth they represent.

Here another difficulty emerges. For what conditions this necessary value-judgement is not intrinsic to the performative modality of its utterance. That in itself cannot make a poem good. If it could, or if Shakespeare and his fellow Elizabethans

[12] Barthes, p. 145.

believed it could, such poet–kings as Marlowe's Edward II, Shakespeare's Richard II, and Ford's Perkin Warbeck, all of whom are magisterial exemplars of performative utterance, would have had to meet different, and better, destinies within their plays. Yet in none of these cases does their performance as poets ensure their historical success. Quite the opposite: their performative rhetoric, brilliant as it is, *fails* to carry the day. The value placed on performative utterance as such, whatever its technical or 'intrinsic' quality, seems to be a function rather than a determinant of historical and cultural circumstance—as the outcome of each of these plays demonstrates, and Barthes' own highly polemical advocacy of it as the preferred modernist or post-modernist mode, itself attests.

But there is another, more formidable obstacle to identifying the claim of *55* to poetic perdurability with its performative status as intransitive or apodictic writing, in Barthes' term, 'inscription'. Far from abandoning the notions of 'recording, notation, representation, "depiction" (as the Classics would say)' in favour of present, personal, and non-instrumental 'inscription', Shakespeare's *Sonnets* generally, and *55* particularly, insistently press their mimetic and empirical claims, their designs upon a prior, non-linguistic 'reality' in order to fix and perpetuate it. How could it be otherwise, when renaissance poetics is invariably mimetic in nature, and seems to know no other way in which to think of itself, to theorize its practice? In contrast to Barthes 'modern scriptor', for whom the intransitive autonomy of writing is to be welcomed with a sense of relief at least, of pleasure or joy at most, the Shakespeare of the *Sonnets*, particularly of the first half of the sequence, consistently regards his writing transitively, as deriving whatever free-standing autonomy it may achieve from the imitation, albeit heightened and hypertrophied, of an original in the way that *55* projects. Very like a monument indeed. This is not to suggest that Shakespeare cannot imagine the mimetic failure of his art, the defectiveness or breakdown of his poetry as representation. He does so often in the sequence. But when he does so, the inadequacy of writing is always measured against a presupposed mimetic norm or ideal.

In the earlier phase of the sequence, especially in the first seventeen sonnets known as the 'procreation series', the priority of nature to art, of the natural to the artistic project, is consistently asserted, and the role of poetry and the poet is conceived as unabashedly empirical or instrumental, to persuade the youth to replicate himself by marrying and begetting children: 'But wherefore do you not a mightier way / Make war upon this bloody tyrant Time?' (*16*.1–2.) Poetry, however relentlessly mimetic, is seen as inferior and subservient—a mere 'barren rhyme'—to the reproduction of nature itself, which is supposedly 'Much liker than your painted counterfeit' (*16*.8), an invidious comparison carried to its self-denigrating and self-denying conclusion in the last of the procreation series, where the poet asks 'Who will believe my verse in time to come?' and finally repudiates that verse on the grounds of its mimetic inaptitude: 'It is but as a tomb / which hides your life, and shows not half your parts' (*17*.3–4). Even in the famous *18* ('Shall I compare thee to a summer's day'), with which the poet's own wooing of the youth seems to begin in earnest, his 'eternal lines' develop their new-found strength in representing their object of desire through a series of comparisons in which natural analogues now prove defective and invidious. The original inadequacy of mimesis has been more than made up in what can only be termed a supermimesis that actually replaces its object with a poetic counterpart capable of withstanding all the destructive elements enumerated in the bold paradoxes of *55*.

But the abandonment of the initial empirical project of the *Sonnets* as persuasion to love, with its justification in a natural, material, and heterosexual reproduction of its object (in all its imperfection and perishability) in favour of the more idealized mimetic or supermimetic project of a transcendent or transmaterial sublimation of or substitution for it, which culminates in *55*, turns out to be a pyrrhic and short-lived victory. This emerging repudiation of the supermimetic ambition to substitute the poem for the object of desire initially expresses itself as moral revulsion at the narcissism it involves: 'Sin of self-love possesseth all mine eye / . . . 'Tis thee, myself, that for myself I praise, / Painting my age with beauty of thy days' (*62*.1,13–14). But it increasingly involves a new consciousness of mimetic embarrassment as well, of the inbuilt frustration of any poetic attempt to transcend the residual materiality of its own utterance. The breath in which it is spoken, or the paper on which it is literally written, is, as we have already seen, an inescapable subversion and ironic self-denial of the claim to transcendent and perdurable supermimesis enunciated in 55.

The sonnets on time that follow and culminate in 65 make even more explicit the contradictions of the supermimetic project by granting Time his full tyrannical due over every nook and corner, every last vestige, of material reality:

> Like as the waves make towards the pebbled shore,
> So do our minutes hasten to their end . . .
> And time that gave doth now his gift confound.
> Time doth transfix the flourish set on youth,
> And delves the parallels in beauty's brow,
> Feeds on the rarities of nature's truth,
> And nothing stands but for his scythe to mow.
>> And yet to times in hope my verse shall stand,
>> Praising thy worth, despite his cruel hand.
>>> (60. 1–2, 8–14)

> Against my love shall be as I am now,
> With time's injurious hand crushed and o'erworn
> When hours have drained his blood and filled his brow
> With lines and wrinkles . . .
> For such a time do I now fortify
> Against confounding age's cruel knife,
> That he shall never cut from memory
> My sweet love's beauty, though my lover's life.
>> His beauty shall in these black lines be seen,
>> And they shall live, and he in them still green.
>>> (63. 1–4, 9–14)

> When I have seen by time's fell hand defaced
> The rich proud cost of outworn buried age,
> When sometimes lofty towers I see down razed,
> And brass eternal slave to mortal rage . . .
> When I have seen such interchange of state,
> Or state itself confounded to decay,
> Ruin hath taught me thus to ruminate,
> That time will come and take my love away.
>> This thought is as a death, which cannot choose
>> But weep to have that which it fears to lose.
>>> (64. 1–4, 9–14)

Since brass, nor stone, nor earth, nor boundless sea,
But sad mortality o'ersways their power,
How with this rage shall beauty hold a plea,
Whose action is no stronger than a flower?
O how shall summer's honey breath hold out
Against the wrackful siege of batt'ring days,
When rocks impregnable are not so stout,
Nor gates of steel so strong but time decays?
O fearful meditation; where, alack,
Shall time's best jewel from time's chest lie hid?
Or what strong hand can hold his swift foot back?
Or who his spoil or beauty can forbid?
  O none, unless this miracle have might
  That in black ink my love may still shine bright.

(65. 1–4, 9–14)

These great 'ruins poems' that dominate the sonnets of the *60*s in Shakespeare's sequence may be read as a dark postscript to the bright promise of *55*. If *55* triumphantly substitutes, by a masterly if narcissistic sleight of hand, its own transcendent textuality for its mimetic object, thereby defeating time, these sonnets envision Time as himself a master-artificer of self-consuming artifacts, a kind of action-sculptor or action-painter gone berserk. For Time's fine frenzy climaxes in that master-stroke of his 'cruel hand' which is the self-destruction of his own great works; his 'transfixing' (*60*.9) of 'the flourish' he himself has 'set on youth' means not permanence but murder, and would have to be countered by a 'strong hand' indeed. The struggle for immortality is now cast as a poetomachia, in which Time himself is seen by Shakespeare as a powerful rival, with the outcome quite uncertain as to which will prove *il miglior fabbro*. The ringing Horatian diction of *55* is still invoked, but the claim of a poetry written in black ink on yellowing paper to outlast time's own favoured media of brass and stone now requires the 'might' of a 'miracle' to make itself good. The poetic imperative of *55*, through which poetry immortalizes by fiat its object and itself, has become in *65* a merely subjunctive 'might'.

III. SPEAKING PICTURES

In recalling attention to the unlikely nature of 'black ink' as a medium of representation—'His beauty shall in these black lines be seen, / And they shall live, and he in them still green'—Shakespeare returns, and returns us, through this radical defamiliarization of his medium, to the questionable mimetic potential of writing in comparison to that of the plastic and visual arts. And as we witness Shakespere wrestling with the full dubiety of that issue, might we not well wonder why he should want or need to do so? Why should renaissance poetry and poetics be unable to think of themselves as anything other than mimetic, despite the difficulties, so explicitly raised and addressed by the *Sonnets*, in maintaining that claim? Were it not better done, as our post-modernist poetics has long since done, to abandon all claims or pretensions to a lifelike mimesis, and settle for a concept of writing as a productive or constitutive, rather than imitative, function, more in line with our more general and modern understanding of the intransitive productivity of signs and sign-systems? After all, even painting and sculpture, apparently so much better adapted to the imitation of an object, have often in this century seen fit to abandon their traditional mimetic function in order to develop their own constructivist and productivist, abstract and expressionist potential.

Such changes in the rationale of the arts, in the discourse that explains and legitimates their function, clearly have at least as much to do with the changing historical and cultural conditions within which the arts are produced as with intrinsic aesthetic issues within and between them. In the case of Elizabethan sonnet-sequences, the system of aristocratic patronage that traditionally supported their production may well remain, as we say nowadays, 'inscribed' in the poems themselves as well as in the Elizabethan poetic theory that surrounds them, and may well help to account for the dubious mimetic ambition they often express in terms of an equally dubious comparison with the visual arts. Even at a point when the poet was turning—and Shakespeare's career coincides with this point—from the service of the aristocracy, as the source of patronage and authority in commissioning works of art designed to confirm and perpetuate its own present power, to the practice of an art which could maintain and authorize itself by· the more independent means made possible by the printing of books, even at such a point, the measure of poetic success was still conceived as the ability to render up a presence, if no longer of the embodied and institutional authority of the culture, at least of the poetic object. The noble youth of Shakespeare's sequence, whether or not he can be identified with the Henry Wriothesley, Earl of Southampton, whose actual patronage Shakespeare seems unsuccessfully to have sought, may be read as just such a sign of transition within the poet's affairs. The authority of Shakespeare's *Sonnets* is conceived from within the *Sonnets* as inseparable from their ambition to represent and perpetuate the active presence of the youth himself, despite the sublimation of his social authority into his power to compel love and devotion, and despite the dubieties that this representation in so unlikely a medium as 'black ink' entails.[13]

If these speculations are at all valid, it follows that Shakespeare's retention of mimesis as the source of his own poetic authority reinscribes in a displaced and metaphoric form an older discourse of artistic authority based quite literally in the artist's proximity to the historical and social—the marxists would say 'real'—sources of power. The classic rationale of mimesis under which poetry and painting were still associated—*ut pictura poesis*—must then be understood as a new self-justification or self-authorization in the adopted terms of the displaced or substitutive presence that is

---

[13] On the system(s) of patronage that supported the arts and letters during the Middle Ages and renaissance in Europe and England, a great deal has been written, and I cite only a few relevant studies. See Karl J. Holzknecht, *Literary Patronage in the Middle Ages* (Philadelphia: University of Pennsylvania Press, 1923); Eleanor Rosenberg, *Leicester, Patron of Letters* (New York: Columbia University Press, 1955); John F. Danby, *Poets on Fortune's Hill* (London: Methuen, 1952); E. H. Miller, *The Professional Writer in Elizabethan England* (Cambridge, Mass.: Harvard University Press, 1959). An incisive reading of the *Sonnets* as representing the 'failure of patronage' is offered by Alvin B. Kernan, *The Playwright as Magician: Shakespeare's Image of the Poet in the English Public Theater* (New Haven: Yale University Press, 1979), Ch. 2, and of the frustrations of patronage implicit in Elizabethan sonnet sequences, by Arthur F. Marotti, '"Love Is Not Love": Elizabethan Sonnet Sequences and the Social Order', *ELH*, 49 (1982), pp. 396–428. Given the frequency with which Nicholas Hilliard's 'Young Man among Roses' is cited in connection with the *Sonnets*, a recent work on Elizabethan miniature-painting is also relevant: Roy Strong, *The English Renaissance Miniature* (London: Thames and Hudson, 1983). The technique of 'limning' directly from life in three sittings to create the illusion of vivid presence, as described by Strong, bears directly on the mimetic and 'metonymic' concerns of this chapter.

metaphor. The access and proximity to 'real' power once enjoyed by the arts under the system of ecclesiastical and royal or aristocratic patronage—a metonymic or literal authority—is giving way in the late renaissance to a recreation in linguistic and poetic terms of that older, now displaced, relation—a metaphoric or figurative authority. Poetic language, as a displaced presence seeking to maintain through similarity the place it once occupied through contiguity, to close the gap of its displacement from centrality, by becoming the self-authorizing object of its own representation, thus takes on a newer metaphoric and an older metonymic aspect, which are blurred together under the concept of mimesis. The metaphoric similarity of poetic language to its authorizing object now becomes an issue, takes on a new and special urgency, in a way it never did before when the authority of poetic language was based on its metonymic contiguity to a 'real', i.e. socially legitimate and authoritative, object. This new urgency becomes all the more intense and troubled when the conventional comparison with painting, slower to emerge into the dubious and anxious freedom from patronage conferred on writing by the printing press, is invoked. The by now familiar questions, raised by Roman Jakobson and others, concerning the relations of contiguity and similarity, syntagm and paradigm, metonymy and metaphor, *within* language and poetic language, could not have been raised until prior questions concerning the contiguity and similarity *of* language and poetic language, in relation to a pre-existing reality had been raised. The relative claims to priority or authority of metaphor and metonymy *within* the functioning of poetic language, could not become an issue until poetic language had been separated from a reality with which it had formerly been identified, that is, until its own relation to 'reality' was conceived as merely metaphoric or metonymic, as in some sense figurative. This seems to occur late in the development of a culture, and in the case of European culture the moment of that anterior rethinking was the renaissance, and its major text, Shakespeare's *Sonnets*.[14]

[14] The idea that words bear not a conventional but natural relation to things was commonplace in classical antiquity and the Middle Ages. Both Plato and Aristotle thought that words retain a natural relation to the things they name, and poetic

Nor is it accidental that this rethinking of the relation between language and 'reality' is conducted, within renaissance poetics and Shakespeare's poetry, in terms of a sustained comparison with the visual and plastic arts in particular.[15] Those sister arts of visual representation, particularly in their monumental forms, still aristocratically commissioned in Shakespeare's culture, would have seemed on the face of it, to enjoy at least two advantages over writing, so it is not really surprising to find writing appropriating their terms and assimilating itself to them. Sculpture and painting are both historically contiguous to their objects, their 'sources' of cultural authority and prestige. They are or were adjacent in time and space to the tyrant, prince, or aristocrat who commissioned and presumably sat for them, or whose remains they commemorate or even literally contain, and with whose

language, according to Plato (*Cratylus*, 418–19), recovers the true form of an original, univocal language given by a divine name-maker but now distorted through usage. Solider Aristotle, locating 'reality' not in transcendent forms but in the phenomenal world, defines the paramount poetic function as a 'command of metaphor', 'for to make good metaphors implies an eye for resemblances' within the natural order (*Poetics*, *XXII*.9). The idea of a divinely sanctioned natural order reflected in language and recovered and revealed in poetic language—rather than constructed by it—is implicit in the medieval commonplace that identifies the 'books' of nature and revelation, both originally scripted or scriptured by God. (See E. R. Curtius, 'The Book of Nature' in *European Literature and the Latin Middle Ages*, tr. Willard R. Trask (Princeton: Princeton University Press, 1953), pp. 319–26.) Such a notion also underwrites the comprehensive taxonomies of natural, social, and psychological reality that modern historians of ideas have labelled 'the great chain of being' and 'the Elizabethan world-picture', those culturally sanctioned systems of correspondence that provided renaissance poets with vast ready-made repositories of metaphoric similarity. The fragmentation during the seventeenth century, under pressure from an emerging empirical science, of these discursive formations, based as they were on the presumed correspondence between language and world as interchangeable texts, is discussed by Michel Foucault in the first chapter of *The Order of Things*, trans. Alan Sheridan (New York: Pantheon, 1970). The present essay argues that this fundamental change is already occurring in Shakespeare's *Sonnets*.

[15] Even music, for us the most abstract and least mimetic of the arts, was regarded in the renaissance as an art of imitation—if not always consistently so—as 'programme music'. Its 'programme', or object of imitation, could vary considerably, according to date, provenance, and commentator, from the physical sounds of the natural world to the mathematical structure of nature, to the 'harmony' that was supposed to inhere in the macrocosm of the sphere and microcosms of society and the individual. The persistent connection made between poetry, particularly lyric poetry, and music served to reinforce this mimetic understanding of music. See, for example, John Hollander, *The Untuning of the Sky: Ideas of Music in English Poetry 1500–1700* (Princeton: Princeton University Press, 1961), pp. 194–206 and Bruce Pattison, *Music and Poetry of the English Renaissance* (London: Methuen, 1948).

actual person they may be, at least for a time, compared.

Their function as a mnemonic device, as a bid for eternal presence, moreover, is not only a matter of historical contiguity, but of material similarity, since stone, brass, and paint have a natural affinity with the human flesh they can be contoured and coloured to resemble, and thereby recall while replacing. The most striking illustration of this double mimetic advantage of monumental sculpture occurs in *The Winter's Tale*, where the similarity of Julio Romano's statue to the 'dead' Hermione—to which everyone present attests—is further reinforced by its contiguity to Hermione's supposedly look-alike daughter, Perdita (conceivably played by the same actress) at its unveiling. 'Had he [Julio] eternity himself, and could put breath into his work,' remarks one of the onlookers, 'he would beguile nature of her custom, so perfectly is he her ape' (V.i.105–8).

The advantage of mimetic contiguity of course fades with time and is always compromised by the inescapable conventionality of art, but these qualifications only allow the conversion of one advantage into the other. Even at a later historical stage, when art no longer directly represents the aristocratic or bourgeois power that commissions it, as in Velázquez's *Las Meninas*, it contrives to exploit its inbuilt implication of presence. Rembrandt's long sequence of self-portraits gain much of their force from the assumption of mimetic contiguity, from the illusion they continue to induce, as self-portraits, of our being as close as his own mirror to the very presence of the painter and of our watching, like a fly on that mirror, the simultaneous progress of his ageing and process of its recording in a kind of ultimate objectification or anatomization of subjectivity. The Egyptian pharaohs, who used to efface the names inscribed on the tombs of their predecessors and substitute their own, could thereby, thanks to the high and accommodating stylization of Egyptian art, enforce the sense of mimetic similarity through sheer historical contiguity. Even in Shelley's 'Ozymandias', despite its ironic denial of the Egyptian conqueror's boast of eternal omnipresence, the speaker none the less feels himself very much in the presence, if not of this particular pharaoh, of the generalized passions of tyranny itself, which yet survive.

Poetry, by contrast, can make no such claim on the basis of its written medium even to the displaced presence that historical contiguity and material similarity confer on sculpture and painting. For writing, unlike the plastic arts, has only an arbitrary and conventional relation to its mimetic referent. Its referential function depends on the constitutive power of a system of signs that have no natural, material, or historical relation of contiguity or similarity to what they signify, but only an arbitrary and conventional one. Poetic representation is thus far more indirect and mediated than iconic representation, in so far as its arbitrary and conventional system of verbal signs requires a more complex and displaced reconstitution or concretization of the represented object. Our initial decipherment of poetic language is always already belated, occurs at a temporal and spatial remove from its putative object, and issues in a concretization of that object that is itself inescapably subjective, a filling-out of the inbuilt and necessary indeterminacies of textuality that is always dependent on prior beliefs, assumptions, and ideologies that vary from reader to reader and are never fully specifiable.[16]

For the contextual and communal norms that might determine our reading of texts are themselves texts that require a further, ultimately elusive, determination. Writing, by putting the original context of language into radical abeyance, renders its objects simultaneously overdetermined and underdetermined in any readerly concretization of it. As a second-order system of representation neither deployed nor deciphered in the presence of its object, writing begins and remains on the far side of its object, remote and alienated from it, while continuing to aspire, at least in classical and

---

[16] The 'concretization' of the text by the reader as a special case of Husserlian 'appresentation' is seminally discussed by Roman Ingarden in *The Cognition of the Literary Work of Art* (Evanston: Northwestern University Press), p. 50 ff. It is further refined by Wolfgang Iser, *The Implied Reader* (Baltimore: Johns Hopkins Press, 1974), pp. 274–94, and Horst Ruthrof, *The Reader's Construction of Narrative* (London: Routledge and Kegan Paul, 1981), pp. ix–xiii, among many other discussions of the phenomenology of readerly response. My adoption of the concept, as will become clear, in no way suggests that the process of concretization can ever fully or definitively 'fill out' the indeterminacies of the text, in so far as those indeterminacies are themselves created by the act of concretization and arise as a function of the prior experience and assumptions that condition it. See Stanley Fish, 'Why No One's Afraid of Wolfgang Iser', *Diacritics*, xi (March 1981) pp. 2–13.

renaissance accounts, to re-present it. All the major Elizabethan sonneteers—Sidney, Spenser, and Shakespeare—recognize within their sequences the manifold difficulties involved in representing an object conventionally or actually 'fair' in so unlikely, estranged, and unverisimilar a medium as the 'black ink' of writing, while continuing to pursue that mimetic ambition. Yet it is only Shakespeare, as we shall see, who apprehends the full difficulty of that project while attempting a fully modern and writerly solution to it, which is to say, a solution that recognizes it is not a solution.

Before considering Shakespeare's distinctive 'solution' to the paradox of writerly representation, let us look first at Sidney's more conventional approach to it. For Sidney's defence of the power of poetic language to represent a sensory world from which it seems to have forever taken leave is cast in precisely the terms we have already seen Shakespeare put into question: its supposed difference from the 'black ink' of writing in general, and its supposed affinity with the visual arts. Contrasting the poet's representation of 'concrete universals' with the particulars of historiography and the precepts of philosophy, Sidney contends that

he [the poet] giveth a perfect picture of it [the general precept] in some one by whom he presupposeth it was done. . . . *A perfect picture I say*, for he yieldeth to the powers of the mind an image of that whereof the philosophers bestoweth but a wordish description: *which doth neither strike, pierce, nor possess the sight of the soul so much as that other doth.*

For as in outward things, to a man that had never seen an elephant or a rhinoceros, who should tell him most exquisitely all their shapes, colour, bigness, and particular marks, of a gorgeous palace the architecture, with declaring the full beauties might well make the hearer able to repeat, as it were by rote, all he had heard, *yet should never satisfy his inward conceits with being witness to itself of a true lively knowledge:* but the same man as soon as he might see those beasts well painted, or the house well in model, should straightways grow, without need of any description, to a judicial comprehending of them: so no doubt the philosopher with his learned definition—be it of virtue, vices, matters of public policy or private government—replenisheth the memory with many infallible grounds of wisdom, which, notwithstanding, *lie dark before the imaginative and judging power, if they be not illuminated or figured forth by the speaking picture of Poesy.*[17]

The language in which Sidney maintains the classic claim of poetry, as distinct from other modes of writing, to the status of pictorial representation, is strikingly similar to that of the most sanguine of the *Sonnets*. For both Sidney and the Shakespeare of *55*, poetry does not so much 'speak' as 'perform' its object. It is a 'perfect picture' that bears 'witness to itself of a true lively knowledge'; it 'illuminates' or 'figures forth' what lies 'dark before the imaginative and judging power'. How close we are to the proclaimed 'power' of *55* to make its object 'shine bright' and 'pace forth' in time to come! And once again, this enunciation of visual and sensory immediacy is made in spite of the abstraction and distanciation, also acknowledged, inherent in the 'wordiness' of its written medium. The paradox with which we began has not so much been resolved by Sidney as restated.

But not 'merely' restated, in so far as Sidney's own language is itself 'performative', or at least 'rhetorical'. The agency Sidney invokes as enabling poetry to bring off the miracle of achieving a representative power equalling that of the visual arts, despite the abstract wordiness of the written medium it shares with philosophy, is also the one he employs, namely, rhetoric or figurative language, the forms of language that George Puttenham terms 'Sensable, because they alter and affect the minde by alteration of sense', i.e. language that violates or disturbs the conventional and normal, and therefore by received cultural association, the *naturalized* relation of sign and signification. The very phrase with which Sidney concludes his account of poetry's superior power of imaging its object illustrates precisely the operation it

---

[17] 'An Apology for Poetry', in *Criticism: The Major Texts*, ed. W. J. Bate (New York: Harcourt Brace Jovanovich, 2nd edn., 1970), p. 89. Italics mine. See also Henry Peacham, *The Garden of Eloquence* (London, 1593), sig. A iii: 'By figures he [the speaker] may make his speech as cleare as the noone day: or contrarywise, as it were with cloudes and foggy mists, he may cover it with darknesse: he may stirre up stormes, and troublesome tempests, or contrariwyse, cause and procure, a quiet and sylent calmnesse, he may set forth any matter with a goodly perspecuitie, and paynt out any person, deede or thing so cunninglie with these couloures, that it shall seeme rather a lyvely Image paynted in tables, then a reporte expressed with the tongue.'

describes. The phrase 'speaking picture' is first and foremost a metaphor, albeit a metaphor that has lost, through its repetition as a commonplace, the root meaning that George Puttenham, Englishing the nomenclature of classical rhetoric, translates as the figure of 'transport', by which the qualities of one thing are transferred to something similar yet distinctly different, in this case the human voice to a mute visual image. Or it might be classified within Puttenham's scheme under the more radical figure which follows and extends metaphor, that of catachresis or 'abuse', in so far as it applies to painting a term 'neither natural nor proper' to 'the thing we would seeme to expresse', a term blatantly inappropriate. Or it could even fall under paradox, or 'the wondrer', since it reports 'of a thing that is marvelous', the suggestion of a wondrous or marvelous power of poetry as all but unmediated vision being the point of Sidney's account.[18] Other figures could also be nominated.

My point in drawing attention to the figurative nature of the renaissance commonplace Sidney employs is precisely that it draws attention to itself; by virtue of its semantic context and emphatic position in it, it begins to exemplify or perform the marvelous function Sidney describes, as the phrase activates in the mind the image of a picture speaking. In so doing, it re-produces the very effect of wonder that Sidney has just claimed for poetic language generally as an invisibly visual mimesis present to the mind's eye. Through Sidney's resurrection of a buried metaphor to active life, his revelation of an unforeseen fit between sign and signification, words and the sensory world they describe, a minor miracle has been performed. This is precisely what occurs in the final scene of *The Winter's Tale*, where Leontes, fancying that the statue of Hermione actually breathes, exclaims in wonder: 'What fine chisel / Could ever yet cut breath?' (V.iii,78–9.) Shakespeare,

---

[18] George Puttenham, *The Arte of English Poesie, 1589* (Menston, Yorkshire: The Scholar Press, Facsimile edn., 1968), pp. 133, 148, 150, 189. Puttenham defines 'figurative speech' generally as 'a noveltie of language evidently (and yet not absurdly) estranged from the ordinarie habite and manner of our dayly talke and writing ... giving them ornament or efficacie by many manner of alterations in shape, sounde, and also in sence, sometime by disorder, or mutation' (pp. 132–3). Similarly Peacham, for whom rhetorical figuration is a means of 'tournying from the common manner and custom of wryting and speaking' (sig. B.i.).

a more excellent carver than either his own Julio or Paulina, has performed his own mimetic miracle in the line itself. Combining catachresis and onomatopoeia (Puttenham's 'new-namer'), he has fixed our sense of wonder on a succession of monosyllables composed of short vowels chopped off by dental stops, and by so doing, has imitated in language the sharp clicks of a chisel tapping through its medium. What fine writing or speech could ever yet cut a chisel in the act of cutting? None other than Shakespeare's, and since it is nothing other than breath itself, i.e. the articulated air of dramatic speech, that is doing the cutting of breath, the art, as these Elizabethans would say, itself is nature, the word has performed its meaning.

IV. THE PUN MADE FLESH

The performative potential of rhetoric, it would seem, can begin to overcome, by altering the customary internal relations of language, its comparative disabilities in the foreign affairs of imitating a sensory world quite alien to it. The *Sonnets* of course offer countless examples of this kind of performative language, of what will later be termed 'enact-ment', in which the normal linguistic relations between signifier and signified, sound and sense, form and meaning, are altered in what Puttenham terms 'figures of disorder' as a way of opening an appeal from language to nature. Roman Jakobson has called attention to onomatopoeia as one of the chief poetic devices through which sound approximates sense, and it represents a classic example of the kind of language in which the differences between sign and referent that charac-terize language as a system are apparently foreclosed from the side of the phonetic signifier, much as they are by metaphor and its variants from the side of the semantic signified. (So much so, that Saussure felt the need to deal specifically with onomatopoeia as an apparent exception to the rule of arbitrary conventionality.) The text-book case of enactment for traditional poetics is Pope's example from Homer in his 'Essay on Criticism': 'When Ajax strives some rock's vast weight to throw, / The line too labours and the words move slow.' But the *Sonnets* offer more striking examples, such as the opening of *129*: 'Th'expense of spirit in a waste of shame / Is lust in action.' There, the sustained sibilance of air escaping past its labial and dental stops mimes the expenditure of vital 'spirits'—the word held multiple Elizabethan meanings, from the physiological to the moral and theological—in the heavy breathing and piecemeal dying entailed in the sexual activity that this sonnet anatomizes.

Or consider another, related 'auricular' figure, the one Puttenham terms 'barbarism', since it depends on the phonetic unfamiliarity and consequent awkwardness of non-native or incompletely naturalized, lexical material, such as we meet in the opening of *116*: 'Let me not to the marriage of true minds / *Admit impediments.*' Here, the tongue-twistingly Latinate phrase 'admit impediments' becomes itself an impediment, through its polysyllabic materiality, to the fluent nativism of the opening line, an obstruction placed in the way of Shakespeare's nimble feet (the word's etymology, in fact) and our tripping tongues, a material reminder that the course of true love can only run smooth through an act of will that transcends all obstacles. Or the recovery of that linguistic materiality which enables language to regain its mimetic affinity and aptitude may take advantage of its graphic, and thereby spatial, dimension. This also occurs in *116*: 'Love's not time's fool, though rosy lips and cheeks / Within his bending sickle's compass *come*'. The displacement of the verb 'come' from its normal position in the middle to the end of the clause—the figure is 'histeron proteron', termed by Puttenham 'the preposterous'—defers comprehension of the line, our gathering or reaping of its sense, in a way mimetic of the action of the reaper's bending sickle, as it gathers to itself roses and youthful flesh at the end of their natural lives. The human lifespan has been mimetically comprehended in Shakespeare's grammatical, i.e. graphic and spatial, dislocation of the conventions of his verbal medium.

Let us return, then, to *Sonnet 55*, in order to try out the skeleton key that the recuperative programme of Elizabethan rhetoric provides, and see whether it will unlock the secret of Shakespeare's claim to poetic and mimetic perdurability. If Roman Jakobson had analysed *55*, one of the things he would have noticed in its first strophe is the high incidence of alliteration on 'm', 'p', and 's', which is repeated in the third strophe. That Shakespeare 'affects the letter' in these stophes, and that they are thereby linked at the phonetic level is not in question. Our question is what performative relation this purely formal linkage at the level of the signifier might bear to the sonnet's signification, its 'contents' as Shakespeare equivo-cally puts it. Here Jakobson can be of little help, taking as he notoriously does, meaning or content for granted or reducing it to the received ideas of other commentators. In the terms of his analysis, the most the empirical fact of alliteration can be is an earnest of poetic power, alerting us that some extra-communicative intention may be at work; in itself, it cannot be a source or explanation of that power. Occurring as it does within a semantic field that the alliteration does not itself generate, the function of alliteration cannot be causal or integral to signified meaning. Rather, it operates here as what Puttenham would call a figure of 'ornament' of the kind Shakespeare designates and illustrates as such in the previous sonnet ('O how much more doth beauty beauteous seem / By that sweet ornament . . .'). As ornament or decoration, alliteration bears the same superficially attractive but func-tionally inessential relation to the poem as 'gilt' does to the 'monuments / Of princes' mentioned at the outset. Gilding is to monumental sculpture as alliteration is to the sonnet.

This analogy, if we allow it to guide our reading, would make the sonnet itself a monument or tomb containing the earthly remains of a prince or noble. Indeed, there is much to suggest, and nothing to deny, just such a reading. We have already seen that several of the *Sonnets* similar to 55 in form, theme, and diction explicitly compare themselves, as monu-ments to the beloved, triumphantly or unhappily to 'tombs of brass' (*10*.7–14) and 'a tomb / Which hides your life' (*17*. 3–4). The editor of the latest, most intelligent edition of the *Sonnets*, glossing the phrase 'in these contents', plausibly suggests that the 'word *in* and the idea of the poem as a receptacle make the phrase ominously reminiscent of *monu-ments*: the phrase carries a suggestion of "in this coffin", a suggestion given scope by the vagueness and imprecision of *these contents* as a means of expressing "this poem" or "these lines".'[19] The suggestion gathers even greater force with the third and fourth strophes, in which the beloved object is said to 'pace forth' and 'still find room' by analogy with a Christian or Christological resurrection that transcends the confinement of the tomb.

This implicit depiction of the sonnet as a coffin or tomb, with the beloved as the body it contains, is an example of the figure Puttenham loosely terms 'icon, or resemblance by portrait, and ymagerie'. Even without an Elizabethan tradition of emblem poetry refined to a fine art by Donne and Herbert to encourage such resemblances, the four-square block of print the sonnet presents on the page would make it easily assimilable to the form of a box. Given this rough resemblance, Shakespeare's opening paraphrase of Horace works to carve it more finely into a verbal icon of the poem as mausoleum or sarcophagus. The economy of inflection lends Horace's Latin—*exegi monumentum aere perennius*—something of the epi-grammatic concision of an epitaph such as might actually appear inscribed on the base of a monument or the lid of a sarcophagus, a pointedness that is of course much harder to attain in the uninflected volubility of English. Yet the syntactical structure of the opening line of *55*, and again of line 7, as well as the opening of *107* on the same theme—the 'Not . . . nor' or 'nor . . . nor' construction—may well represent Shakespeare's attempt to reproduce in English something like the epigrammatic symmetry of Latin by adopting and translating its classic '*nec . . . nec*' construction. This impression of latter-day Latinity may be further reinforced within the 'nor . . . nor' clause of line 7 by the inclusion of a Latinate metonymy ('Nor Mars his sword'), whereby the name of the Roman war-god and its archaic genitive is paralleled with its modern English equivalent ('nor war's quick fire').

These latinate usages suggest, particularly in the context of the Spenser/du Bellay sonnet quoted above, a kind of double resurrection at work. On the one hand, Shakespeare's pseudo-latinity lends his sonnet something of the quality of an epitaph proclaiming the resurrection of the body contained within the mausoleum or sarcophagus of the sonnet itself. On the other,

---

[19] Booth, p. 228.

it performs a resurrection of the dead language of Latin poetry into the life of a modern European vernacular. The effect is analogous to that produced at the climax of *Julius Caesar*, a play dense with internal reference to monumental sculpture and carving, when Caesar breaks into Latin at the moment of death—'*et tu Brute*'—only to return to English, but an English cadence closely modelled in its dying fall upon that patch of Latin—'Then fall Caesar.' The lapse into Latin and relapse into English dramatize the time-transcending claim made earlier by the play's co-carver of Caesar's fate, Cassius, that their bloody scene will be re-enacted 'in states unknown, and accents yet unborn' (III. i, 113), a claim analogous to that of *55*, and one that similarly depends on the performative potential of the poetic medium to reproduce a 'living record'. 'When you entombed in men's eyes shall lie', Shakespeare writes in *81*, 'Your monument shall be my gentle verse / Which eyes not yet created shall o'er-read, / And tongues to be your being shall rehearse.' In so far as the monumental statuary, mausoleums, and sarcophagi of the classical world have been mimed in the poetic form of the sonnet itself, as well as in some of its phonetic and syntactical units, the classical world has here been literally and fully textualized, rendered into a 'speaking picture'.

And if such a project of performative reappropriation is indeed at work in the poem, it is entirely fanciful to read the transition from its third quatrain—in which the beloved is envisioned as about to 'pace forth' and 'find room'—to its closing couplet—in which a last judgement of Christian resurrection is proleptically invoked—as enacting the change of state promised at the outset, the release of the beloved from imprisonment in the tomb of history into the liberty of textuality? Is it entirely fanciful to read the final couplet as a turning of the hinges of the poem, an unsealing of the tomb or swinging open of the coffin-lid through which the youth is released from the box of the sonnet's four-square quatrains in order to live and roam abroad, even increase and multiply, in the free, lively, and endless reflection of the 'lovers' eyes' that will read the poem? Indeed, is this entire exercise in reading the sonnet, as a sustained attempt at hyperconcretization, at substantiating the claim of poetic language to equal mimetic power with the visual arts by recalling attention to poetry's own carving of its phonetic and graphic materiality, no more than an exercise in metaphor-making, a fallacy of imitative form, however seriously encouraged and underwritten it may be by Elizabethan poetics?

Before reaching that conclusion and dismissing the entire project of enactment, what Shakespeare himself terms 'speaking in effect', as a kind of writerly pathetic fallacy, it is worth pointing out that the poetics of enactment are not a peculiarly Elizabethan superstition or caprice but seem to persist, in modified but still recognizable, versions into this century. The Russian formalists, for example, like the Elizabethans, see language as aboriginally poetic, and similarly identify its performative potential in the storehouse of metaphor that lies buried within it. Words, in the highly metaphoric words of Viktor Shklovksy, 'complete the journey from poetry to prose', lose their visual and sensory value, their metaphoric density, through time and use, and wear away into thin and transparent counters of thought.[20] The poetic project then becomes 'the resurrection of the word', its 'rebarbarization' through such tactics as 'defamiliarization', 'retardation', 'staircase-effect', and a general strategy of 'baring the device'. This heightening of technical consciousness is in the service of enabling us to see and hear again through poetic language what ordinary language has obscured and abstracted into mere recognition, much as people who live by the sea do not hear the waves, or a man does not notice the walls of his own room. How far is this, after all, from the claim of sensory presence advanced by Sidney and the Elizabethans?

Similarly with the poetics of F. R. Leavis, who independently advanced the criterion of enactment as the touchstone that distinguishes poetic authenticity. Leavis's enactive poetics takes the form of a series of practical value-judgements, whereby a poetry of sensuous concreteness, such as we find in Eliot, some of Keats, Blake, Pope, and Milton, but pre-eminently in Shakespeare, Donne, and the Metaphysicals carries the day against the abstraction of Shelley and most of Milton. It is through enactment, the term Leavis regularly

---

[20] 'The Resurrection of the Word', in *Russian Formalism*, eds. S. Bann and J. E. Bowlt (Edinburgh: Scottish Academic Press, 1973), pp. 41–7.

employs, that the best poetry recovers for language an emotional and moral integrity with the 'real' and 'human' world that has been rendered increasingly precarious since the 'dissociation of sensibility', of thought from feeling, that supposedly occurred during the seventeenth century. The synthetic, sensuous wit of metaphysical, as opposed to romantic, poetry becomes the model of poeticity itself in its attempt to recover a full mimetic presence and univocality, all but lost yet still recuperable. Like that of the Russian formalists, though without a thoroughgoing theoretical pro-gramme to support it, Leavis's poetics of enactment is a polemic in the service of a certain contemporary poetic practice that legitimates itself in a myth of lost linguistic origins, an essentially religious or sacramental or superstitious view of language as a bygone original presence now fallen into abstraction, alienation, and division.[21] Once again we do not seem to be very far from Sidney, Puttenham, and the Elizabethans.

V. THE FLESH MADE PUN

Or perhaps more accurately, we seem to be so near and yet so far from them. So near, in the residual belief, superstitious or religious as it may be, that the poetic word once possessed and can still recuperate its lost integrity and univocality with the world, through some version of the enactive or performative process. And yet we are so far from the Elizabethans in that our post-Saussurian understanding of language, with its foregrounding, not to say fetishizing, of inbuilt structural difference and deferral—both that between signs themselves and that between the sign and any fully determinate meaning, let alone external reference—is so radically and unrecuperably *counter-enactive*. In the work of Shklovsky, for example, it is never fully clear whether the revivifying power ascribed to poetic language is directed toward reviving our perception of the world or merely of the word. The process of reinvesting

[21] See Peter Barry, 'The Enactment Fallacy', *Essays in Criticism*, xxx. 2 (April 1980), pp. 95–104. Barry's critique of enactment turns on the same point as Saussure's of onomatopoeia: 'If we did not understand English, yet knew its sound and stress patterns, we would not instinctively say the lines in such a way as to echo the sense' (p. 101).

language with its lost density by defamiliarizing it, and thereby concentrating our attention on it as language, cannot help but render it opaque, not more but less transparent upon or reflective of, a signified world. Our access to any prior, non-linguistic reality that might exist is jeopardized, not enhanced, by that programme. The referential value of language must, as modernist poetics is well aware, decrease in proportion to its self-referentiality. It is the constitutive and generative, rather than the reflective or mimetic, power of poetic language, as Trotsky understood only too well, that Shklovsky and the formalists are asserting and giving new priority. Form, after all, generates content, and not *vice versa*.

For even if the supposedly aboriginal metaphoricity of language could be fully resurrected, its mimetic power would not be all that is recovered. Would it not carry with it a renewed sense of insuperable difference and duplicity, since metaphor is not natural magic but word-magic, not the recovery of hidden connection between words and world but continuing linguistic difference masquerading as identity? The persistent reinvestment of the poet with Orphic or Adamic powers of restoring to language a primal univocality is itself a rhetorical gesture. Similarly with Jakobson's model of language as communication, in which poetic language concentrates attention upon the message and its internal relations, thickens the medium, as it were, to the point where sender and receiver virtually drop out of the picture, as they in fact do in Jakobson's analyses of poetic texts. The paradox that haunts all performative accounts of poetic language, Elizabethan and modern, is that the means of recovering lost integrity and univocality is a further linguistic disturbance, a shattering of accustomed internal linguistic relations that can be recodified at a higher level but never reunified under any rhetorical programme, however elaborate. Rhetorical figuration, far from repairing the putative rift between sign and meaning, becomes only an encyclopedic record of the possibilities of this dislocation, which when applied in practice, only re-enacts that dislocation. This paradoxical condition cannot be dialectically resolved from within the logic of an enactive poetics. Defect cannot be made up by more defect, by what Puttenham classifies as 'figures of disorder' and 'figures of default'.

Or can it? Perhaps there is still some means available to language to repair its own defect as a mimetic medium, to enable it to achieve the legendary supermimesis of Apelles' Venus, invoked as analogy for Shakespeare's Cleopatra, which supposedly makes 'defect perfection'. It is just such an interrogation of the adequacy of any rhetorical programme to reproduce an object at all that lies at the core of Shakespeare's sequence, the poems from *76* to *106*, and that issues in the partial solutions embodied in the figures of the rival poet and ultimately of the dark lady herself. At this stage, the sequence turns self-consciously metamimetic, questioning from within itself, even to the point of 'tongue-tied' silence, its own capacity, and that of the rhetorical repertory generally—'What strained touches rhetoric can lend' (*82*.10)—to represent the youth at all.

The problem is now conceived as twofold: not only is the youth's beauty so transcendent as to strain to the limit the resources of Shakespeare's own rhetoric, but the inadequacy of that rhetoric has been revealed by its having been imitated and exceeded at the hands of rival poets, 'As every alien pen hath got my use / And under thee their poetry disperse.' (*78*.3–4.) Let us leave aside for the moment the punning allusion to literary patronage and sexual infidelity and confine ourselves to the rhetorical implications. A rhetoric that derives its performative capability from its disturbance of conventional usage has itself become conventional usage, thereby requiring a further disturbance to maintain its mimetic advantage. This heightened awareness of rhetorical limitation is doubly difficult to transcend, since what has been revealed to Shakespeare is at once 'How far a modern quill', despite the eager ingenuity displayed around him, 'doth come too short' (*83*.7) and the essential poverty of his own rhetorical invention, its inability to overgo itself and thereby overgo his imitators and rivals: 'Why is my verse so barren of new pride, / So far from variation and quick change?' (*76*.1–2). In these sonnets, Shakespeare comes up against the paradox of a self-superseding modernity: 'Finding thy worth a limit past my praise, / and therefore [am] enforced to seek anew / Some fresher stamp of the time-bett'ring days' (*82*.5–8). If rhetoric, as Hopkins remarked, 'is the teachable part of poetry', then some new and unprecedented rhetorical resource beyond the present state of the art, must continually be found.

Shakespeare meets this double dilemma with a two-pronged strategy. On the one hand, he bequeaths to other poets 'What strained touches rhetoric can lend' (*82*.10), ascribing to them—pre-eminently to that red herring of biographical research, the 'rival poet' (the dark lady being its Loch Ness monster)—an embodied fullness of rhetorical powers he claims no longer to have himself, or have any use for ('Was it the proud full sail of his great verse', *86*.1), and which in any case miss the mark of mimetic adequation, however effective they may be in seducing the youth. And on the other, he pursues a new self-conscious minimalism in his own writing, a wavering between plain speech and tongue-tied silence, which claims to hit the mark precisely because of its acknowledged inadequacy:

> This silence for my sin you did impute,
> Which shall be most my glory, being dumb;
> For I impair not beauty, being mute,
> When others would give life, and bring a tomb.
> There lives more life in one of your fair eyes
> Than both your poets can in praise devise. (*83*.9–14)

> Truth needs no colour with his colour fixed
> Beauty no pencil, beauty's truth to lay:
> But best is best, if never intermixed?
> Because he needs no praise, wilt thou be dumb?
> Excuse not silence so, for't lies in thee ‹the muse›,
> To make him much outlive a gilded tomb,
> And to be praised in ages yet to be. (*101*.6–12).

But this neo-platonic or Keatsian approach—heard melodies are sweet, but those unheard are sweeter—has its own inbuilt poetic handicap, and as Shakespeare fully recognizes, a certain defeatist potential.

In setting up the rhetorical eloquence of the rival poet as a foil to his own more eloquent understatement, Shakespeare does not so much transcend the problem of rhetorical defect as defer it: 'Where art thou, muse, that thou forget'st so long / To speak of that which gives thee all thy might?' (*100*.1–2). The ingenious solution of abjuring rhetoric and 'speaking in effect'—'Then others for the breath of words respect, / Me for dumb thoughts, speaking in effect' (*85*.13–14)—turns out to be no solution at all, in so far as it is still speaking and still rhetoric, albeit a self-deprecating or self-denying rhetoric of understatment. What Shakespeare has done in this phase of the sequence is to exchange one rhetorical programme for another, a rhetoric of presence, fullness, immediacy, and enactment—now ascribed to and personified by the hypothetical rival poet—for a rhetoric of difference, deferral, indirection, and counter-enactment, involving a new set of dominant figures—those Puttenham terms 'figures of default' —and generating a new set of thematic oppositions and contrasts—between himself and his rivals, poetry and its object, past and present poetry. The rationale for this new programme is that of *reculer pour mieux sauter*, that rhetorically less is mimetically more, as if a fault in the medium of representation can still be made fortunate. The earlier project of poetic fullness, of rivalling or replacing through a poetics of enactment the fullness of 'great creating nature'—set out in the initial 'procreation sequence'—a 'second nature' that rivals and replaces the first, fallen one, has not so much been abandoned as reconceived.

It remains to be seen, however, whether this latest programme of 'speaking in effect' can recuperate the enactive project, can make effective, let alone perfect, the 'defect' in which it seems to be based, or whether its promise of enactive recuperation is haunted by linguistic bad faith from the beginning. For this latest turn in Shakespeare's search for a rhetoric of mimetic adequation, as the phase that names it suggests, seems to be rooted in nothing more than a pun. 'Speaking in effect' can mean either 'speaking effectively' or 'speaking by default', or 'defectively', i.e. 'not speaking at all'. We have already seen how, in Shakespeare's earlier and more straightforwardly enactive practice, so much depends on those figures which work to overcome conventional difference, to reinforce our sense of the shaky resemblance and relation between sign and signification, such figures as metaphor, catachresis, icon, and pre-eminently onomatopoeia, Puttenham's 'new namer'. Yet all of these devices, as they work locally to bring likeness out of conventional difference, also draw attention to themselves as devices, and thereby re-represent difference and deny resemblance. They act, as Puttenham might say, as 'double agents' who betray the cause of enactment and play into the hands of its mighty opposite, a poetics of counter-enactment, nowadays known as decon-struction. The poetics of counter-enactment also has its master-trope, its chief figure, the very opposite of onomatop-oeia, the 'new-namer', and that figure is paranomasia, in Puttenham's scheme, 'the nick-namer', or as it is better known to us, word-play, pun, or quibble.

If the figures of enactment, of 'speaking in effect' in Shakespeare's phrase, work cumulatively to integrate the jigsaw puzzle of language into a concrete replica of the sensory world, the pun is precisely that piece of language which will fit into several positions in the puzzle and thereby confound attempts to reconstruct the puzzle into a map or picture with any unique or privileged reliability or fidelity of reference. Whereas metaphor and onomatopoeia attempt to bridge the precipitate fissures between signs and their meanings, parano-masia effectively destabilizes further whatever conventional stability the relation between sign and meaning may be thought to possess. The pun is the concealed fault-line that reticulates the landscape of language, hardly visible until it slips, but once it does, the serene linguistic landscape is suddenly and totally transformed. Doubly anarchic, the pun can and often does collapse not only the horizontal differen-tiations in the outstretched panorama of signs that hold the system of language in place, but the hierarchical structures of 'high' and 'low' discourses or styles erected upon it as well.

Whereas metaphor tends to operate across discourses, while enforcing class distinctions within them, the pun is well suited to turning these vertical structures topsy-turvy, and hence, as Puttenham is well aware, especially useful for comic and carnivalizing effect. It brings low the conventionally high and upraises the conventionally low. It is no wonder, then, that the pun is proverbially regarded as the lowest form of wit, subversive as it is of second-order conventions of decorum, of the socially determined relations that are at once reflected and reinforced in daily linguistic usage, so that the laughter it

provokes is often reluctant, uncertain, anxious, or disapprov-
ing. We are not always pleased to be reminded, as the pun
reminds us, that the socio-linguistic house in which we dwell
is not so well constructed as we might wish to think, that not
only the individual bricks of which it is made, so firmly
separated by mortar joints, but the floors on which we stand,
may suddenly, handy-dandy, change places around us. At the
very least, it reminds us of the arbitrariness of language as a
system of differences, and at most of the conventionality of the
social relations that system reflects and reinforces.

Now if Shakespeare is the poet whose power of metaphor
and enactive language is generally acknowledged to be
unsurpassed—a traditional view which my technical analysis
of these effects so far only confirms—he is also the poet most
notoriously given to the counter-enactive subversions of the
pun. 'A quibble was the golden apple', wrote Samuel Johnson,
'for which he would always turn aside from his career, or
stoop from his elevation', 'the fatal Cleopatra for which he lost
the world, and was content to lose it.'[22] The anxiety that
speaks through Johnson's strictures doubtless arises from the
threat posed by Shakespeare's wordplay to the 'natural order'
that any poetic classicism and social conservatism, however
flexible, must presuppose. 'Take but degree [i.e. hierarchical
difference] away, untune that string,' as Shakespeare's Ulysses
puts it, 'And hark what discord follows.' If princes and
gentlewomen can quibble indecorously with and like fools and
clowns, even at moments of the highest passion and deepest
pathos, then two 'natural' orders are simultaneously threatened by this blurring of difference, one *by* language and the
other *of* language.

The neo-classical social and moral ideals of sincerity and
integrity, the virtues of the 'honest soul', are simultaneously
undermined as criteria of poetic value, since they depend on a
reliable correspondence between sign and meaning. The
destabilization and fragmentation of meaning effected by the
pun, in which the material similarity or identity of two or
more signs dissolves into two or more distinct and often
antithetical meanings, can only reflect a disintegrated con-

---

[22] 'Preface to Shakespeare', in Bate, p. 213.

sciousness destructive of traditional moral and mimetic claims. Any attempt to read *Sonnet 129*, for example, as a moral tract against concupiscence, is defeated precisely by its puns, as such words as 'spirit' (i.e. 'sprit') and 'heaven' (i.e. 'haven') oscillate dizzily in Swiftian fashion between their abstract and concrete, sublime and ridiculous, religious and genital meanings. Similarly, any attempt to read it as philosophical poetry in the lofty, generalizing vein of 'An Essay on Man' is undone by the puns of the final couplet on 'well' ('will', and 'Will' Shakespeare) on which the poem turns from impersonal pronouncement into a curiously resigned or bemused, even somewhat sordid, personal confession.

What with its demonumentalization of fixed or 'natural' meaning, Shakespeare's wordplay would seem to be the ultimate 'figure of disorder'. From the viewpoint of an enactive poetics, it is counter-productive in the extreme, a denial and demystification of the lofty claims to poetic monumentality advanced in *55*. If anything, the pun seems to play into the hands of the enemies, Time and Death, not only in the structural sense that it undermines the monumental integrity of the word by fracturing its meaning and thereby 'roots out the work of masonry', but also in the historical sense that the connotations it activates, particularly its lower ones, are often of a local or colloquial nature—as with the Elizabethan 'sprit' ('erect phallus')—and therefore likely to be lost on posterity, while its root, etymological meanings are often already lost on all but the most historically and philologically erudite, as modern readers of Shakespeare's comedies will attest. The cult of etymology and etymological puns in the renaissance as a favoured means of concentrating present meaning by recovering supposed origins can counter-productively turn the poet, as in the case of its foremost practitioner Spenser, into a poet's poet at best and a scholar's poet at worst—a destiny quite the opposite of the timeless and universal immediacy projected by an enactive poetics.[23] Yet Shakespeare notoriously and unremittingly puts his enactive poetics at risk by cultivating the pun, and often the etymological pun.

[23] See Martha Craig, 'The Secret Wit of Spenser's Language', in *Elizabethan Poetry*, ed. Paul Alpers (London: Oxford University Press, 1967), pp. 447–72.

There is no better example of a sonnet rooting out its own masonry, risking its monumentalizing immediacy, and counteracting its own enactment, than *107*, already cited as a companion piece to *55* in its self-monumentalizing theme and its ringing 'Not . . . nor' opening. Leaving aside the radical wordplay of 'the mortal moon hath her eclipse endured', with its all but infinite variety of reference assiduously and unsatisfactorily explored by scholars—does the phrase not epitomize the restlessness of reference itself, the ebb and flow of phonetic and semantic flux?—let us proceed to the third quatrain, in which the triumph of writing over the historical mutability of time and death is asserted:

> Now with the drops of this most balmy time
> My love looks fresh, and death to me subscribes,
> Since spite of him I'll live in this poor rhyme,
> While he insults o'er dull and speechless tribes.
> And thou in this shalt find thy monument
> When tyrants' crests and tombs of brass are spent.

Though more provisionally than in *55*—for here the poem refers to itself as a 'poor' rather than 'powerful' rhyme, whose monumental status is no longer apodictic but remains to be found—the triumph over Time and Death is none the less proclaimed, and more remarkably still, it is proclaimed as having been wrought with their own weapons.

For the etymological puns on 'subscribes' and 'insults' revivify the old Latin senses of those words, which work here to reinforce their more modern and abstract meanings. Death 'subscribes' to Shakespeare not only in the abstract sense of 'submits' or 'enters into agreement' but in the concrete, enactive sense of writing one's name at the bottom of a document, in this context a lease on life or peace treaty, and Death is forced to do so with the 'drops' of Shakespeare's own ink! After such terms of surrender, the only victory remaining for Death is the hollow one over those hypothetical 'speechless tribes', whom he will continue to 'insult'—in the older sense of 'leap against' or 'assault' and in the later sense of 'verbally abuse'—without any possible comeback. By reactivating through wordplay these decayed senses and pressing them into the service of his writing, Shakespeare imagines himself defeating Time and Death at their own war-game, temporarily arresting the historical fluctuations of language that undermine masonry, and fixing these words permanently into place within his poetic monument.

It seems that even the most potent weapon of counter-enactment and destabilization, the pun, can be pressed into the service of poetic enactment and presence, and victory snatched from the jaws of devouring Time himself! Indeed, the very next sonnet ('What's in the brain that ink may character') self-consciously celebrates, through a series of writerly puns, just such an improbable victory:

> So that eternal love in love's fresh case
> Weighs not the dust and injury of age,
> Nor gives to necessary wrinkles place,
> But makes antiquity for aye his page,
> Finding the first conceit of love there bred
> Where time and outward form would show it dead. (*108*.9–14)

If puns—and these lines contain several: on 'case', 'injury', 'age', 'antiquity', 'aye', 'page', 'conceit', 'would'—and particularly etymological puns, are the wrinkles carved by Time on the once clear face of meaning, what Shakespeare has done is to include the work of time within his own work in such a way as to arrest flux and pre-empt obsolescence. 'Wrinkles' may be an organic necessity in the progress of nature toward death, but by giving them a place in his work he denies them priority or pride of place.

This was his practice, as far back as *18*—'Nor shall death brag thou wand'rest in his shade / When in eternal lines to time thou growest'—though here in *108* it has become fully and self-consciously foregrounded. Lines of living become lines of verse; classical antiquity, the freshly written page; the tomb or coffin of the love-sonnet, the tome or show-case from which love rises afresh to the reading eye for aye. The most astute modern reader of the *Sonnets* is surely—and quite uncharacteristically—under-reading this sonnet, when he demurs over earlier editors's paraphrasing of its closing strophes as a 'continuation of the discussion of literary invention in lines 1–8', suggesting that it 'exaggerates the purposefulness and continuity of *this secondary train of thought.*'[24] Only by maintaining the priority of the sonnet's, indeed the sequence's, empirical or mimetic over its writerly and metamimetic enterprise could Booth relegate this train of thought to a 'secondary' status.

Such a demurrer, coming as it does from a reader on whom few of Shakespeare's puns are lost, forces us to look again at that wordplay—which is precisely what wordplay invites us to do anyway—and reconsider whether it serves the triumph of enactment after all. In calling this writerly train of thought in the *Sonnets* 'secondary', Booth implies that some other train of thought, presumably their empirical design as persuasion to love poetry or their mimetic design on representing the beauty of the youth, his worth, truth, or love, or perhaps those of the poet, is primary. But whatever primacy an empirical project may initially have held in the *Sonnets*, or may be maintained in such Elizabethan sonnet sequences as Spenser's or Sidney's, it has long since given way in Shakespeare's, first to the mimetic project so confidently proclaimed in *55*, and then to the exploration of the equivocal potential of poetry itself, which we have been tracing.

Shakespeare's primary concern seems to have shifted from the object to the process and medium of its representation, even to the point where the very capacity of his language to represent anything other than falsehood, betrayal, or 'lying' will become an open and pressing question, particularly so, once the mimetic duplicity of the pun has been accepted. Yet Booth, attentive as he is to Shakespeare's ubiquitous wordplay and assiduous as he is in tracking down its connotations, is reluctant to grant it priority either as destroyer or preserver of mimetic effect. The puns are recognized as 'there', but their importance is downplayed, precisely because their multiple meanings must be tracked down, and it is hard to know, once this pre-eminently *readerly* process is activated, where to stop.

For wordplay thrives in the dilated duration of response opened up by reading; hence it is a *writerly* device that demands our full *readerly* attention. Spoken puns we either

[24] Booth, pp. 350–1. Italics mine.

catch or we don't; it is written puns we have the leisure and opportunity to go back to and retrace the trains of meaning they set in motion. Hence Joyce's remark that his ideal reader would devote a lifetime to his work. In this sense only, that the pun exists in the mode of afterthought, can its multiple meanings be thought of as secondary. Booth often remarks, in fact, on the way the flexibility of Elizabethan grammatical pointing works to serve multiple references and meanings. But so too does Elizabethan spelling. For it is the distinctive character of the pun that it enjoys its fullest expressive life in the written or printed, over and above the spoken, medium of language, and the relative freedom of Elizabethan orthography, its heterography as it were, plays directly into the writer's hands. Shakespeare's spelling of 'tombe', for example, brings out its conflation of 'tomb' and 'tome' through the appended grapheme ('e') more forcibly to the eye than the sliding phoneme ('o') could to the ear, since the latter must be voiced one way or the other,[25] much as the theatrical performance of a Shakespearian play must always generate a more limited field of meaning, by virtue of the interpretative options it must leave unexpressed, than the printed text.

The pun, by foregrounding its character as the privileged resource of writing, thus works against any notion of poetic enactment that presupposes the presence and immediacy of spoken language—hence Booth's quite traditional deprivileg-ing of its effect—but at the same time it makes possible another kind of enactment beyond the reach of spoken language, with its hit-or-miss, here-and-gone rapidity, its momentary materiality. The relative transience, the short time available for the construction and concretization of meaning, in spoken as distinct from written wordplay, would thus seem to be a control upon its counter-enactive effect. But the written pun, by making available a longer, potentially endless, time for the construction of possible meanings, and hence the deconstruction of fixed or monumental meaning, reveals this control to be arbitrary and illusory, merely a momentary stay against multivocality. The overplus of time allowed by writing and reading for potentially endless

---

[25] The case for a 'tomb/tome' pun is argued by T. Walter Herbert, 'Shakespeare's Word-play on Tombe', *MLN*, 64 (1944), p. 235–41 and supported by Booth, p. 283.

construction and multiple concretization allows interpretation to do its deconstructive, fragmenting, counter-enactive work. The cultural authoritarianism that deprivileges or criminalizes wordplay, in the attempt to save a univocal or unified reading is thus always a losing battle, a rearguard action fought against time in the name of a mimetic or supermimetic project that Shakespeare certainly states, in accordance with the poetic and rhetorical theory of his time, but also undermines and disowns as a function of his own writerly practice.

VI. THE DARK LADY IDENTIFIED

The abandonment of the mimetic or supermimetic project of reproducing the beloved object for all time, implicit in Shakespeare's foregrounding of the flaws and tricks of his written medium, however, only makes room for another project. This latest project is also enactive, but enactive with a difference, and it is still mimetic—since all signs must always signify something, and signification, though it can be complicated, multiplied, and embarrassed can never be made to cease, not even in 'nonsense' verse or symbolist poetry, and certainly not in the poetic figures of understatement, irony, or ellipsis. But this latest project, which occupies the last fifty or so poems of Shakespeare's sequence and carries the process of writerly self-consciousness we have been tracing to an uneasy cadence, is mimetic with a difference, or more accurately, mimetic *of* a difference. For this is the 'metamimetic' project of representing nothing other than linguistic difference itself. Its mimetic object is language in the act, always imperfect or defective, of representing, and it depends on precisely the hyperactivity of the sign epitomized in the pun and such related figures as irony, litotes, and ellipsis, all of which share a constitutive capacity to mean more than they say, or say more than they mean.

Now if Shakespeare's scepticism toward the empirical and mimetic attempts to render or replace the youth in so unlikely a medium as 'black ink' has generated a new rhetoric, or counter-rhetoric, of disability and default, it also generates a new object better suited to metamimetic representation. That is, if the medium of black ink cannot ultimately be appropriated to its conventionally 'fair' object, one potential solution—the only one remaining to be explored—is to appropriate the 'object' to the medium. Why not an object whose physical complexion, being dark, would make her as representable in the medium of ink, as any traditional 'fair' might be in the media of paint or marble? But while this 'solution' may restore a certain superficial material compatibility and similarity between medium and message, it cannot make up for the more profound differences and instabilities in the linguistic medium that the sonnets of the 70s and 80s have already uncovered. After such self-consciousness, there can be no return to a naïve realism that presupposes the mimetic adequacy of the medium. But even that problem can be solved by making the lady's character as shady as her complexion, indeed as dark and ambiguous as the characters that inscribe it. What more writerly solution to the problem of the insuperable difference of writing than to have writing generate its own best—or worst?—object, an object as dark and different as writing itself?

Yet this fanciful invention of a writerly dark lady, visual and moral negative to the countless, colourless fairs of sonnet tradition, while it may well have seemed to bid fair toward resolving the problem of mimesis, offers no final solution for Shakespeare. For the representation of even a dark lady is still a function of rhetorical duplicity, of irony and negative comparison ('My mistress' eyes are nothing like the sun'), and as such, can only expose, rather than transcend, the impostures of prior convention and the artifice, the 'false compare', of all verbal art, even that which exposes its own falseness and imposture. It cannot close the distance or repair the unlikeliness of the written medium in relation to its object, or deliver up even a dark and unlikely presence. But if this new extralinguistic object cannot be poetically imitated any more effectively than the old extra-linguistic object, she can embody and foreground a still newer and more truly congenial object for poetic representation: the duplicity and discrepancy, lying and betrayal of poetic representation itself:

> In the old age black was not counted fair,
> Or if it were it bore not beauty's name. (*127*)

Why should my heart think that a several plot,
Which my heart knows the wide world's common place?
Or mine eyes, seeing this, say this is not
To put fair truth upon so foul a face?
In things right true my heart and eyes have erred,
And to this false plague are they now transferred. (*137*)

Therefore I lie with her, and she with me,
And in our faults by lies we flattered be. (*138*)

My thoughts and my discourse as madmen's are,
At random from the truth vainly expressed;
For I have sworn thee fair, and thought thee bright,
Who art as black as hell, as dark as night. (*147*)

O me! what eyes hath love put in my head,
Which have no correspondence with true sight! (*148*)

For I have sworn thee fair: more perjured eye,
To swear against the truth so foul a lie. (*152*)

What is striking in these late sonnets is not just how openly Shakespeare confesses the mimetic invalidity of his art in order to assert its metamimetic validity, but how fully this confession of poetic misrepresentation has been re-thematized and re-embodied, i.e. represented, in the dark lady's and the poet's interactions. An untrustworthy textuality and an untrustworthy sexuality now mirror one another in the perfection of defect of the pun on 'lie': 'Therefore I lie with her, and she with me, / And in our faults by lies we flattered be.' It is no longer possible to tell which came first or has ontological priority, language or action; which 'mirrors' which, the betraying pun or the betraying flesh; or which is the signifier and which the signified, dancer or dance in this old gavotte. The relationship now represented—or is it generated—is as unstable, polymorphous, and perverse as the language which represents, or generates, it.

In this last phase of Shakespeare's *Sonnets*, where the shifting triangulations of representation become the object of representation, we find ourselves in a situation not unlike that of the opening scenes of *The Winter's Tale*, where Leontes' suspicion of the word at once reflects and generates suspicion of his wife and friend. Hermione is of course no shady lady, and we are used to thinking of that play as one in which everything, pre-eminently the relations of nature and art, is restored to a pristine integrity. Indeed, in its final scene, surely the locus of poetic self-consciousness in Shakespeare, the movement of the *Sonnets* from enactment to counter-enactment, from performance to pun, from mimesis to metamimesis would seem to be well and truly reversed, as time and death are defeated through art and a living monument of flesh and blood, wondrously fair, is bodied forth.

Yet the scene also recapitulates, with dizzying concision, the movement from mimesis to metamimesis we have been tracing in the *Sonnets*. It begins with an assertion of direct mimetic correspondence when Paulina reveals Hermione's 'statue' and rhetorically asks, 'Comes it not something near?' Leontes qualifies his amazed agreement with a demurrer: 'But yet, Paulina / Hermione was not so much wrinkled, nothing / So aged as this seems.' Paulina meets this just criticism of the statue at the mimetic level by appeal to a higher, supermimetic fidelity analogous to that claimed by *Sonnet 55*:

> So much the more our carver's excellence;
> Which lets go by some sixteen years and makes her
> As she lived now. (V. iii. 24–32)

The palpable mimetic difference between the living Hermione and the 'statue' that aspires to represent her is supposed to have been repaired at the supermimetic level, through the time-defeating pre-emption of time's effects, the wrinkles that defeat the youthful perfection of human flesh in the way linguistic fluctuation defeats the univocal perfection of language as a representing medium. But because the traces of time's touch are imaginable, indeed enactable within the work, a kind of supermimesis still seems possible by which included imperfection becomes, through its anticipation of obsolescence, the condition of a new perfection, a timeless contemporaneity.

Yet we soon discover that the 'statue' that represents Hermione, wrinkles and all, is not a statue but the living Hermione; that this supposedly supermimetic art does not even exist; that its perfection of imperfection turns out to be only the old imperfection of imperfection that is nature; and that Paulina's claim to a redemptive supermimesis is only an admission of artistic inadequacy or sleight-of-hand. But the phenomenology of Shakespearean representation does not stop here, in a resigned subscription to the traces of time, the wrinkles of flesh, the differences of language. For if Paulina's celebration of that 'excellence' which carves time into the work is misapplied to the supposedly supermimetic art of Julio, which does not exist, it is fully instinct with the metamimetic art of Shakespeare, which is the play. 'Our carver's excellence' consists precisely in Shakespeare's ultimate unconcealment of all those differences that no poetic art can overcome; the differences between some purely hypothetical, super-realist Julio and Shakespeare himself; between a breath-takingly lifelike statue of Hermione and the actual Hermione; between the 'actual' Hermione and the actor or actress who plays the role; in sum, between the aspirations of art to the flawless condition of immortal diamond and its acknowledge-ment, through such devices as puns and wordplay, of its own wrinkles, i.e. of its historical and displaced status. In the dialectical play of Paulina's lines among mimetic, supermimetic, and metamimetic reference—a fluctuation that is only fully available, incidentally, when the play is conceived as a textual rather than theatrical event—Shakespeare's entire poetic project lies compressed.

VII. THE REIFICATIONS OF READING

Whether the lady in question is fair or dark, morally irreproachable or reprehensible, Hermione or Cleopatra, her perfect representation in the medium of black ink would seem to be impossible, except at the metamimetic level of the pun, and that is to foreground defect and defeat perfection: 'Therefore I lie with her, and she with me, / And in our faults by lies we flattered be.' The point cannot be made too strongly, however, against those textualists and grammatolo-gists who would like to proclaim the end of representation, that representation does not, because it cannot, cease. What ceases is the dream of univocal representation, which now becomes multivocal, in something of the way the Roman

Empire does not so much cease as become Europe. The foredoomed project of univocal representation, based on enactment and aspiring to the perfect realization of a single object of desire, now gives way to a multivocal representation, arising from the hyperactivity of the pun and generating numerous objective correlatives.

It is no longer possible to specify the erotic and ethical duplicities and disloyalties represented in the later sonnets, because the language in which they are represented so openly acknowledges its own duplicity and disloyalty. But neither is it possible to deny that anything is being represented at all. For the Shakespeare of the later sonnets, unlike Leontes, this condition of multivocality is neither a nightmare of anxiety nor a utopia of bliss—as their tone of detached engagement attests—but a kind of bemusement at the irrepressible power of language to keep on signifying beyond any particular significance, to work overtime, as it were, producing an overplus of signification that cannot be brought to rest in any definitive act of interpretation, either positive and humanist or negative and deconstructive.

But not even Shakespeare's metamimetic art, which tells us in one and the same breath that univocal representation and definitive interpretation are impossible, can prevent us from trying to restore the monumentality of the printed sign, so apparently stable and permanent on the page, to full mimetic integrity. The modernist authenticity of the *Sonnets*, as distinct from their traditional mimetic authority, arises precisely from Shakespeare's exertions, against the grain of his medium and against his foreknowledge of ultimate frustration, to test to the limit of its potential monumentality the figurative potential of language, of writing and print in particular. We, in our turn as readers, go directly against their acknowledgement of imperfection and betray the authenticity of this acknowledgement by attempting to re-monumentalize writing through that systematic reification of it we name interpretation, the repeated attempt to discover within or project on to his poetry a mimetic coherence it knows it cannot have, as I have just done in the foregoing interpretation. Or perhaps it is just such a foreknowledge on Shakespeare's part of such vain efforts at interpretive remonumentalization that enables his equally vain claim of poetic monumentality in the first place. Perhaps he resembles none of the characters projected in his own sonnets so much as that fair lady of Spenser's *LXXV*, who rebukes her poet's repeated attempts to inscribe her name in sand: 'Vayne man, sayd she, that doest in vaine assay, / A mortall thing so to immortalize.' Yet it is only because of this work of repeated, frustrated, but irrepressible re-monumental-ization, through the repeated reifications of reading across history, that time, the destroyer of the gilded monuments of princes, can become the ally and preserver of the printed monuments of poets.

6

Beyond Theory

The theory of poetry is the theory of life.

Wallace Stevens

I. THE DEATH OF THE AUTHOR

The foregoing chapter attempts to identify a major change in the cultural condition of art, already in process at the turn of the seventeenth century, a new consciousness of the literary text as a written or printed object, which was to undermine its traditional status as a transcription of experience and its author's claim to control the meaning of that transcription. This change in the status of the text and of the author can be seen not only in such auspiciously self-reflective 'sports' of earlier literary history as *Don Quixote*, *The Tempest*, or *Tristram Shandy* but, thanks to recent poststructuralist speculation, even in those pre-modern texts where the mimetic impulse and claim seem most strong, texts such as Shakespeare's *Sonnets* or Balzac's 'Sarrasine'. The recent paradigm-shift toward theory, which has enabled such texts to be read as never before, and writerly modernity to be radically backdated, may itself be only the latest phase of that larger change in the status of writing which enabled such self-critical and self-destabilizing texts to be produced in the first place, the academic institutionalization of a textual self-consciousness long since in train. The present chapter attempts to account for this latest mutation in the institution of literature, through which theory has all but caught up with a clairvoyant past practice, reading with writing's foreknowledge of its own manifest and manifold destiny.

But not even Shakespeare's prophetic soul could have foreseen fully the consequences that this new potential of printed books for endless and diverse remonumentalization at the hands of a vastly enlarged but newly dispersed readership, and the more recent academic institutionalization of their study, would hold for the author himself. Once the mimetic authority deriving from the poet's proximity to a given and privileged object of representation had given way to a metamimetic authenticity arising from a new and strenuous self-reflection on the poem's own free-standing but precarious textuality, the role and status of the author himself could be put radically into question or into brackets. The modern intransitivity of writing, its open acknowledgement that it can speak only for and of itself, was made possible by the independence from patronage that the widespread dissemination of printed books conferred upon writers.[1] But their interpretive re-monumentalization was now in the hands, and at the mercy, of this newly literate, more scattered readership remote from the author and the immediate support-system of his culture, and newly open to an unforeseen transitivity.

While the mimetic, classic, or readerly text—to retain Barthes' terms—may have guided or repressed the reader with the shared conventions, literary and cultural, of a 'parsimonious pluralism',[2] the metamimetic, modernist, or writerly text could be reinvested by the now unrepressed reader with unforeseeable motivation and guided in unpredictable directions. Provided he is willing to put in the strenuous interpretive labour of displaced remonumentalization that now falls to him, the power and authority once claimed by and ascribed to the author now devolve upon the reader and the community, or special interest group within that community, for which he speaks or which speaks him. In the case of Shakespeare, we have seen how a characteristic renaissance claim to poetic authority based on the mimetic enactment of its object gives way in the course of the *Sonnets* to a redefined and qualified, indeed strikingly modernist, claim to authenticity arising from the metamimetic productivity of writing itself. A poetic of unitary and present effect, associated

---

[1] Samuel Johnson's famous letter of rebuff to Lord Chesterfield's belated offer of patronage is the classic document of this transition. See Alvin B. Kernan, *The Imaginary Library: An Essay on Literature and Society* (Princeton: Princeton University Press, 1982), pp. 3–36.

[2] See Barthes, *S/Z*, trans. Richard Miller (London: Jonathan Cape, 1975), pp. 4–5.

with the instantaneous availability of speech, has given way to a poetic of plural and deferred meaning, issuing in the endless interpretability of textuality. Such a change must alter the status of the author, if not render him altogether etiolated and anachronistic.

Clearly it is no longer possible to conceive of the author, not even when the author in question is Shakespeare, in the same terms as the renaissance, or even the romantic age, conceived of him. In a pluralist culture whose source of social authority is hard to locate, shifting as it now seems to do between special interests and the impersonal system that loosely binds them together, the claim of a particular voice, let alone of a privileged poetic language, to literary and cultural authority seems hollow or marginal. Hence the rumours of 'the end of man', 'the end of representation', 'the death of the author' that echo within our contemporary literary critical discourse. No longer sanctioned by a shared liberal-humanist, i.e. upper bourgeois, vision of culture, for which he is the highly placed spokesman or even the unacknowledged legislator, the author has fallen prey to the enveloping cultural pluralism, with its concomitant relativization of creative and interpretive authority. Within the logic of the secular protestantism of which pluralism is the product, the interpretive authority once ascribed to the hieratic author has devolved upon the individual reader. 'The birth of the reader', writes Barthes 'must be at the cost of the death of the Author', the Brutus-like justification for this quasi-political assassination being 'to give writing its future'.[3]

Barthes' polemical and peremptory tone notwithstanding, the event he heralds seems already to have occurred. The Author as an originary, definitive source of timeless and univocal meaning, as the ultimate or stable signified on which interpretation could come to rest, would seem—if our reading of Shakespeare's *Sonnets* carries any conviction—to have long since self-destructed. What had not yet or not fully occurred at the time Barthes wrote was the critical recognition of this event. The Author may have been kept artificially alive within the authoritarian and repressive confines of French institutional

[3] 'The Death of the Author', in *Image-Music-Text*, tr. Stephen Heath (New York: Hill and Wang, 1977), p. 148.

literary study—hence Barthes' anxiety to preserve an 'open-ness for writing'—but within the more permissive and pluralistic institutions of Anglo-American liberal humanism, the Author has already been displaced by the author, the 'persona', and the 'unreliable narrator', as reinterpretation of the classics in terms of changing ideology has been taken for granted and even encouraged. The latest stage of this process of displacement has now occurred—the replacement of authorial with readerly authority—and Barthes' essay is symptomatic of it. For cultural differences aside, what is striking about Barthes' polemic is precisely its own authoritar-ianism. This new reader sounds very much like the old Author whose death he is announcing, his authoritarian tone itself symptomatic of the authority vacuum left by the demise of the Author and the communal sanctions that authorized Him. *Le roi est mort! vive le roi!* It is paradoxically fitting that this great reader, the cacangel of the Author's death, should have published his own autobiography in a series styled by its publisher '*Écrivains de toujours*'![4]

Yet readers too, as we have come to understand, speak for the interpretive communities that constitute them, and in so doing, promote the attitudes, beliefs, and interests of particular social groups, whether they know it or not, which are then projected on to the texts they read and reinvest with a new authority and monumentality. In a society whose chief, perhaps only, shared assumption is that a plurality of assumptions, cultural and educational, must be tolerated, it is inevitable that means replace ends, which are seen as all relative anyway. Technique becomes the measure of all things, including read-ing, which is now reified into 'schools' of interpretation—feminist, marxist, structuralist, etc.—'approaches' or 'method-ologies' that seek to justify, indeed 'authorize', their own special interests by interpreting the texts they take up in the only terms that command anything like wide cultural prestige, the specialist jargons of presumed technical expertise.

Yet it is deeply ironic, to say the least, that the yearnings for a quasi- or pseudo-scientific discourse, which we have seen at work in all the dominant theoretical discourses, and which

---

[4] *Roland Barthes par Roland Barthes* (Paris: Seuil, 1975).

aim at attracting to themselves some of the supposed cultural prestige and centrality of science and technology, arise at the very moment when science and technology—as a result of the disastrous side-effects of their long cultural hegemony—are themselves losing the prestige and centrality they have so long enjoyed. And it is no less ironic that the search for a quasi-scientific or theoretical 'ground' on which the various schools hope to found their practice seems to turn up only an infinitely varied groundlessness, as each 'ground' can be relativized and demystified in relation to some other.

II. THE BIRTH OF THE READER

Since the death of the godlike author, any number of idols have been erected in His place under the names of our diverse theoretical schools as the ultimate reference of literature and resting-point for its study. Each of these schools promises its own version of salvation through correct interpretation in a grounded, and by that token valid, reading of texts. The analogy between contemporary theory and an older theology is not fortuitous. Just as God was once the ground of being, from Whom all things come and to Whom they return, the transcendental Signified toward which all textuality—the 'books' of nature and of revelation—points and on which it was based, so our theoretical schools, while generally denying the divine or metaphysical basis of the textuality they study have displaced but by no means dispensed with the notion of a transcendental signified, a kind of bottom-line for reading, that justifies and guides their operations.

For structuralism and semiology, which may well lay claim to having founded the new religion of theory which has replaced that religion of literature which replaced religion itself, the ground of textual being is of course language, at once the lexical material of which texts are made and the structural model for understanding their operations. If all cultural texts, as second-order sign-systems, were only read in accordance with the set of rules based on and deriving from those that underwrite the operation of the first-order sign-system of language itself, then all our interpretive problems would be solved. Such was the bright promise of structuralist poetics. Salvation was to be found in methodology—linguistic methodology—alone, in the rigours of tracing out the chain of signification that points to the metalanguage of semiotics itself as the transcendent signified. Yet as we have seen, this process of 'transcoding' is only a more technocratic version of what used to be called interpretation. Its 'meanings' may be more depersonalized or anonymous but no less transcendentally 'authorized'. And it is no accident that the appeal of structuralism, like that of linguistics, reached its peak in the sixties, at a time when confidence in the promise of technology for the material transformation of our culture was most widespread. Literary study was to be fully methodized, even routinized to conform with the methods of the other 'human sciences'. Our students were to pass through the communal *rites de passage* of extrapolating the binary oppositions and underlying grammars from the texts they studied, in something of the way students of engineering learn to form and solve differential equations, in order that our institutions of learning could qualify them at once to build much-needed bridges between disciplines and to attain upward mobility in a technocratic society.

But the technological optimism of the structuralist adventure soon developed its own shadow-side in deconstruction, in which its original brightness was soon eclipsed. Because it shared with structuralism the premiss of language as the ground of being (and reading), deconstruction could engage structuralism directly and turn into the severest critic of its new methodism. For even though it took, like structuralism, language as the material and model of all textuality, it was a very different aspect of language that deconstruction foregrounded: not the linguisticity that determines social construction and communication but the rhetoricity that puts those enabling structures into question and renders them radically problematic or indeterminate, the inbuilt figuration that suspends grammar and logic and indefinitely defers present meaning. As a ground of being, this linguisticity is so plastic and slippery that it hardly qualifies as a ground at all. Proceeding on so infirm a basis and informed by so doctrineless a faith, the blind and strenuous persistence of the reader can be described as charismatic at best, a dark 'progress' illumined by haphazard advents of grace along a mystical *via negativa* leading to the anxiety, or bliss, or bliss of anxiety—depending on sectarian emphasis—of losing oneself in a textuality without bounds, a world without end or beginning.

Even when that state of grace is achieved, as it so often is by the masters of deconstruction, what is discovered in the literary text is a 'foreknowledge of criticism' that turns out to know only that it cannot know.[5] However adept the deconstructive practitioner, however complete his mastery of humanist and hermeneutic tradition, his practice, working in the voids and abysses of language, can never in theory find a new ground on which to reconstitute the *disjecta membra* of that tradition into a newly found unity or totality. Nor does deconstruction, except at odd moments of blindness to its own insight or of repression of its own negative knowledge, profess or promise to do so. For it to do so would be somewhat like the Professor of Classical Philology at Basel, after remarking how curious it is 'that when he wished to turn author, God learned Greek, and that he did not learn it better,'[6] proclaiming that He is none the less alive and well and living in the sacred text.

For the marxists, on the other hand, the problem of what knowledge is inscribed in the text and liberated by its systematic study is not really a problem. 'Literature', for the marxists as much as the deconstructionists, is the foreknowledge of criticism, but there is nothing mystical or self-negating about this foreknowledge. On the contrary, it is palpable, positive, and present, nothing other than history according to Marx, a history, that is, of material relations and class struggle. And while reading that history out of the 'literary' texts on which it is inscribed may require, in the latest marxism, a new and meticulous methodism owing something to structuralism, its reason for being is not linguistic or metalinguistic. The marxist fideo-materialism, with its fundamentalist ground of History and utopian goal of socialism to

[5] Paul de Man, *Blindness and Insight* (New York: Oxford University Press, 1971), pp. 30–1.

[6] Friedrich Nietzsche, *Beyond Good and Evil*, 'Apopthegms and Interludes', 121, in *The Works of Friedrich Nietzsche* (New York: Tudor Publishing Co., 1931), p. 82.

support and guide its reading of texts, is rather a dogmatism, another secular theology in which the old transcendental signifieds of God and the Bourgeois Author may have been superseded or sublated by History but certainly not dispensed with.

So a new problem arises, or perhaps it is the old one in disguise, namely that of the communal faith required to maintain any dogmatism. For the historical subtext upon which marxist criticism is grounded now appears as unstable and deconstructible as the older authority-structures of God, the Author, and Literature once were. Unless one is a true believer, how can he have faith in the reading of history that supports all our other reading, when that reading proves to be repeatedly in need of correction or revision, as capitalism continues to survive every crisis, including its latest, that was supposed to mark its demise? To what more fundamental ground do we appeal to make those corrections? As Terry Eagleton himself sees, the problem is not to formulate an internally coherent marxist criticism—no more than inventing Esperanto is a problem—but to establish the marxist society that would support it.[7] If the latter task could be done, the former would take care of itself.

In this respect, the marxist dilemma is paradigmatic of that of all the current theoretical schools. With such diverse heterodoxies in the field, each with its chosen ground of reading, it seems unlikely that any one will be able to persuade or co-opt the others and thereby emerge as a new institutional orthodoxy, an authentic interpretive community as against the sectarian 'communities' that exist at present. For this problem of assent bedevils not only the major schools that form the subject of the present study, but the more recent movements that have grown out of them by combining or displacing the diverse grounds or goals of their interpretive practice: Lacanian psychoanalysis, feminist criticism, and reader-response criticism. Indeed, the more often those

---

[7] Explicitly stated by Eagleton in a paper, 'Toward a Socialist Criticism', delivered at the University of Melbourne in July, 1983, and implicit in the argument of his recent *Literary Theory: An Introduction* (Oxford: Basil Blackwell, 1983) that the ideological dispositions of criticism, like those of 'literature', are always a function of political and cultural ideology.

grounds and goals are recombined or displaced, the more apparent it becomes that they never were—except rhetorically —grounds or goals in the first place; the more relative each appears, and the more elusive becomes the *sine qua non* of communal assent. Each attempt to centre or centralize theoretical discourse reveals how decentred it has become.

Consider Lacanian psychoanalysis. Like its marxist counterpart, this latest freudianism is an attempt to update an older tradition of reflection by filling a gap within that tradition that has become increasingly visible, its absent mindedness *vis-à-vis* a general theory of language as distinct from the special theories formulated by Freud concerning wit, jokes, slips, and poetry. It has attempted, that is, to articulate a silence in Freud's account of the development of the psyche or self—the ground of all freudian theory—with the twentieth-century problematic of language. In the attempt, the self has been decentred and depersonalized, in so far as it is no longer a traditionally given subject forged out of the interpersonal relations of family and social life, but a function of language, an imaginary projection or symbolic construct. Hence the Lacanian affiliation with structuralism. But in so far as language is discourse, so many historical formations embodying and transmitting cultural ideology, the individual ego is further displaced or dispersed into a function of the discourses and cultural apparatuses that constitute him or it. Here its interrelations with Althusserian marxism emerge. It is no longer possible to decide which ground has priority or authority. The attempt to articulate the subject within the interstices of cultural discourses, has had the effect of derealizing it as a given and redefining it as a construct. The effect, if not the intention, has been to undermine the authoritarianism, and much of the authority, of freudian discourse, certainly its traditional claim to scientific authority, since scientific discourse requires an already formed and given object about which it is in a position to speak.

Feminism too has sought to extend methods derived from marxist and freudian models, in this case toward establishing gender as a new or neglected ground of literary study. As the literary arm of a political movement, feminist criticism remains internally divided in its aims and methods. Fluctuating among a para-marxist materialism, a post-freudian metaphysics of the female, and a semiological critique of cultural patriarchy—in proportions varying with the side of the Atlantic or the Channel one has in view, feminist criticism has yet to generate a theory or a practice comparable to those of its models in intellectual coherence or explanatory power. Its appropriation of marxist manœuvres to its special interest, particularly its extension of the marxist critique of class-distinction and colonial exploitation, and of the cultural ideology that maintains them, into the domain of gender, sits uneasily with the metaphysics of its ambivalent freudianism. It is hard to tell whether its transcendental signified of gender is finally located in the mind, in culture, in language, or in biology. After more than a decade, feminism has yet to define a mode of existence for itself that transcends political cause or religious cult, and a method that addresses the special demands and problems of literary texts.[8]

Of reader-response criticism or 'affective stylistics' more needs to be said. In the wake of the new-critical hypostatization of the text and an older and more traditional privileging of the author as source or ground of meaning, the demand that the newly born reader be given his due is, as we have seen, a rhetorical inevitability. So a new ground for theoretical exploration would seem to have emerged. But is it so new, and is it a 'ground'? For the trail-blazers of this school, Stanley Fish and Wolfgang Iser, a continuing matter of dispute turns on the questions of who is 'the reader' and how much is 'his/her due'? On these questions, Fish offers the more radical answers. Whereas Iser retains such historical and phenomenological categories as 'text' and 'world', 'horizon of expectations', and 'determinate' and 'indeterminate' meaning in defining the reader's role in the process of constructing the text, Fish claims that such distinctions are presumptuous and unreliable in so far as they are themselves a function rather than a determinant of the reading process, that they beg too many anterior questions or offer circular answers, and finally,

---

[8] For an excellent account of the divisions and problems internal to feminist criticism, see K. K. Ruthven, 'Male Critics and Feminist Criticism', *Essays in Criticism*, xxxiii. 4 (October 1983) pp. 263–72.

that in allowing for all responses and constructions, they explain and challenge none.[9]

Yet Fish himself has been forced back, in developing his own theory of response over more than a decade, upon similar expedients.[10] Having adopted and abandoned the successive presumptions of speaking for the 'fit' reader, the 'informed' and 'ideal' reader, Fish now claims to speak only for 'himself', to bear witness only to his own response and report only on his own reading experience. But to speak for oneself, it turns out, is not the solipsism or glossalalia it might appear to be, since the self that reads and reports on its reading is constituted by the assumptions and beliefs of a prior 'interpretive community'. The text, which for Iser is partly determinate and partly indeterminate, partly 'there' and partly 'not there', has become for Fish wholly indeterminate, the projection of the reader's prior belief-structure, which is in turn constituted by the interpretive community to which he or she belongs, whether or not he or she is aware of belonging to it.

Such an infinite regress from text to constitutive reader to pre-constitutive community seems to be open to the same charge of inconsequentiality for which Fish indicts Iser. As long, that is, as the particular interpretive community which constitutes a particular reader who constitutes a particular text remains hypothetical and unspecified—a state of affairs that Fish, in the interest of maximum theoretical reach and generality, is content to let it remain. Having denied the existence of any textual meaning, or any text, independent of the reader's constitution of it, and the existence of any reader independent of his interpretive community's constitution of him, Fish is in the position, as one commentator puts it, of allowing 'criticism to go on as before but with this difference, [that] one must acknowledge that [one's interpretations] are the result of the interpretive strategies one possesses'.[11] Who

---

[9] 'Why No One's Afraid of Wolfgang Iser', *Diacritics* (March, 1981), pp. 2–28.

[10] The landmarks and turning-points in Stanley Fish's ten-year pilgrimage toward the horizon of his own assumptions and beliefs are collected, complete with autobiographical sub-text, in *Is There a Text in this Class? The Authority of Interpretive Communities* (Cambridge, Mass., 1979). In the last four essays of this pilgrim's progress, which represent the latest stage of the reader's self-reading, that horizon turns out to be not only unreachable but not even 'his own'.

[11] Jane P. Tompkins, ed., *Reader-Response Criticism: From Formalism to Poststructuralism* (Baltimore: Johns Hopkins University Press, 1980), p. xxiii.

would argue with, or be afraid of, that? If Fish's tail-chasing 'theory' avoids the pitfalls of that large body of contemporary theorizing that seeks to prescribe practice, it does so at the high cost of withholding any practical guidance whatever in doing what we would do anyway, since the reader's operations are quite literally beyond 'his' control. Who needs or wants a theory that is, in this strict sense, inconsequential? In the absence of any attempt to specify the particular forms and pressures of the historical interpretive communities whose continuing existence it presupposes, it is a 'thin' description indeed of readerly practice. And if it did attempt to specify them? Well, it might just turn into a version of marxism, or at the very least, of literary sociology.

III. *QUO VADIMUS?*

With so many contending heterodoxies in the field, it seems unlikely that any one of them will be able to persuade or co-opt the others and thereby emerge as a new institutional orthodoxy of reading, the shared ideology of an authentic interpretive community, as distinct from the sectarian 'communities' that exist at present. Such a vision is surely utopian within a historical institution, and the historical culture that surrounds and supports it, whose only discernible common assumption is that we agree to disagree. The sheer minimality of the pluralist ideology that so loosely binds together both the institution of literary study and its sponsoring culture does not hold much potential for generating some new sense of common purpose, let alone cultural mission, for the institution of reading, not even if the institution were to turn, as it now seems to be doing, relentlessly theoretical. For the institutional turn toward theory as the new common denominator of our activity only re-enacts the divergence of interests, beliefs, and attitudes which conditioned it. Rather than reintegrating those diverse cultural interests at a higher level, it relapses into the pluralism or fragmentation it was supposed to repair.

In so far as theory turns out to be only so many theories, each a monument to the interests of a particular interpretive community, the claim to authority of any particular theory must be so limited and relative as to amount to hardly more than a rhetorical gesture. 'The authority of interpretive communities', the grandiose sub-title of one recent work of literary theory, illustrates the point. There, a skilful rhetorical strategy, signalled in the paradox or oxymoron of the sub-title, is mobilized to resolve or mediate the logical contradiction between the social consensus Fish perceives to be necessary for authoritative interpretation and the pluralist dissent he sees vitiating such authority. The immediate aim of his rhetoric—to promote his own critical discourse to a position of institutional dominance—is furthered by its adoption of the trappings of a foundational logic—it presents itself as addressing basic, instituting conditions, the first principles, of interpretation, and flaunts the logical rigour and essentializing vocabulary of traditional philosophical argument. By so doing, Fish directs his formidable rhetorical arsenal at a further, less self-interested objective: to form an authentic interpretive community united by its common study of the ideological and rhetorical inauthenticities and relativities, the acts of faith, of past and present interpretive 'communities'. But his strategy is also circular in so far as it is doing, and can only do, what those past communities have done, while pretending to have attained, by taking their tendentiousness of belief and interest as his subject, a position that transcends them.

In the circularity of this position, Fish is not alone. The best definitions of textual study that theory—still operating (whether it realizes it or not) on the minimal social contract available within a pluralist culture that can agree only to disagree—can hold out are themselves minimal, reductive, and circular: 'the function of literature is to keep us functioning'; the function of criticism is 'to continue the conversation of the West.'[12] Textualist study, whether in its deconstructive or pragmatist forms—those schools, that is, which are complicit with the present pluralism—cannot transcend the cultural situation that enables—and debilitates—them: their institutional marginality. But neither are they immune to the anxiety of their

---

[12] Geoffrey Hartman, 'The Fate of Reading', in *The Fate of Reading and Other Essays* (Chicago: University of Chicago Press, 1975), pp. 248–74, and Richard Rorty, 'Problem about Fictional Discourse' in *Consequences of Pragmatism* (Minneapolis: University of Minnesota Press, 1982), pp. 136–7.

position and the desire it generates to regain a lost centrality. That desire manifests itself in a rhetoric that pretends or aspires to be logic, and nowhere more so than when these schools turn to the study of rhetoric itself, a system of tropes in the service of persuasion, as their chosen subject. But the study of textual rhetoricity does not transcend rhetoricity; it merely calls attention to the anxiety on the part of its students over their own rhetoric.

A more promising deliverance from this vicious circle is envisioned by those theorists I have termed contextualist, for whom the study of texts is justified in other than institutional terms, as a means of transforming material, political, or sexual relations within the wider culture. In such a context, the inescapable rhetoricity of theory is not necessarily a crippling handicap, as long as the rhetorical strategies of literary theory are employed to good and progressive effect outside it. In fact, the recent institutional turn toward theory is explained and justified in precisely these political terms by those theorists who came of age, if not to full maturity, in the late sixties, and whose work retains the ideological imprint of that period. Terry Eagleton, for one, explains our current preoccupation with theory as the mature offspring of a wild seed sewn at that time, an interest 'born in response to a deep-seated social crisis which, unusually, found its focus in the academic institution.'[13] The challenge to liberal-humanist critical ortho-doxy now marching under the banner of poststructuralist theory arose out of the prior challenge to the established authority-structures that produced an era of political assassin-ation, unjust war, and civil demonstration. Presumably, it would bear out its promise in proportion to its effectiveness in changing those older authority-structures by changing the collective cultural reading habits that have held, or helped to hold, them in place.

That is one account of the origin and object of our new theoretical consciousness, and even in so rough-and-ready a form, it would be difficult to say it is wrong. Literary theory may well be a displacement or refinement of politics, certainly of the politics of high culture, but if it is, it could be regarded

[13] Terry Eagleton, *Times Literary Supplement* (May 27, 1983), p. 546.

as an over-refinement even by those political critics who locate its origin in the culture of social protest. 'Being political is now', wrote Lionel Trilling in the late sixties, 'what being literary used to be.' Can it be only a decade and a half since our students were demanding microphones to turn lecture courses on Shakespeare into protest rallies against the Vietnam war, since professors of English counselled the burning-down of universities, and the MLA itself moved its meeting-place to register its disapproval of the treatment of protesters at the hands of the Chicago police? How remote we now seem from the political violence of that erupted, or threatened to erupt, in such havens of academic serenity as the Sorbonne, Cornell, Columbia, and Yale—the very same centres where all that disturbs the peace nowadays are theoretical disputations of an almost medieval abstraction! One might update Trilling's dictum: being theoretical is now what being political recently was, to be of the moment, at the cutting-edge of change, avant garde, but without the promise, or the danger, of immediate political consequences. In so far as the theoretical critique has taken for its object the institutional discourse, its cutting-edge has moved to the margin of society, and its social and political implications will be long-term, uncertain, and difficult to measure. It is impossible to decide, even by the lights of those contextualists who see theory as politically motivated, whether it represents an advance or regression in 'real' political terms.

For even if the political explanation and rationale for theory is accepted, it is difficult to decide, given the pluralism of theory, *whose* politics it serves or advances. Consider the case of deconstructive textualism. Though not overtly political in its concerns, deconstruction can none the less be read as deeply political in its origin and effect, in Eagleton's terms, as a 'response' to the political conditions within which it emerged and to which it continues to answer. But in the relentlessness of its textualist focus, it would have to be viewed as a negative response, whose political effect, if not intention, is at least quietism, at most anarchism, *vis-à-vis* the status quo. For the critique of established authority that characterized the oppositional discourse and practice of the period in which deconstruction emerged—epitomized perhaps in the ritual burning of draft-cards—while it represented new political hope for some, was also viewed by others as having brought western culture very near to anarchy. It certainly came close to destroying the conditions of academic discourse altogether. While carrying over the structuralist, phenomenological, and marxist destabilization of given or self-evident signification, of some natural and authoritative framing of the world, deconstruction carried that process further than any of its precursors wanted, or could afford, to carry it. Deconstruction thereby signalled the danger of the destabilizing process itself, if never quite naming it as such. Let the semioclasts beware, lest there be no signs or idols left to break. Is it any wonder that deconstruction, though no friend to the literary culture of liberal humanism, has maintained an uneasy alliance with and within it?

This is not of course what deconstructive textualism would say of its own origins and aims. As deconstruction never tires of pointing out, the attempt to fix cultural paternity uncannily draws out the unwanted and repressed implication of the biological metaphor it employs, that paternity is always uncertain. For an alternative account, no less plausible, could be offered, one that locates the 'origins' and 'causes' of our current theoretical moment, not in public, political events, but in the retentions and protensions, the traces and spaces as it were, of institutional discourse itself. After all, even the most avant-garde theoretical rhetoric can be seen as occupying the gaps created by a proto-theoretical discourse already in place in such still centers of academic contemplation as Wimsatt's and Wellek's New Haven of the forties, or Frye's Toronto of the fifties. Those august and 'apolitical' titans cannot be ruled out among the possible fathers of today's powerful imps. In this respect, the textualist and contextualist poststructuralisms of today are postscripts or glosses upon a proto-theoretical text that seems in retrospect defective, uncompleted, or indeed, barely begun.

Indeed, the theoretical impulse can be traced back further still to the work of such post-romantic giants as Marx, Nietzsche, and Freud, whose discourse fell between the compartmentalizations of the classical academic disciplines, and begat the new discourse that now goes by the name of

Theory. That discourse may even be said to have thrown up a new institutional dwelling-place, and created a new set of material relations within the academic institutions that house it, as departmental structures and appointment policies are accordingly transformed. It may ultimately do the same within the wider culture, however unpredictable the shape of that transformation may now be. For one common denominator of all the schools of theory is the conviction that their thought, and the language of their thought, is consequential in real social terms, that their relation to society is not that of a passive reflex or mechanistic response. Even such recent contextualists as Althusser and Foucault recognize that the discursive formations and conformations of ideology are uneven in origin and unpredictable in development, and have a life and momentum of their own that defies direct description of their social aetiology or reliable prediction of their cultural effect. It is no longer possible to say, even from within marxism—so subtle has it become—whether Marx was right in claiming that social being determines consciousness, or whether Hegel, the theoretical precursor whose thought he was supposed to have inverted, may not also have been right in the view that consciousness determines being. Once dismissed as 'idealist', Hegel has uncannily returned to inhabit or haunt all the major schools of contemporary theory. And given its intimidating effect on overconfident political action, such an inhibiting self-consciousness may not be altogether a bad thing.

IV. THE CRITICAL CATS

That, given our pluralism, is for the individual and the future to decide. What is clear at present is that 'the critical cat is now so far out of [the] bag that one can no longer ignore its existence.'[14] If this is the case, the question that must weigh on the institution—or temple—of literary study within which the cat—or leopard—is all but loose, is how to meet this menace to its existence? Is there life after poststructuralism, and if so, what form might its institutionalization take? How

[14] Paul de Man, 'Professing Literature: A Symposium on the Study of English', *Times Literary Supplement* (Dec. 10 1982), pp. 1355–6.

may we carry on our critical and pedagogical practice under the pitiless gaze of deconstruction in particular, a doctrine that desanctifies our once sacred texts, destabilizes our secure hierarchies of authors and readers, classics and criticism, out of reliable relation, and demystifies our humanist vision of high cultural and moral purpose? With the cat so far out of the bag, what is our best strategy for survival?

While no general strategy for meeting the crisis has yet emerged, at least three particular tactics have, each with its own strategic implications, and each to my mind unsatisfactory. There has been the reaction voiced by a number of representatives, not all of them old or established, of our old and established humanist tradition. This course, usually couched in a moralistic rhetoric and often based on gross misunderstanding or anxious caricature of its antagonist, amounts to little more than a counsel of willful ignorance of the enemy's ways, as if the threat to established institutional practice posed by the emergent poststructuralist cat, or rather 'cats'— for, as we have seen, there are more than one—would disappear if only we bury our heads deeper in the sand.

One is reminded of F. R. Leavis's reaction, during an earlier 'crisis', to the novels of C. P. Snow: 'to read them would be to condone them.' Apart from its ineffectiveness as self-defence—for the cats show no sign of withdrawing back into their bags—this ostrich-like reaction can only deprive the institution of whatever insight is offered by poststructuralism generally and deconstruction specifically, or by the institution's historical and dialectical engagement with it. Paradoxically, the humanist exponents of the institution's historical function and cultural mission thus put themselves in the position of attempting to arrest its historical development by denying the institution's own changing historical status and turning it into an antiquarian museum. Even the temple has been wiser than that. After such knowledge, what retreat?

If we cannot scare the poststructuralist cats into retreat through self-blinded polemics, an alternative course for the institution has been to attempt to domesticate them. In the case of deconstruction, what was once perceived as an oppositional practice subversive of the historical and hermeneutic labours of humanism is now regarded by many as merely a new corrective conscience or even a 'constructive' criticism, which may in time become a new institutional norm. After all, as the only poststructuralist practice addressing itself to maintaining the traditional canon of literature as a privileged and distinctive category, deconstruction, suitably adapted, may well become the means of saving the classic texts and recuperating the traditional institution of their study. That process of domestication is already well under way, as the canonical works of European and American literature are subjected to an increasingly predictable and programmatic set of methodological reflexes and routines.

Lost in this process of routinization, however, is precisely the oppositional, anti-methodical character that lent deconstruction its peculiar potency, its power to disturb institutional complacency by forcing recognition of insuperable textual alterity, the uncanny 'difference' that at once tempts and bedevils all our textual dealings. Having undermined the monism of new-critical practice by bringing out into the open the necessary and absolute pluralism, the inbuilt overdetermination or indeterminacy, of textual meaning, deconstruction now bids fair, having been duly domesticated at the hands of its epigones and disciples, to become a new methodological monism, another 'paradigm' under which the canon can be more or less normally re-read until it is 'filled out', much as the older paradigms of historical, practical, and formalist criticism were before it. This process, already under way, will no doubt generate much useful labour, the production of a thousand theses, articles, and monographs unsaying the old 'truths' about the great works of time under the imprimatur and in the jargon of deconstruction.

But the recuperative programme of working with deconstruction by domesticating it to existing institutional norms, and in effect neutering it, will not please everyone. It has, in fact, already generated a counter-programme. This is the course prescribed by deconstructive textualism's mighty opposites within poststructuralist theory, the various contextualisms which recognize that taming the deconstructive cat poses a subtler but greater danger than allowing it to ravin freely. While the routinization of deconstruction's negative labour may in the short term strengthen the institution by providing work for us all and a new textual technology for performing that work, it also represents a further trivialization and marginalization of the institution of textual study within the wider discourses and practices of culture.

Taming the deconstructive cat is not enough; worse yet, it may be the real danger. In so far as it only continues the aestheticization of literature and literary study into the playthings of a privileged élite that they have long since become, the exercise of real power for good and ill in society is permitted to go on elsewhere with the institution's connivance or indifference. The cat must be declawed, at the very least belled, in order that the institution may recover its political consciousness and reassert the power of texts in terms of a will to social change. Unless that happens, the institution of literary study, of literacy itself, is doomed to be relegated to the marginal status currently enjoyed by departments of classics and philosophy, the historical progenitors to which it is heir. Any new-found and much-needed reinforcement of the institution accruing from its wholesale adoption of the technical procedures of deconstruction—what one of its critics has called its 'diddling-around with texts'[15]—will only hasten its historical relegation.

The agenda, then, is to bell the cat by historicizing or contextualizing it—by posing such questions as 'why deconstruction now?' or 'what are the conditions that determine deconstruction?' or 'what is the cultural question to which deconstruction seems an answer?'—and by so grounding deconstruction in or against something else, to see it as an epiphenomenon and demystify its seductive allure. Such a project could be mounted from any of several contextualist standpoints—Althusserian, Foucauldian, feminist, even Freudian—though this last, to my knowledge, has yet to be tried.

Despite my extensive sympathy with such a project, I fear that the deconstructive cat cannot be so easily belled. The problem is not simply that the contextualist opposition must meet deconstructive textualism on the latter's own ground, where the textualists have all the advantages of wit, style, elegance, and rhetorical agility that derive from their unre-

---

[15] E. D. Hirsch, in discussion after a paper delivered at Melbourne University in July 1982.

pentant literariness, but that they are fully capable of denying, i.e. deconstructing, the metaphoric and metaphysical notion that there is any 'ground' at all on which they can be met, particularly the historical or contextual ground on which their opponents claim to stand. If deconstruction can be historicized or contextualized, so can any historical context be deconstructed, according to the former has always already deconstructed itself. One system or anti-system can always critique another, because each begins from different premises, premises that remain themselves ultimately groundless, a leap of faith without foothold in an *a priori* truth.

In so far as the contextualist critique of deconstruction is a theoretical one, it is itself deconstructible—of making many theories there is, as we are coming to see, no end—and in so far as it is a practical or textual one, it operates at a serious disadvantage in relation to the more sophisticated textual practices of the deconstructionists themselves. Moreover, to remain within theory is to allow deconstruction to carry the day by default. For deconstruction, as the only poststructural-ist definition and defence of literature on offer, is also the only textual practice attempting to specify and engage the 'literari-ness', as distinct from the historicity, of our canonical literature, albeit in a way so uncanny and perverse as to shake to its metaphorical foundations the traditional institution of its study.

What remains to be seen is whether a literary criticism at once poststructuralist and institutionalizable is even possible, a poststructuralist practice that neither clutches blindly at the straws of given, present, and positive meaning, as our older historical formalism did, nor attempts pseudo-scientifically to predetermine meaning, or the conditions of meaning, in contextual terms as the latest Althusserian and Foucaultian historicisms would, nor forgets its own reason for existence in textual difference by becoming itself homogenized and routine as deconstruction itself is rapidly becoming, nor remains so resolutely theoretical as to abstract itself altogether from the texts it was supposed to illuminate, as all the going 'isms' threaten to do.

It is worth recalling at this point a lesson drawn by some historians of science, that when one paradigm replaces another it does so without argument; the process is not one of logical demonstration or proof but of practical expedience. But perhaps that analogy is misleading in its wishful or purist premiss of a succession of 'paradigms'. Do we really want a new monism to underwrite our practice? And with so many contenders in the field competing for that dubious standing, is it even reasonable to expect one to emerge? Are not the literary, historical, and philosophical communities, as distinct from those of science, characterized by an unprogrammatic, though not undisciplined, pluralism, by a rigorous diversity of institutional practice? Does not the appeal that remains, in Samuel Johnson's phrase, always open from criticism to 'nature', remain open only because the human 'nature' that forms the object of literary study as distinct from that of science, is never given and autonomous, or even consensually or conventionally agreed? If this is the case, changes in literary-critical practice come about through the appeal of strong example, and not through the methodical unconceal-ment of *a priori* truth. This may well be the case in the sciences as well, even if the scientists themselves, as distinct from the philosophers and historians of science, have yet to realize it.

Where, then, are we to find examples strong enough to restore a sense of common purpose into our institutional practice, given its necessary and desirable diversity? What does it take, nowadays, to make a good critic? In answering that question more than half a century ago, to the effect that one must be 'very intelligent', T. S. Eliot might have seemed to be speaking for all time. But even *ex cathedra* pronounce-ments are historical, and the intelligence Eliot recommended and embodied was very much of its time, a time when the highest critical intelligence was devoting itself, doubtless for historical reasons, to the practical, indeed empirical, challenge of anyalyzing texts in a manner seemingly untouched by theoretical principle. Though all has changed—even to the point where Frank Kermode can now bear witness to the compatibility of intelligence and theory[16]—it would be ahistorical in the extreme to invest the future intelligence of the institution in practice or theory exclusively. Our practice

[16] 'Intelligent Theory', *London Review of Books* (7–20 October, 1982), pp. 8–9.

has become, willy-nilly, theoretical. It is too late for intelligent criticism to remain persistently and unself-consciously intuitive and late enough to foresee the institutional dead-end of going relentlessly theoretical. It cannot avoid contact with theory as if the latter were some latter-day 'French disease', a contagion imported from the foreign field of European philosophy. After half a century of literary modernism, an insistence on nationalism or nativism cannot help but seem provincial as well as anachronistic.

But neither can criticism continue to feed itself on grand illusions of any first or final rationale, some pure good of theory or system on which it might 'ground' itself and guarantee its practice, some foundational philosophy that would lend it authoritative support and restore the prestige it has lost to science, technology, and material productivity and acquisition. If, under pressure of cultural marginalization, our practice has turned theoretical, so must our theory turn practical, which is not to say complacent or intuitive or blind. Any discipline worthy of the name must offer its reasons for saying and doing what it does, reasons which will be deemed valid or invalid, embraced or rejected, only according to the norms of the historical community within which they are offered, and not according to those of some utopian order of ultimate rationality or imminent socialism. This counsel of liberal scepticism—some would call it pragmatism—may not enable us to avoid the gross, obvious errors of interpretive subjectivity and cultural ideology that have beset criticism, as its historical condition, from the beginning. But what counsel for criticism could do that? Certainly none of the dreams of system currently abroad in the land, of some monistic and overarching theory of theories.

What can we reasonably expect, then, as the outcome of the institution's twenty-year involvement with literary theory? Not a common methodology, as was first hoped, for the ideologies from which methods are inseparable, as meanings are from signs, are too many to allow any one method to dominate, least of all a 'scientific' method. Certainly not a common ideology: the political interests within and outside the academy are much too diverse for that to happen. And not a meta- or master-discourse either. The most we can expect—perhaps it has already occurred—is a new historical dialect, more like Pidgin than Esperanto, that draws on the lexicons and grammars of several existing languages, holds diverse connotations for its speakers, and is sufficiently, though still imperfectly, shared to enable the haggle of exchange to go on more or less as usual, the dialect not of an interpretive community but of a mercantile tribe. Whereas literary critics not long ago would haggle passionately in the market-place over the value of their goods in terms of its 'complex sensibility' and 'life-enhancing richness', the new tribe of literacy theorists, more multinational and entrepreneurial in spirit, will negotiate their mergers and puff their products in terms of their 'implied readers', 'discursive formations', and 'textual difference'. The measure of that discursive shift, the still centre of that turning world, the virtual focus of our changing critical discourse will be the great classic texts, which continue to repay so richly each historical construction and deconstruction they attract.

Index